CO-AWV-596

C H A W A
N O
R G O I
O K
I A
Ramushonock
Ohanoock
Moratuc
Tandaquomuc
Metquien
Catokinge
Waratan
Mascoming
Skicoak
Chepanun
Chepioc finus
WEAPE
MEOC
Chesepioc
Apasus
guepen
asquiewock
Pasquenoke
pare
Roanoac
25
Trinety harbor
Matorask

OCCIDENS
MERIDIES
ORIENS
SEPTENTRIO

HISTORY

OF

NORTH CAROLINA:

WITH

MAPS AND ILLUSTRATIONS.

BY

FRANCIS L. HAWKS, D.D., L.L.D.

VOL. I.,

EMBRACING THE PERIOD BETWEEN THE FIRST VOYAGE TO THE COLONY IN
1584, TO THE LAST IN 1591.

FAYETTEVILLE, N. C.:
PUBLISHED BY E. J. HALE & SON.
RALEIGH: H. D. TURNER—W. L. POMEROY.
1857.

1

N. C.
9 75.6
H

Volume - 1

"History Of North Carolina", by Dr. Francis L. Hawks (two volumes), is a set being produced in a series on the Basic History of the Original Colonies.

The Reprint Company is specializing in Colonial and Revolutionary period history in two distinct divisions: (1) Basic material on the Settlement and Colonial periods and (2) Major Battles and Campaigns of the Revolution.

Basic histories available include: Georgia — Author, Jones; Maryland — Authors, McSherry, McMahon, Bozman; New York, — Authors, O'Callaghan and Lossing; North Carolina — Authors, Hawks, Creecy; New Jersey — Authors, Smith, Barber & Howe; Pennsylvania — Authors, Proud, Gordon; Virginia — Authors, Stith, Campbell; South Carolina — Authors, Hewatt, Ramsay, Landrum, Logan and Gregg.

Revolutionary period volumes include: Draper's King's Mountain; Stryker's Trenton and Princeton; Tarleton's Campaigns in Southern Provinces (N. C., S. C. & Va.); Schenck's Campaigns and Battles in North Carolina, South Carolina and Virginia; Landrum's Battles in Upper South Carolina; French's and Murdock's Concord, Lexington, Bunker Hill and Siege of Boston.

Also completed and available is the 12-volume Heads of Families, First Census of the United States, 1790, with volumes for the States of South Carolina, North Carolina, Virginia, Pennsylvania, Maryland, New Hampshire, Maine, Rhode Island, Vermont, Connecticut, Massachusetts and New York.

The Reprint Company has completed and has available a six-volume set on Women of Colonial and Revolutionary Times. The books are: "Martha Washington" and "Dolly Madison" of Virginia; "Eliza Pinckney" of South Carolina; "Catherine Schuyler" of New York; "Margaret Winthrop" and "Mercy Warren" of Massachusetts.

Volumes on Colonial America and the Revolutionary Battles and Campaigns are constantly being added to our list of reprints.

THE REPRINT COMPANY
154 W. Cleveland Park Drive
Spartanburg, S. C., 2930 3

First Printing — May, 1961
Second Printing — March, 1966
Third Printing — March, 1969

C. 3
· MLib

TO THE

NATIVES OF NORTH CAROLINA;

AS WELL

TO THE DWELLERS AT HOME AS TO THE DISPERSED ABROAD;

TO ALL ALIKE,

WHETHER WITHIN OR WITHOUT HER BORDERS :

THIS ATTEMPT TO PRESERVE THE STORY OF THEIR CHILDHOOD'S HOME

IS AFFECTIONATELY INSCRIBED,

BY THEIR COUNTRYMAN,

THE AUTHOR.

ENTERED, according to act of Congress, in the year Eighteen Hundred and Fifty-six,

BY E. J. HALE & SON,

In the District Court of the United States, for the District of North Carolina.

JONES & DENYSE,
STEREOTYPERS AND ELECTROTYPERS,
183 William-Street.

Standard Book Numbering:
No. 8715 2006 0
Library of Congress Catalogue Number: 61 3775

CONTENTS.

PAGE

No. 1. The Letters Patent granted by Queen Elizabeth to Sir Walter Raleigh, in 1584.. 11

   Biographical sketch of Raleigh appended thereto................. ... 18

No. 2. The First Voyage under Raleigh's directions, made by Amadas and Barlowe, in 1584.. 69

No. 3. The First Voyage, made for Raleigh, by Sir Richard Greenville, in 1585.. 89

No. 4. An account of the employments of the colonists left by Sir R. Greenville, 1585–6 : By Ralph Lane... 103

No. 5. Voyage of a Relief-ship, sent by Raleigh, in 1586.................... 142

No. 6. A brief and true Report of the Country, by Thomas Hariot, one of the colonists under Lane ; founded on a twelvemonths' personal observation, 1585–6.. 146

No. 7. A Voyage with three ships in 1587, made to establish a colony under the charge of John White..... 191

No. 8. The Voyage of John White, made in 1590, to Roanoak, for the relief of the Colony left by him in 1587............................... .. 213

Historical Narrative founded on the preceding............................. 232

PREFACE.

In the execution of a purpose long and warmly cherished, the author and compiler of this volume offers to his countrymen, with all humility, this commencement of the history of their native State, North Carolina. The volume is complete in itself, as furnishing the most full account that existing materials at this day afford of the first attempts at colonization on our shores. The period embraced extends from the year 1584 to 1591, and includes the five voyages made, under the charter to Sir Walter Raleigh. It is a distinct portion of our history. an isolated chapter, having little connection with what is to follow: for, after the failure of all the efforts made under the Charter to Raleigh, a long interval of time, more than half a century, elapsed before any permanent settlement was made within our borders.

In entering upon his work, the writer avails himself of the opportunity briefly to explain his proposed plan, as in some of its features, it departs from established historical models. A mere chronologically accurate narrative of important public events does not in his view constitute history; though of it, such a narrative properly forms a part. He has supposed that the real history of a State is to be read in the gradual progress of its *people* in intelligence, refinement, industry, wealth, taste, civilization, &c. The public events that transpire are but the exponents of the condition of the inhabitants, in these and other particulars.

The "people" constitute a nation, not the legislature merely, nor the courts, not the army nor the navy. These are all but parts of the whole; and yet many so called histories tell us little else save the changes of dynasties, and "the wars and fightings" of ambitious rulers. We would gladly see there beside, something of the inner life of the *people* themselves. And the thought has occurred that in the effort to catch and present a picture of this, classification is a valuable auxiliary : its advantages are obvious in some of the earlier English histories, such, for instance, as those of Mortimer and Henry ; while in the latest imitation of their example in Knight's Pictorial History of England, many portions are almost invested with the interest of an agreeable romance. Now it is true that in our short career, we cannot have had as much variety as is to be found on the broader field that spreads over centuries in the history of the other hemisphere ; and yet even we have room for classification. We must speak of various subjects. The "religion," "laws and legislation," "education," "agriculture," "industrial and mechanical pursuits," "commerce," "extent and advance of settlements," "wars with native or foreign foes," "manners and customs of the people," &c., all demand their share of notice, and will be better understood as well as remembered, if they receive distinct treatment. Hence we divide the time through which the State has passed, particularly in its more recent career, into periods or epochs, and endeavor to present in all respects, as full and perfect a picture, or rather series of pictures, as we can make of each period.

Another feature in our work, of which this volume will afford a specimen, is to be found in the reprint and consequent preservation of the rare and valuable old documents, tracts, &c., which furnish part of the material for our history. We know very well that such documents generally have but little interest save for the historical antiquarian ; but we are writing more especially for North Carolinians ; and we cannot but believe that for them, such early and authentic memorials of their country will possess an interest, independent of all antiquarian taste or study. To the extent of our humble abilities, we shall endeavor to enliven the dullness and relieve the quaintness of these worthy old chroniclers by such notes and remarks as may serve to link pleasantly together the past with the present. And if in this we fail, as we fear we sometimes shall, still an important end will be answered. The soul of history is TRUTH: the reader will have in the reprint of these old publications, all the means extant of eviscerating the truth for himself; while the writer voluntarily shuts out the possibility of his substituting invention for the sober realities of history: in his narrative of *facts* he must conform to the early testimony which he has placed in the hands of the reader; his deductions, suggestions, reflections, &c., are his own, and will pass for what they are worth with the intelligent, without the risk of being confounded with the *facts* of early records. But, of course, this use of earlier documents will be constantly diminishing as we travel upward in the story, through period after period, because of the diminished necessity of reprinting that which, beside being generally known, is easily accessible in other forms. One exception to this, however, will exist in the case of important and *hitherto unpublished manuscripts.*—An appendix of documents with notes is not an uncommon suffix to a volume of history; we merely make of them a prefix.

With this brief outline of the chief features of our work, it only remains to be added that we shall issue the volumes successively, as fast as they can be properly prepared; and, soliciting from all our countrymen such aid as they can render in furnishing us with family papers, local traditions, old documents, or otherwise, we can say no more than that, embarking in our undertaking as a labor of love, our first effort shall be to tell the simple truth; and our highest ambition, so to tell it that North Carolinians will not be ashamed of the narrative.

HISTORY OF NORTH CAROLINA.

THE

LETTERS PATENTS

GRANTED BY THE QUEEN'S MAJESTY

TO

M. WALTER RALEGH,

NOW KNIGHT,

FOR THE DISCOVERING AND PLANTING OF NEW LANDS AND COUNTRIES:
TO CONTINUE THE SPACE OF SIX YEARS,
AND NO MORE.

[This grant was made in 1584, and constitutes the first step in the work of English colonization in America. Our reprint is from the copy preserved by *Hakluyt*, and published on page 243 of the third volume of his "Voyages" in the edition of 1600. It may also be found in Hazard's State Papers, vol. 1, page 33. In this as in all the early documents we reprint, we have accommodated the orthography to the usage of our own times.]

ELIZABETH, by the Grace of God of England, France, and Ireland, Queen, defender of the faith, &c. To all people to whom these presents shall come, greeting. Know ye that of our special grace, certain science, and mere motion, we have given and granted, and by these presents for us, our heirs and successors, we give and grant to our trusty and well-beloved servant, WALTER

RALEGH, Esquire, and to his heirs and assigns forever, free liberty and license, from time to time, and at all times forever hereafter to discover, search, find out, and view such remote heathen and barbarous lands, countries and territories not actually possessed of any christian Prince, nor inhabited by christian people, as to him, his heirs and assigns, and to every or any of them shall seem good, and the same to have, hold, occupy and enjoy to him, his heirs and assigns forever; with all prerogatives, commodities, jurisdictions, royalties, privileges, franchises, and pre-eminences, thereto or thereabouts, both by sea and land, whatsoever we by our letters patents may grant, and as we or any of our noble progenitors have heretofore granted to any person or persons, bodies politic or corporate : and the said WALTER RALEGH, his heirs and assigns, and all such as from time to time, by license of us, our heirs and successors, shall go and travel thither, to inhabit or remain there to build or fortify, at the discretion of the said WALTER RALEGH, his heirs and assigns, the Statutes or Acts of Parliament made against fugitives, or against such as shall depart, remain or continue out of our realm of England without license, or any other statute, act, law, or any ordinance whatever to the contrary, in any wise notwithstanding.

And we do likewise by these presents, of our special grace, mere motion, and certain knowledge, for us, our heirs and successors, give and grant full authority, liberty and power to the said WALTER RALEGH, his heirs and assigns, and every of them, that he and they, and every or any of them, shall and may at all and every time, and times hereafter, have, take and lead in the same voyage, and travel thitherward, or to inhabit there with him, or them, and every or any of them, such and so many of our subjects as shall willingly accompany him or them, and every or any of them to whom we do also by these presents, give full liberty and authority in that behalf, and also to have, take, and employ, and use sufficient shipping and furniture for the transportations and navigations in that behalf, so that none of the same persons, or any of them, be such as hereafter shall be restrained by us, our heirs, or successors.

And further, that the said WALTER RALEGH, his heirs and assigns, and every of them, shall have, hold, occupy and enjoy to him, his heirs and assigns, and every of them forever, all the soil, and all such lands, territories, and countries, so to be discovered and possessed as aforesaid, and of all such cities, castles, towns, villages, and places in the same, with the rights, royalties, franchises, and jurisdictions, as well marine as other, within the said lands, or countries, or the seas thereunto adjoining, to be had, or used, with full power to dispose thereof, and of every part in fee simple or otherwise, according to the order of the laws of England, as near as the same conveniently may be, at his, and their will and pleasure, to any persons then being, or that shall remain within the allegiance of us, our heirs and successors, reserving always to us our heirs and successors, for all services, duties, and demands, the fifth part of all the ore of gold and silver that from time to time, and at all times after such discoveries, subduing or possessing, shall be there gotten and obtained: All which lands, countries and territories, shall forever be holden of the said WALTER RALEGH, his heirs and assigns, of us, our heirs and successors, by homage, and by the said payment of the said fifth part, reserved only for all services.

And moreover, we do by these presents, for us, our heirs and successors, give and grant license to the said WALTER RALEGH, his heirs and assigns, and every of them, that he and they, and every or any of them, shall, and may from time to time, and at all times forever hereafter, for his and their defence, encounter and expulse, repel and resist, as well by sea as by land, and by all other ways whatsoever, all and every such person or persons whatsoever, as without the especial liking and license of the said WALTER RALEGH, and of his heirs and assigns, shall attempt to inhabit within the said countries, or any of them, or within the space of two hundred leagues near to the place or places within such countries as aforesaid (if they shall not be before planted or inhabited within the limits as aforesaid with the subjects of any christian Prince being in amity with us), where the said WALTER RALEGH, his heirs or assigns, or any of them, or his or their or any of their associates or company, shall within six years (next ensuing) make their dwellings or abidings, or that shall enterprise or attempt at any time hereafter unlawfully to annoy, either by sea or land, the said WALTER RALEGH, his heirs or assigns, or

any of them, or his or their, or any of his or their companies ; giving
and granting by these presents further power and authority, to
the said WALTER RALEGH, his heirs or assigns, and every of them,
from time to time, and at all times forever hereafter, to take and
surprise by all manner of means whatsoever, all and every those
person or persons, with their ships, vessels, and other goods and
furniture, which without the license of the said WALTER RALEGH,
or his heirs or assigns as aforesaid, shall be found trafficking into
any harbor or harbors, creek or creeks, within the limits aforesaid (the subjects of our realms and dominions, and all other
persons in amity with us, trading to the *new found lands* for fishing as heretofore they have commonly used, or being driven by
force of a tempest, or shipwreck only excepted) ; and those persons, and every of them, with their ships, vessels, goods and furniture, to detain and possess as of good and lawful prize, according to the direction of him the said WALTER RALEGH, his heirs and
assigns, and every or any of them. And for uniting in more
perfect league and amity, of such countries, lands, and territories,
so to be possessed and inhabited as aforesaid with our realms of
England and Ireland, and the better encouragement of men to
these enterprises, we do by these presents grant and declare that
all such countries, so hereafter to be possessed and inhabited as is
aforesaid, from thenceforth shall be of the allegiance of us, our
heirs and successors. And we do grant to the said WALTER
RALEGH, his heirs and assigns, and to all and every of them, and
to all and every other person, and persons being of our allegiance,
whose names shall be noted or entered in some of our courts of
record within our realm of England, that with the assent of the
said WALTER RALEGH, his heirs or assigns, shall in his journeys
for discovery, or in the journeys for conquest, hereafter travel to
such lands, countries and territories, as aforesaid, and to their and
to every of their heirs, that they, and every or any of them,
being either born within our said realms of England or Ireland,
or in any other place within our allegiance, and which hereafter
shall be inhabiting within any the lands, countries and territories
with such license (as aforesaid), shall and may have all the privileges of free denizens, and persons native of England, and within
our allegiance in such like ample manner and form, as if they

were born and personally resident within our said realm of England, any law, custom, or usage to the contrary notwithstanding.

And forasmuch, as upon the finding out, discovering, or inhabiting of such remote lands, countries, and territories as aforesaid,
it shall be necessary for the safety of all men, that shall adventure themselves in those journeys or voyages, to determine to live
together in Christian peace, and civil quietness each with the
other, whereby every one may with more pleasure and profit enjoy
that whereunto they shall attain with great pain and peril, we for
us, our heirs and successors, are likewise pleased and contented,
and by these presents do give and grant to the said WALTER RA-
LEGH, his heirs and assigns forever, that he and they, and every
or any of them, shall and may from time to time forever hereafter,
within the same mentioned remote lands and countries in the way
by the seas thither, and from thence, have full and mere power
and authority to correct, punish, pardon, govern, and rule by their
and every or any of their good discretions and policies, as well in
causes capital, or criminal, as civil, both marine and other, all
such our subjects as shall from time to time adventure themselves
in the said journeys or voyages, or that shall at any time hereafter inhabit any such lands, countries, or territories, as aforesaid, or
that shall abide within 200 leagues of any of the said place or
places, where the said WALTER RALEGH, his heirs, or assigns, or
any of them, or any of his or their associates or companies, shall
inhabit within six years next ensuing the date hereof, according
to such statutes, laws and ordinances, as shall be by him the said
WALTER RALEGH, his heirs and assigns, and every or any of them
devised, or established, for the better government of the said people as aforesaid. So always as the said statutes, laws, and ordinances may be as near as conveniently may be, agreeable to the
form of the laws, statutes, government, or policy of England, and
also so as they be not against the true Christian faith, now professed in the Church of England, nor in any wise to withdraw
any of the subjects or people of those lands or places from the
allegiance of us, our heirs and successors, as their immediate
sovereign under God.

And further, we do by these presents for us, our heirs and successors, give and grant full power and authority to our trusty and

well beloved counsellor Sir WILLIAM CECILL, Knight, LORD BURGH-
LEY, our high Treasurer of England, and to the Lord Treasurer of
England, for us, our heirs and successors for the time being, and
to the privy council, of us, our heirs and successors, or any four
or more of them, for the time being, that he, they, or any four
or more of them, shall and may from time to time, and at all
times hereafter, under his or their hands or seals by virtue of these
presents, authorize and license the said WALTER RALEGH, his heirs
and assigns, and every or any of them by him, and by themselves,
or by their, or any of their sufficient attorneys, deputies, officers,
ministers, factors, and servants, to embark and transport out of
our Realms of England and Ireland, and the dominions thereof,
all, or any of his, or their goods, and all or any the goods of his
and their associates and companies, and every or any of them,
with such other necessaries and commodities of any our Realms,
as to the said Lord Treasurer, or four or more of the privy council, of us, our heirs and successors for the time being (as aforesaid)
shall be from time to time by his or their wisdom or discretions
thought meet and convenient, for the better relief and support of
him the said WALTER RALEGH, his heirs and assigns, and every or
any of them, and of his or their or any of their associates and
companies, any act, statute, law, or other thing to the contrary in
any wise notwithstanding.

Provided always, and our will and pleasure is, and we do here-
by declare to all Christian Kings, Princes and States, that if the
said WALTER RALEGH, his heirs or assigns, or any of them, or any
other of their license or appointment, shall at any time or times
hereafter, rob or spoil, by sea or by land, or do any act of unjust
or unlawful hostility, to any of the subjects of us, our heirs or
successors, or to any of the subjects of any the kings, princes,
rulers, governors, or estates, being then in perfect league and
amity with us, our heirs and successors, and that upon such injury,
or upon just complaint of any such prince, ruler, governor, or
estate, or their subjects, we, our heirs and successors, shall make
open proclamation within any the ports of our Realm of England,
that the said WALTER RALEGH, his heirs and assigns, and adherents,
or any to whom these our letters patents may extend, shall within
the terms to be limited, by such proclamation, make full restitu-
tion and satisfaction of all such injuries done: so as both we and

the said princes, or other so complaining, may hold us and themselves fully contented. And that if the said WALTER RALEGH,
his heirs and assigns, shall not make or cause to be made satisfaction accordingly, within such time to be limited, that then it shall
be lawful to us, our heirs and successors, to put the said WALTER
RALEGH, his heirs and assigns and adherents, and all the inhabitants of the said places to be discovered (as is aforesaid) or any of
them out of our allegiance and protection, and that from and after
such time of putting out of protection of the said WALTER RALEGH,
his heirs, assigns and adherents, and others so to be put out, and
the said places within their habitation, possession and rule, shall
be out of our allegiance and protection, and free for all princes
and others, to pursue with hostility, as being not our subjects, nor
by us any way to be avouched, maintained or defended, nor to be
holden as any of ours, nor to our protection or dominion, or allegiance any way belonging; for that express mention of the clear
yearly value of the certainty of the premises, or any part thereof,
or of any other gift, or grant by us, or any our progenitors, or
predecessors, to the said WALTER RALEGH, before this time made
in these presents be not expressed, or any other grant, ordinance,
provision, proclamation, or restraint to the contrary thereof, before
this time given, ordained, or provided, or any other thing, cause
or matter whatsoever, in any wise notwithstanding. In witness
whereof, we have caused these our letters to be made patents.
Witness ourselves, at *Westminster*, the five and twentieth day of
March, in the six and twentieth year of our reign.

[The portion of time back to which this charter carries us, embraces one
of the most exciting as well as brightest periods of English history in
the reign of the "Virgin Queen;" and of the characters presented to
our notice, the most interesting to North Carolinians is that of the very
remarkable man whose enterprise first planted on our shores a colony
of Englishmen.

The State in which he placed the little handful of men who were the pioneers in America, of English colonization, has rendered its tribute of
respect to the name of RALEIGH by conferring it upon her capital; and
we would fain justify our countrymen by showing that they have but
rendered honor where it was due. It is therefore hoped that to a story
of which North Carolina is to be the subject, a brief sketch of the life and
character of Sir Walter Raleigh will form no inappropriate introduction.]

VOL. I.—2.

BIRTH-PLACE OF RALEIGH.

THERE is ever to a generous mind something painful in contemplating the fallen fortunes of a man who once has "towered in his pride of place." Our sensibilities are touched when we look upon the buried greatness even of one whose own unworthiness has made him "totter to his fall." Who, for instance, can dwell unmoved upon the picture of a Bacon illustrating the truth of a sentiment penned by himself almost as if with prophetic vision—"Of all men he is most miserable who follows at the funeral of his own reputation?" The contrast is so great between the honors rendered to elevated station, and the insult and neglect attendant upon altered fortunes, that in its contemplation even this world's pity divests itself for a time of its hypocritical mockery, and for once is honest in the expression of its sympathy. And if this be so, when "even-handed justice" is constrained to mingle condemnation with our pity, how much more is there to touch the sensibilities of our nature, when envy and persecution, fraud and falsehood, have all combined to drag a noble spirit to the dust, and in their infernal success call upon us to look on the decayed, nay, ruined fortunes of one whose heaviest crime has been that God made him a greater man than his fellows? Such was the treatment that Sir Walter Raleigh received; and one might almost think that like his illustrious contemporary Bacon, he too was endowed with the spirit of prophetic anticipation. In his early offerings to the muse, he has left on record a sentiment which his own sad history proved to be no poetic fiction:

> "Tho' sundry minds in sundry sort do deem,
> Yet worthiest wights yield praise for every pain ;
> But envious brains do naught, or light, esteem,
> Such stately steps as they cannot attain :
> For whoso reaps renown above the rest,
> With heaps of hate shall surely be oppress'd."

Of the earlier years of Raleigh, no more need be said than that he was born in the year 1552, of an ancient and reputable family in Devon, and was sent to Oxford for his education. One of the wisest men that England ever produced has borne testimony to the genius and wit of the young student, and it is therefore no waste of time to follow the fortunes of one whose powers commanded the admiration of Bacon. His college life, however, exhibited little more than that remarkable union of the habits of a scholar with those of an active man of the world, which through his whole career characterized him. In his case, too, as in that of other distinguished men, his early reading gave color to the future complexion of his life.

The conquest of the Spaniards in this hemisphere furnished in his day a new story. Raleigh was much too imaginative not to be pleasurably excited by the romance embodied in the tales of Montezuma and the Inca, the chivalric boldness of Cortes and Pizarro ; and as he was pre-eminently fitted for action, he felt that a field was open on this yet unknown continent for the exercise of his loftiest powers. Thus was he unconsciously preparing himself to become one of the boldest maritime adventurers of his age and nation.

Young, handsome, brave, accomplished and intelligent (for he was all this), the first field in which we find him playing the part of man, was France. It was at the period when the Protestants,

2

under the great Prince of Condé and Admiral Coligni, were struggling for religious liberty. Elizabeth, on more accounts than one, was not an indifferent spectator of this contest. She gave permission to Henry Champernon, who was a near kinsman of Raleigh, to raise a troop of a hundred gentlemen volunteers, and to pass over to the continent. The French historian, De Thou, has left a description of the appearance they made in the camp of the Protestants : " A gallant company," says he, " nobly mounted and accoutred, and bearing for a motto on their standard, ' Let valor decide the contest.' " Of this troop was Raleigh, and one who knew him then, speaking of his education and bearing, writes, " it was not part, but *wholly gentleman—wholly soldier.*" In this school he remained for more than six years, bearing well his share in some of the most memorable actions of the times, until the peace of 1576, when he returned to England. Very soon after this we find him in the Netherlands, a volunteer under the Prince of Orange against the Spaniards.

Raleigh must not, however, be considered a mere soldier of fortune, ready to draw his sword in any quarrel. Both in the Low Countries and in France, the principle for which he contended was the same. He was armed in the cause of liberty, and in both instances he was indirectly defending his country; for in both he had gone forth under the sanction of Elizabeth, and fought under the English standard.

Among his fellow-soldiers was one who, remarkable as much for his eccentricity as for his valor, had traveled far and fought in many lands, and in whom great versatility of genius was not without its usual accompaniment, a wonderful facility in devising multifarious projects. One of his many schemes was the establishment of a colony in America. When he adverted to this, he touched a chord in Raleigh's bosom which instantly gave a responsive vibration. Amid the toils of the camp, the young volunteer had never neglected the cultivation of his mind: he was a soldier student, and had mastered all that was then known on the subjects of cosmography and navigation. His half-brother, Sir Humphrey Gilbert, had obtained a patent for colonizing in North America : leaving the army, Raleigh joined him to try his fortune on our shores. A combination of disasters, however, defeated the undertaking, and he returned home without having seen this country, and with no other advantage than that derived from the lessons of his brother, one of the most experienced seamen of his age. Scarcely had he reached England, however, before he found himself in another scene of activity and war. Spain had stirred up the spirit of rebellion in Ireland. Raleigh now had a name as a soldier, and we find him at the seat of war in command of a company. Here it was that his remarkable talents first shone forth with a lustre that challenged notice. He found himself in various important trusts, and well did he execute them all. Uniting the sagacity and ripe judgment of age with the daring courage and uncalculating generosity of youth, he would now defeat the enemy by superior tactics, and now rush single-handed to the rescue of a friend, and bring him off in triumph at the peril of his life. The rebellion was suppressed, and Raleigh, with a reputation of the highest order among those who had stood by his side as soldiers, returned with no recommendations but those his own talents and attainments had procured, to play his part at a most eventful period among men, more splendid than any other court in Europe at that day could boast.

And now we must digress from our narrative long enough to present a picture of the "Virgin Queen," and those whom she had gathered around her for the support of her throne.

Of Elizabeth herself, perhaps no more comprehensive character was ever sketched than that which came from the pen of her secretary, the younger Cecil, after the grave had secured him against the possibility of her resentment. She was, as he said, "more than a man, and in troth somewhat less than a woman." In the masculine vigor of her understanding, and the lion-hearted boldness which she inherited from her father, she exhibited qualities belonging to the sterner sex; and was often more than many men would have been under the circumstances;—while her feminine weaknesses went far beyond those of most women. The distinguishing features of the better part of her character were her admirable power of discriminating true mental strength; and of attaching to her service the devoted labors of the best minds in her kingdom. The individual who can do these things belongs not to the ordinary class. When seated at the council board, we see none of Elizabeth's womanly follies. She had an opinion of her own, and was prepared with reasons to sustain it : she never forgot the dignity belonging to her station, and permitted not the greatest man before her in the slightest degree to entrench upon it. She knew no favorites in the discussion of great questions of state policy, and no reign presented more of such questions than her own. Her agents in important enterprises were always judiciously selected ; no gilded court butterfly was ever sent to execute a difficult duty. She tolerated no fools about her when she was deliberating on the interests of her throne.

These are facts which deservedly place her among the very first of female sovereigns. But her weaknesses stand out in sad contrast to all these high qualities. She was vain much beyond the ordinary limits allowed to the weaker sex by the courtesy of the stronger. With features so plain that not even self-love could persuade her she was handsome, she yet was exceedingly anxious to be thought beautiful. A passionate admirer of beauty in the other sex, she exacted most mercilessly the homage of the handsomest men in her kingdom, and no miser was ever more covetous of gold than she was of admiration. When the frosts of sixty winters had whitened her locks, and the ploughshare of time had traced many a furrow in the wrinkles of her shriveled cheeks; so that ugliness had not even the small merit of healthy youth to redeem it from the loathings of disgust ; she affected all the romantic sensibilities of love-sick sixteen. The smiles and sighs and tears and thousand interesting "femalities," so pretty and engaging in tender damsels who fall in love; all these derived an added lustre from the parchment face of sixty, agonizing for a blush and striving to torture the indurated muscles into an expression of sentimentality. With all a woman's dexterity would she play off one of her favorites against another, and so admirably equalize her tokens of regard that each had just enough of hope to save him from despair, and quite enough of fear to stimulate him to renewed devotion. With a jealousy as cruel as the grave, she allowed no man about her to bestow the affections of his nature upon an object worthy of them, but with lynx-eyed vigilance tracked him in his love, and construed it into an insult to herself. Envious of her own sex, if a lady of the court acquitted herself well in the lively dance, it was the royal pleasure to enter the lists in a saltatory contest, and the agility of youth yielded the palm to the stately dignity of sixty-nine years, walking with becoming gravity through the slower paces of a minuet. Vindictive when the slightest personal reflection had been made, the fate of Essex (favorite though he was) was sealed from the unfortunate moment when, sick of her caprices, he remarked that her counsels were " as crooked as her carcase." Treacherous toward her rival, the unhappy queen of Scots, the policy of state which called for her murder was none the less acceptable because it gratified also the envy that sickened at her beauty.

Such was Elizabeth, and such the strange intermingling of kingly qualities and womanly weaknesses that made her, as Cecil said, "more than a man and less than a woman."

The next character in importance to the queen was the sagacious and wary Burleigh. A more unimaginative creature than William Cecil, perhaps, never lived. A heart less likely by its generous impulses to mislead the judgment never beat in a human bosom. Spenser, the poet, came recommended to him by his royal mistress herself; he had no sympathy with the beautiful creations of his fancy, and treated him with neglect. Military reputation he valued at no more than he could find in the tangible results of a victory. He estimated the genius of a commander by the security the country derived from his conquests, or the coin they brought into her coffers. Calm and taciturn in every condition of state affairs, with a judgment imperturbably cool, and a rigidity of muscle that never betrayed the slightest feeling, he swayed the destinies of England for years in one of the most trying times of her history, and from first to last possessed the confidence and respect of one of the most capricious old women that ever fancied herself lovely. Elizabeth as little thought of flattering Burleigh into a dream of love, or binding him to her interests by the occasional affectation of tenderness, as if he had been chiseled out of marble. This was a game to play with such spirits as Essex and Leicester; but Burleigh was much too sagacious to permit her majesty to think it possible that he knew there was any such thing as love. His abilities made him indispensable, he was aware of it, yet never acted as if he thought so

The only object he had in view through a long life, was the glory and aggrandisement of England. For these he toiled with indefatigable labor. Take him for all in all, his country never had a better minister of state, and yet his mind was not of the highest order. There was none of the brilliancy or originality of genius belonging to him. There was no enthusiasm which enabled him to appreciate it in others. Still Burleigh was a great man. A survey of the measures of his government, and the consummate prudence with which he conducted them, all stamp him with the impress of true greatness. The difficult questions involved in the establishment of the Protestant faith, the triumphant resistance to the untiring hostility of the then powerful court of Spain, the dexterous opposition to the Papal power exhibited in the professed support merely of liberty of conscience in France and the Netherlands ; the far-reaching sagacity that liberally encouraged voyages of discovery and colonization, because it saw that England's strength was to be in her marine ; all these, with many other particulars, attest that William Cecil has had few equals among statesmen. This man appreciated Sir Walter Raleigh, and was his friend : probably he was ignorant that the knight had ever been guilty of what has been termed " the vagabond-like occupation" of perpetrating poetry.

Far different from Burleigh was the proud and profligate Dudley, Earl of Leicester. The appreciation of his character that may be made from the representation of the great novelist will not be entirely erroneous. The sad story of Amy Robsart, which has been invested by Scott with so much of melancholy interest, is not all fiction. Utterly unprincipled, Leicester never scrupled at the means necessary to accomplish his end. He hated Burleigh because he could not undermine him in the confidence of Elizabeth : Burleigh repaid his hatred with contempt, but was too politic to betray it by overt acts. Leicester acted for himself primarily. When Raleigh came to court, he found him a royal favorite, possessed of immense influence and power, for a subject. And Leicester loved power not as a means of doing good for his country, but as gratifying pride and furnishing opportunities for revenge. He never scrupled to destroy that he might build himself on the ruins of his victim. He was one of the most profound dissemblers that ever lived. Professing devoted attachment to his queen and country, and bearing no small share in her counsels, he yet was secretly intriguing with Spain and the members of the Church of Rome, because he wished to destroy the protestant interest of Cecil. Notoriously profligate in morals and abandoned in his habits, he could again, when occasion required, lay aside his pretended sympathy with Rome, and with the deepest hypocrisy, assume the language of puritanism, and wear the mask of a most self-denying christianity. He wished the aid of Puritans to prostrate Cecil's labors in building up the Church establishment. No man was ever better fitted by nature to play off the plausibilities of insincerity. Of remarkable personal beauty, uncommon gracefulness of manner, ready address, and no deficiency of understanding, he claimed rank by his noble birth, and sustained the claim by his thorough breeding. Perfectly aware of the foibles of the queen, he plied her with a delicate flattery and a devoted gallantry, complimented her caprices as evidence of her wisdom, and, with a dexterity as cunning as it was secret, contrived, under the seeming show of homage rendered to his sovereign, to strengthen his power, by acting on the principle that Elizabeth was a woman before she was a queen. It was as a woman that she made the handsome Leicester a favorite—it was as the queen that she never allowed her confidence in Cecil to falter. Hence, both stood high in her regard, though they were utterly unlike in all things, and never loved each other.

The only individual who can be said to have shared with Leicester the particular favor of the queen was Essex. We are inclined to think that less than justice has usually been done to his character. He is ordinarily considered as one who became a favorite rather from personal beauty than from real merit, and sharing the fate of most favorites, but little sympathy has been felt in his misfortunes or his fall. Had he been less honest, he had probably escaped the scaffold at the early age of thirty-four. Essex possessed many noble traits of character, and with some it will be deemed enough to redeem his memory from reproach, that he was too proud to be the slave of a woman's whims, though that woman was a queen. He was sick of the perpetual alterna-

tions from lover-like tenderness to royal rage. One day it was all
the nauseating affectation of female fondness that a withered old
woman of sixty-eight could lavish ; and the next, perchance, some
tigress-like outbreak of ferocity sentencing him to banishment.
He would not, like Leicester, compromise his own dignity by
eternally playing the hypocrite and offering the incense of flattery
to the queen ; and, as has already been stated, it was the honesty
of his language giving offence to a woman's self-love that made
her relentless and sent him to the block.

Between Essex and Raleigh there were strong bonds of sympathy. Both loved letters, both were generous, both were brave,
both were fearless in speech. In the collisions of a court, it happened at times (as might be expected) that they came together in
conflict ; but each respected the other. When Essex had the
command in an expedition that proved disastrous, Raleigh, who
served under him, with a noble generosity rejoiced in his own
partial success, because it would in some degree mitigate the
censure which he knew awaited Essex from his royal mistress.
So, too, when Essex and that arch deceiver Robert Cecil (Burleigh's son) were at variance, and the cunning of the latter was
an overmatch for the rash frankness of the former, it was Raleigh
who stepped in and reconciled them. It has, indeed, been supposed that Raleigh contributed to the condemnation of Essex.
He was far less instrumental than Robert Cecil in the production
of that event, and at the execution it was Raleigh, not Cecil, who
wept at the untimely end of a noble spirit. But all the courtiers
around the queen could not have saved Essex from the resentment of Elizabeth's wounded vanity. He had called her carcase
crooked, and so it was, but that only sealed his fate.

These were some of the men with whom Raleigh was now to
act ; but these belonged to one class only. There were others
whose pursuits were more in unison with some of his tastes. He
was always a student ; never did he go upon the sea without his
books, and in the camp his library was always a part of his equi-
page. Even in the most active periods of his life, it was his custom to read four hours a day, and the uncommon versatility of
his mind enabled him to find interest in every path over which
he traveled in the wide field of letters. Skilled in mathematics,

familiar with all that in his day was known of chemistry, and adding by experiments to his stock of knowledge, deeply read in history, one of the best cosmographers of his age, an admirable navigator, and well versed in military tactics; better informed than any of his contemporaries as to the power of his country's enemies—master of several languages, conversant with natural history, and one of the sweetest of England's early poets, he was a fit companion for men of letters, nor was he without such associates. History makes little mention of them however, for the quiet pursuits of literature afford no attractive theme for the man who, under the name of historian, can find no causes operative in the progress of nations, but the tricks of statesmen and the carnage of war. Enough, however, may be gleaned (and to the student the task is pleasant labor) to let us know that in letters Raleigh held companionship with Shakespeare, Sir Philip Sydney, Spenser, Ben Jonson, Drummond of Hawthornden, Bacon, Hariot the mathematician, Beaumont, Fletcher, Selden, Cotton, Carew, Donne, and many others, whose names are consecrated in the history of English literature. At a later period of his life than that of which we are now speaking, Raleigh formed a literary club, which combined all the genius of the metropolis, and in its meetings, in the unreserved and friendly intercourse of scholars, doubtless many a scintillation of fancy sparkled, many a keen encounter of playful wit set the merry students in a roar, many a *jeu d'esprit* gave life to the social meeting. It is hard to curb the imagination in the thought of such a scene. We can fancy Shakespeare then simply the successful dramatist, all unconscious of the deathless renown that awaited him. He is perchance engaged in a pleasant play of wit with Ben Jonson, when suddenly the club-room in the Mermaid tavern rings with the shouts produced by some successful sally. But though it be easy to fancy the laughter, who, alas! shall fancy the wit that produced it? None; for none may venture now to find meet words for the mouth of Shakespeare.

As we shall not have occasion again to advert particularly to the literary tastes of Raleigh, it may here be mentioned, that to him we are indebted for that beautiful production of Spenser, the " Faëry Queen." Raleigh became acquainted with the poet in

Ireland, and an intimate friendship was the result. Years before, Spenser had prepared the first three cantos of his poem, but had been induced by the criticisms of a school anxious to expel rhyme from English poetry, to lay the work aside. Of these critics, it may occasion some surprise to know that Sir Philip Sydney was one, and indeed the only one whose name has come down to our day as associated with the history of English literature. Raleigh heard the first three cantos; he had a soul too truly attuned to real poetry not to perceive that his friend possessed " the faculty and gift divine." His commendation operated as a stimulus to the gentle spirit of Spenser. He returned with Raleigh to England, and published what he had written, dedicating it to the " Most High, Mighty and Magnificent Empress Elizabeth." Ushered into the world under such auspices, it attracted notice, and this was all it needed, for its own merits were sufficient to sustain it. The poet was then induced to complete what Raleigh's discriminating taste had shown him to be so worthily begun; and thus were our language and literature enriched with a poem, which despite its faults, is surpassingly beautiful, and has confessedly supplied a model to one of the modern masters of English verse.

We now return to Raleigh's history. It was after his arrival from Ireland with his well-earned reputation that he first was brought into the presence of his sovereign. The well known anecdote of the gorgeous cloak which, with such ready gallantry, he threw upon the ground to serve as a foot-cloth for the queen, is said to have been the means of his introduction to her notice and regard; and the story is probably true. Be this, however, as it may, he was immediately employed in honorable offices at court, and acquitted himself with reputation in all. His spirit, however, was too active to be content in this situation. He was not without ambition, but it had a loftier aim than that of rising to distinction by the intrigues of a court. He would carve out for himself a nobler path to renown and fortune, and he turned to America as the fit field for his efforts. The patent of his brother, Sir Humphrey Gilbert, originally granted but for six years, was now near expiring. Two years of it only remained, and Raleigh, acting in concert with his brother, fitted out a fleet of five

ships and barks which, in 1583, sailed for America. Gilbert was
the leader, while Raleigh remained to watch over interests at
home. The expedition was unfortunate almost from its commencement, and proved fatal to its commander. Thus was he
twice unsuccessful, and one would suppose that this double failure
would have discouraged him from further attempts. But Raleigh
was not acting on the mere chance of discovery. He studied the
probabilities of success and proceeded on certain data. He had
read the accounts of the Spanish voyagers, he let no skilful mariner escape his examination, and knowing as he did that the ships
of Spain entered the gulf of Mexico by Hispaniola, and on their
return, sailing eastward from the coast of Florida, left a coast on
their west trending away to the north; he was convinced, from
his knowledge of the sphere, that there was a large extent of
unexplored land between Florida and Newfoundland, and it was
this on which he desired to enter. Having satisfied himself, he
laid the subject before the queen, and in 1584 obtained the patent
we have presented, granting him a title to his discoveries, and
authority to plant colonies. The queen, however, was not willing
that he should go in person on the voyage of discovery, because
she required his services at home. He dispatched, therefore,
Amadas and Barlow with minute instructions, and the result
was the discovery of what is now the State of North Carolina.
They returned, bringing with them two of the natives, and afford-
ing to Raleigh, by their success, the proud gratification of finding
ample confirmation of opinions which he had 'reached by reason-
ing, and the truth of which he had established at his own expense.
The queen, no less delighted than Raleigh, named the newly-dis-
covered region Virginia, and conferred the honor of knighthood
on the man whose sagacity and enterprise had added to the extent
of her dominions. At this period, also, we find him representing
his native county in parliament, and enjoying valuable grants of
monopolies the better to enable him to carry on his work of discovery and colonization. Ere long he had, in company with others, another fleet upon the seas, bound to his American possessions. This squadron left a governor and colonists on Roanoke
Island, to make a permanent plantation; they however unfortunately became embroiled with the natives, and from a variety of

SIR WALTER RALEIGH.

FROM AN ORIGINAL AT WEST WICKHAM, IN KENT COUNTY, ENGLAND.

calamitous events, were glad to return to England with the fleet of Sir Francis Drake, which had touched at the settlement. Scarcely, however, had they departed before another fleet of four vessels, laden with abundant supplies, and sent by Raleigh, reached the coast and found, to their astonishment, everything deserted and in ruins. Fifteen men were left with provisions for two years, and the fleet returned home.

Most men would have abandoned forever an enterprise marked by such a succession of discouragements; but the zeal, enthusiasm and perseverance of Raleigh were indomitable. At this very moment he had two other vessels ready, and sent them forth for a cruise against the Spaniards. They took more prizes than they could bring into port, and added materially to Raleigh's wealth.

Possessed now of the confidence and regard of the queen, who was wonderfully taken with his eloquence, and by whom he was regarded as in some sort an oracle; in the enjoyment, also, of many valuable offices by her gift, a member of parliament, and with wealth to sustain him in his magnificent undertakings; to outward seeming it would appear that, so far as earth was concerned, there was but little left for his desire: but these very circumstances were silently operating to his injury; for they aroused envy and malice to a sleepless vigilance and determined resolution, to seize the first opportunity of dragging him from an elevation which he honored, and his right to which he had fairly earned, and which he forfeited by no fault. Ignorant, probably, of the extent of that malignity which watched for his ruin, he pursued his plans, buoyant with the anticipations shadowed forth by his sanguine spirit, and sent out another colony to Virginia. On reaching Carolina, they sought in vain for the fifteen men who had been left on the former voyage. The only vestiges they ever found of them were their bones, bleaching amid the ruins of their dilapidated and forsaken habitations. Of this last colony about one hundred remained, while the governor, at their request, sailed for England for further supplies. When he arrived, all England was alive to the apprehension of the threatened invasion of the far-famed Spanish Armada. Apprehension was not groundless, for Spain was not then what she is now. It was her day of glory and of strength. Her monarch, Philip, had many causes powerfully operating to stimulate him in his intended blow against England.

There were reasons political, personal, and religious. Elizabeth had espoused the cause of the Netherlands, she had refused the offers of marriage made her by Philip, and she was also a protestant. In all these particulars the King of Spain found causes of offence, and hence long meditated vengeance. His preparations for a descent upon England occupied him during three years, and his resources made him a most formidable enemy. Beside the wealth derived to his exchequer from the precious metals of America, he drew largely on the private fortunes of his nobility, and the result was a prodigious armament of nearly 140 ships, having on board 30,000 men, with 30,000 more under the Duke of Parma, ready to embark at a moment's warning from the Netherlands, with an additional 12,000 under the Duke of

Guise on the coast of Normandy. England never saw a moment
of greater peril, and England never met danger with a braver
spirit. The nation felt that under God, they must prove the bul-
warks of liberty of conscience and liberty of person to Europe.
The queen was now all queen, her lion heart was roused, and she
forgot all her woman's nonsense. It was no time to be fancying
herself beautiful and beloved, and to make herself a ridiculous
old fool in court pageants. She had a kingdom and a crown at
stake. She formed immediately a council of war, of which Raleigh was perhaps the most conspicuous member. Burleigh says
that the course pursued was chiefly on Raleigh's advice. No
man was more competent than he to give counsel. Intimately
acquainted with the resources of Spain, he was at the same time
a skilful admiral and an experienced general. In an incredibly
short period, so extensive and complete were the military preparations, that (according to the testimony of an eye-witness and
Spanish spy) the maritime counties were so furnished that upon
any one spot where a landing might be made, within 48 hours an
army of 20,000 men fully provided could be assembled, under the
command of the most experienced officers. The queen was as
cheerful as she was brave. It is enough to move the spirits, like
the trumpet's call to battle, when we read the heroic words of
Elizabeth at Tilbury. She was of the true Tudor blood—"My
loving people," (thus she spake) "we have been persuaded by
some that are careful of our safety, to take heed how we commit
ourselves to armed multitudes for fear of treachery; but I assure
you I do not desire to live to distrust my faithful and loving
people. Let tyrants fear! I have always so behaved myself.
that under God, I have placed my chiefest strength and safeguard
in the loyal hearts and good-will of my subjects; and, therefore.
I am come amongst you at this time, not as for my recreation or
sport, but being resolved in the midst and heat of the battle to
live or die amongst you all: to lay down for my God, for my
kingdom, and for my people, my honor and my blood, even in the
dust. I know that I have but the body of a weak and feeble
woman, but I have the heart of a king, and of a king of England
too, and think foul scorn that Parma or Spain or any prince of
Europe should dare to invade the borders of my realms."

Raleigh, though he had a command on land, determined that his services should be rendered on the sea. It would bring him first into contact with the enemy, and beside, his adventurous spirit better loved the ocean for the very dangers that attended it. In the midst of all his activity he found time hastily to dispatch two ships to his colonists, and then all his thoughts were for England. And yet in the face of all these facts, a modern English writer of deserved celebrity (Southey), states that the abandonment of his poor colonists in Carolina "must ever be a reproach to Raleigh." He says that no "attempt was made to relieve them, nor to ascertain their fate." He might have found proof of his inaccuracy in the volumes of Purchas. This writer informs us, under the date of 1602, that "Samuel Mace of Weymouth, a very sufficient mariner, who had been at Virginia *twice* before, was (in this year) employed thither by Sir Walter Raleigh, to find those people which were left there in 1587, *to whose succor he had sent five several times at his own charges.*"—Purchas, vol. iv., 1653.

It was on an evening in the latter part of July that the English first descried the enemy, which had entered the British channel the day before. The Armada came on majestically, the ships forming a semi-circle of seven miles in extent. The battle soon commenced, and lasted with intervals until the 1st of August (a period of ten days), when fairly vanquished in every engagement of the ships and sorely handled by the storms, the remainder of this proud navy, consisting of fifty-three vessels, was glad to escape to Spain, and there presented an appearance so shattered, and crews so exhausted, that its very presence was as mortifying as the capture of its companions. Raleigh shared in all the dangers of this protracted sea-fight, and the Lord High Admiral was happy to follow his counsel. After the victory, England found fresh cause for thankfulness in the revelations afforded by some of the prizes of the humane intentions of the Spaniards. Superstition and bigotry had not been unemployed in the great work of preparation to subdue England. The thumb-screws and iron boots with wedges, and whips, and manacles, with divers other ingenious devices to punish heresy and promote conversion, were dragged to the light of day, and their purposes explained by some of the pious ecclesiastics who were made prisoners. These instruments of torture were preserved as trophies, and are yet in the tower of London. In the midst of them, at least such was the fact not many years ago, was placed the instrument by which the gallant man of whom we write suffered death. It was hard to look upon the trophies and the axe, and in their unfortunate juxtaposition not to read a comment on worldly renown, and a satire on royal gratitude.

Amid all these exciting vicissitudes of war, by sea and by land, with the cares of his colonies and the duties of his many offices, Raleigh proved himself to be a wonderful man in the eyes of many, because he found time to address himself to the promotion of the interests of science, and to form a plan for the ready communication and correspondence of the learned among themselves. He is thus supposed to have laid the foundation of those national societies that have contributed so largely to the diffusion of scientific discovery. The secret of his accomplishing so much, however, was very obvious to all those who to activity of mind united *method* in the arrangement and dispatch of business.

His next enterprise was an expedition to restore the King of Portugal to his throne, from which he was excluded by Spain, and his services were deemed worthy of reward by Elizabeth.

Immediately after, we find him proposing to her majesty an expedition against Panama with a plan for intercepting the Plate fleet. On this, having embarked all his private fortune, he sailed in person, and was called back by a messenger from the queen almost as soon as he had reached the open sea. Alas! his sin was that he had ventured to love, and had not made her majesty the object. The queen sometimes granted monopolies to others, but there was one particular in which she tolerated no monopoly but in herself. She thought herself entitled by royal prerogative to all the love, and, like most of her sex who are exacting in that particular, she obtained none that was sincere. Raleigh had seen enough of the ladies of the bed-chamber to induce him to say that "they were like witches, who could do hurt, but could do no good." There was, however, among the queen's maids of honor one between whom and Raleigh there was formed a devoted attachment. Unlike the queen, Elizabeth Throckmorton was young and beautiful. It is probable that she was privately married to Raleigh before his departure on the Panama expedition, and when the story of the attachment of this young couple came to the knowledge of her majesty, she showed how far she herself was capable of understanding or feeling real love, by the sympathy she exhibited toward two of her fellow creatures, who loved and were worthy of each other. She sent Raleigh to the tower, and banished his wife from the court. His enemies now supposed that his ruin would be easy; but Raleigh understood the queen's character, and by a flattery of her vanity, which was altogether unworthy of him, was released from his confinement. The sunshine of the royal favor, however, rested not on him as brightly as before; yet we find him very soon in parliament, taking an active and wise part in its discussions.

The queen, notwithstanding her resentment, could not but appreciate the talents and services of the member for Devon, and had no wish to deprive herself of his really valuable aid. She therefore partially relented and made him a grant of the manor of Sherborne in Dorsetshire; but she permitted not his presence at the court. He retired to his new estate, and without wasting his strength in the vain attempt then to breast a current that was too strong for him, he was willing for the time to be forgotten by his enemies; but with the policy of true wisdom, determined, by the accomplishment of some great enterprise for his country's glory, far beyond the reach or ambition of the minions of a court, at once to regain the favor of the queen, and, placing himself on a loftier eminence than he had occupied before, to defeat the malice of his enemies. He turned his thoughts to conquest in America. Aware of what the Spaniards had done in the southern part of our continent, he resolved to rival their boldest achievements, and make the conquest of Guiana. His imagination was excited by the Spanish stories of El Dorado, as they termed it, and fabulous as they were, his was not the temper to indulge incredulity when he remembered that Cortes had proved Mexico to be a golden reality. The historians of Spanish conquests in this hemisphere had left on record tales of the city of Manoa and its wealth, depicting the gorgeous splendor of more than oriental luxury and riches; and Manoa, as yet unvisited by Englishmen, invited a

3

genius like that of Raleigh to its discovery and its conquest. There can be no doubt that he fully believed in its existence himself. In 1594, he dispatched an officer who had long been in his service to explore the territory. He, on his return, though he represented the enterprise as one full of difficulty, shook not Raleigh's resolution for a moment. In 1595, he fitted out a fleet of five vessels, and taking the command himself, sailed from Plymouth.

It would occupy too much time to speak particularly of this expedition. Suffice it to say, that its commander accomplished, probably, all that any man could do in his situation. It was not, however, done without cost. He thus touchingly describes his condition to the Lord High Admiral and Robert Cecil :—" Of the little remaining fortune I had, I have wasted, in effect, all herein. I have undergone many constructions ; been accompanied with many sorrows, with labor, hunger, heat, sickness and peril. From myself I have deserved no thanks, for I am returned a beggar and withered." To add to his misfortunes, his enemies had availed themselves of his absence to prepossess the queen's mind against him ; and his reception (notwithstanding his discoveries) was marked by coldness and suspicion.

The unfortunate victim of defamation and distrust found, however, a few who could appreciate what he had done, and although Elizabeth, in the spirit of parsimony, refused to colonize Guiana, they assisted him in his purpose of at least keeping up a communication with his distant discoveries until the arrival of brighter times. He was thus able to dispatch two vessels, under the command of an officer who had served with him on his first expedition.

Scarcely, however, had he sailed before Raleigh found work to do near home. Spain was still powerful ; the hatred of Philip had been slumbering only, since the defeat of the Armada. He had collected a formidable fleet at Cadiz, and meditated a descent upon England. The bold spirit of Raleigh conceived the daring design of not even permitting these ships to reach the open sea, but of destroying them within the very harbor of Spain. He had indeed recommended this plan in the case of the Armada, eight years before. The queen now saw, as she supposed, its wisdom, and determined to adopt it. Raleigh was appointed one of the four officers to execute it. The English fleet came on the coast of Spain after a very short run, and took the enemy completely by surprise. The harbor was commanded by extensive fortifications, and filled with vessels of war. The English dashed boldly in, Raleigh taking the lead in his ship, the Warspite, and disregarding the guns of the fort, which he answered only by a trumpet-blast of defiance as he passed, and making straight for the two largest ships, he anchored between them and opened upon them with alternate broadsides. For three hours the fight continued hotly. The Warspite was dreadfully shattered, and fearing that she would not float much longer, Raleigh went on board of the ship commanded by Essex, and told him that if he did not send the boats with men prepared for boarding, he would board from the Warspite at all risks. Essex told him he would second him in any step he took. Immediately Raleigh rowed back to his own vessel, and this seemed to be the signal for boarding to the English fleet. It was not more than fifteen minutes that Raleigh had been absent, but during that time some of the ships had got ahead of him. Resolved to be the first throughout the day, he immediately slipped his anchor, and passing the other vessels again, had the lead, and came within twenty yards of the San Philip. Here he anchored athwart the channel, so that no ship could pass him, and on attempting, by means of warping, to bring himself along side for boarding, the enemy slipped their cables and ran aground, and two of their largest vessels took fire and blew up. Raleigh succeeded, however, in capturing two others before their crews could either ground them or burn them. The history of naval warfare does not present a more remarkable achievement. Sir William Monson, who was in the engagement, speaks of it in his naval tracts, as the most disgraceful overthrow Spain ever received from England. In a battle which lasted from ten in the morning till late in the afternoon, fought in one of the harbors of Spain, and under the very guns of one of her best forts, seven ships, led by Raleigh in the Warspite, destroyed a fleet consisting of six galleons, three frigates, seventeen galleys, and the Mexican squadron, (in all fifty-five,) so completely that the bay of Cadiz was cleared and left in possession of the English.

The merit of this victory was due to Raleigh, and on his return the nation would have been gratified to see him once more restored to the royal favor; but the vindictive and capricious queen would not yet recall him to court.   In two months after his return from Cadiz, this ever active man had another vessel fitted out and on her way to Guiana, and during her absence he employed himself in projecting another naval expedition against Spain. He employed himself also in reconciling Essex and Robert Cecil, who were then the leading favorites of the queen, and the result was that by their joint agency he was recalled and reinstated in his offices at court.

And here we must pause long enough to describe Robert Cecil. Under the eye of his father Burleigh he had been bred a statesman and a courtier. What wonder is it then that he was the embodied representation of duplicity? Deformed in person, he was malignant in heart and splendid in intellect:—possibly the faults of person may have contributed to produce the qualities both of heart and head. Soured by the deformity which made it painful to associate with others, he brooded in the bitterness of his feelings over his condition, and studying the vices only of his fellow-men, learned to cherish a sarcastic contempt for his kind, which ended in an almost total disbelief of the possibility of human disinterestedness or virtue. Cautious, calculating, cunning, and forever intriguing, he cultivated, with incredible labor, a naturally fine mind, determined to achieve, by means of his understanding, a distinction which he could never hope to gain by personal grace or prowess. His suspicious temperament was doubtless increased by his consciousness of deformity. Clarendon has remarked of him that " it was as necessary for Cecil there should be treasons, as for the state that they should be prevented. And though he created none, yet he fomented some conspiracies that he might give frequent evidences of his loyalty."

Possessed of wonderful self-command, he never betrayed passion under any provocation, was the mirror of placid politeness, and as smooth a hypocrite as ever lived. If he had a rupture with a rival, he would glide into reconciliation seemingly most sincere, when interest required it ; but with a vengeful spirit that never slumbered he brooded over his hatred, and secretly preparing means to gratify it, he waited patiently for the day of reckoning. Never man better understood than Cecil, the worst parts of human nature; and never man had in his own heart, a better school in which to study them. It will readily be perceived that such a man as we have described was alike dangerous as a friend and an enemy. It was in the former character that he wished to be considered by Raleigh, when the knight was once more enjoying the favor of the queen and the honors of the court. Cecil, then, was but using Raleigh for the ruin of Essex: when he had finished that work, in the execution of the fallen favorite, he, with the most perfidious villainy sought, as we shall see, to destroy Raleigh.

It was about this period that Elizabeth aimed another blow at Spain, in which Raleigh bore his part on the sea, and returned not without success; though to an extent less than that which marked the memorable fight at Cadiz. And now we are to contemplate him in a new aspect. Wearied with the long and hard service through which he had passed, Sir Walter was glad to find repose for a time at his seat of Sherborne. But with him repose implied not idleness. He turned to his studies, and in the prosecution first of one subject and then of another, found all the rest he needed in the variety of his occupations, yet never lost sight of the busy world he had left for a time behind him. Mathematics, metaphysics, music, poetry, painting, history, antiquarian researches, ornamental gardening, these all, at times, occupied his attention; and it was one of the characteristics of this remarkable man's mind that amid all this diversity of subject, his genius was as powerful as it was varied. We confess that we look upon this great man with most pleasure, in these his hours stolen from ambition. Here (great and important as had been his achievements) we find him effecting triumphs, in our view, not less important, and in a more peaceful field. Here he held converse, not with crafty statesmen, who looked on language, as Talleyrand did, as an ingenious invention to hide men's thoughts; but with those who had found in letters a purer enjoyment than statesmen ever knew. His associates were such men as Sir Henry Spelman, learned John Selden, Camden, and the old chronicler Stowe—all honored names in the memory of the student of antiquities. Here, too, he communed with the minds of the poets of his day, and found enjoyment in the then fresh numbers of Shakespeare and Ben Jonson, Beaumont and Fletcher, Carew and Donne, before yet they had been cast before the world for its judgment. Here, too, his own muse was not idle, and the severity of graver studies alternated with the lighter play of his exuberant fancy. Nor wanted he a pupil in this pleasant retirement. Robert Cecil had for a son a youth of great promise, and was glad to confide him to the care of such a man as Raleigh. The young man was a visitor at Sherborne, and the constant associate of its hospitable owner: what (we must ask in a parenthesis,) what must have been the consummate villainy of his detestable father, when he could be secretly plotting the destruction of the man who with unsuspecting confidence and friendship was at that very moment acting the part of a father to his child?

Here he taught young Cecil to appreciate the loveliness of nature, and exposed the corruption of a court in the language of a poet:

" Heart-tearing cares and quiv'ring fears—
  Anxious sighs—untimely tears ;
    Fly—fly to courts—
    Fly to fond worldlings' sports :
  Where strain'd sardonic smiles are glosing still,
  And grief is forced to laugh against her will :
    Where mirth's but mummery,
    And sorrows only, real be.

" Fly from our country pastimes, fly,
  Sad troop of human misery !
    Come, serene looks,
    Clear as the crystal brooks,
  Or the pure azured heaven that smiles to see
  The rich attendance of our poverty.
  Peace and a secure mind,
  Which all men seek, we only find.

" Abused mortals, did you know
  Where joy, heart's ease and comforts grow,
    You'd scorn proud towers,
    And seek them in these bowers ;
  Where winds, perhaps, our woods may sometimes shake,
  But blustering care could never tempest make,
    Nor murmurs e'er come nigh us,
    Saving of fountains that glide by us "

In a more playful, though not a sweeter strain, does he give to his young companion his lessons in the poet's never-failing subject —love.

> Shepherd, what's love ? I pray thee, tell !
> It is that fountain, and that well,
> Where pleasure and repentance dwell :
> It is perhaps that saucing bell
> That tolls all in to heaven or hell ;
> And this is love, as I heard tell.
>
> Yet, what is love ? Good shepherd, saine !
> It is a sunshine mixed with rain ;
> It is a toothache or like pain :
> It is a game where none doth gain.
> The lass saith *no*, and would full fain !
> And this is love as I hear saine.
>
> Yet, what is love ? Good shepherd show !
> A thing that creeps—it cannot go—
> A prize that passeth to and fro,
> A thing for one, a thing for moe ;
> And he that proves shall find it so ;
> And, shepherd, this is love, I trow.

Hear him next sing his high thoughts of scornful disdain in the contemplation of female fickleness :

> Shall I, like a hermit, dwell
> On a rock or in a cell—
> Calling home the smallest part
> That is missing of my heart,
> To bestow it—when I may
> Meet a rival, every day ?
> If she undervalue me,
> What care I how fair she be ?
>
> Were her tresses angel gold—
> If a stranger may be bold,
> Unrebuked, unafraid,
> To convert them to a braid,
> And with little more ado,
> Work them into bracelets too !
> If the mind be grown so free,
> What care I how rich it be ?
>
> Were her hands as rich a prize
> As her hair or precious eyes,
> If she lay them out to take
> Kisses for good manners' sake,

And let every lover skip
From her hand unto her lip :
If she seem not pure to me,
What care I how pure she be ?

No—she must be perfect snow,
In effect as well as show ;
Warming, but as snow-balls do,
Not like fire, by burning too ;
But when she by change hath got
To her heart a second lot,
Then, if others share with me,
Farewell, her, whate'er she be.

These, however, must suffice as specimens of Raleigh's hours of tuneful idleness, and yet the temptation is not small to linger yet longer in his garden of poesy. But much yet remains to be told, and we will therefore now return to the rougher realities of history, which ordinarily possesses no quality belonging to poetry, unless it be fiction.

The time had now come for the leaf that had faded and wilted, and was now withered to dryness, to fall from the tree. Elizabeth had heard herself called to follow poor Essex into that eternity whither she had capriciously and prematurely sent him. It was to her a sad summons, for the proud woman hated to die. If one could envy royalty, the spectacle of the dying queen would be no bad cure for his malady. She had said, after many years of experience, "to be a king and wear a crown, is a thing more glorious to them that see it, than it is pleasant to them that bear it." Her death gave utterance to the same truth with more eloquent emphasis still. There was the once wise, brave and proud daughter of the Tudor race, sunk in a melancholy so profound that no entreaties could prevail on her to take food or medicine. She refused to be placed upon her bed because she thought that if once laid there, she should never rise again. Cushions were arranged on the floor of her chamber, and there she sat day and night for a week, refusing food, rejecting sleep, entirely indifferent to everything around her, and breathing forth the burden of her soul in groans and sighs. Death was her companion, and with him her spirit held secret communings, reserved for the revelations of another day. The only case in which she could be roused occurred when her council spoke to her of the succession to the throne. The last flash of her old queen-like spirit shot up into a blaze, and then the light went out forever. "I told you," (thus she spoke) "that my seat had been the seat of kings, and I will have no rascal to succeed me! Trouble me no more. He who comes after me, must be a king. I will have none but our cousin of Scotland." Posterity, alas! has furnished those who have thought, not without reason, that in her successor she had both king and rascal combined.

When Elizabeth died, Raleigh lost his best support, for she knew his value and would not permit his ruin. Possibly her shrewdness might have discovered the hypocrisy of the friendship which Cecil professed for him. The cunning secretary had foreseen her death, and with characteristic villainy had opened a secret correspondence with James, who he knew must be her successor. With no little industry had he taken pains to be informed of the peculiarities of the pedantic fool who then held the throne of Scotland, and he accommodated his conduct to the whims and follies of the future king of England. True, Cecil had murdered Essex, and James had no love for any who were concerned in that deed of blood: true, Cecil had borne no small share in sending the mother of James, the lovely queen of Scots, to the block: but what were obstacles like these in the way of such a man as Cecil? An ordinary being, possessed of nothing but the mere instincts of humanity, would have been led by those instincts alone to retire in despair from the task of conciliating and becoming a favorite with the man whose own mother he had helped to murder: but the instincts of Cecil were hardly those of humanity; and when we find that he had actually succeeded, and became the confidential adviser and secretary of James, one scarcely knows which to pronounce most wonderful, the cool effrontery of the murderer and the villain, or the unfilial forgetfulness of the unnatural wretch, who took to his confidence his mother's murderer.

In the secret correspondence of Cecil with James (which would have cost the former his head had it been but suspected by the proud old queen), he took care to play upon his cowardice and arouse his prejudices by anticipation against those who were at all renowned in war. The miserable old woman who, though he wore a crown, yet shuddered at the sight of a naked sword, and cried out "*treason*" when his carver accidentally nicked his finger, which, with royal politeness he had thrust into the dish, was easily led to believe that Raleigh, and men like Raleigh, would keep his kingdom perpetually embroiled in war.

James, therefore, had scarcely mounted the throne before it was plain that the sun of Raleigh's prosperity had set. The deprivation of his offices was among the first acts of the new king's reign : this was the secret work of Cecil, but little did the victim suppose that the deep-laid schemes of the cunning secretary, whom he now found to be his enemy, reached far beyond the mere loss of office, and were destined to find their consummation in his ignominious death. To say that James was an egregious fool, is not necessarily to say that he was either mischievous or dangerous, for a mere fool may be harmless and call for our pity as one of heaven's innocents, but to say that James was a *conceited* fool is at once to pronounce that he was a very dangerous man ; for as a king he had power enough to do harm, and as a fool he was wiser in his own conceit than seven men who could render a reason ; so that he presented the fearful union of oracular stupidity with irresponsible power. It was not difficult to create in such a mind as that of James a dislike of such a man as Raleigh. The one, profoundly impressed with a sense of his own sagacity, loved, by secret, though clumsy management, to astonish the court, as he supposed, with some magnificent outbreak of royal wisdom, as asinine as it was pretending ; while the other, who had naturally "high thoughts seated in a heart of courtesy," knew not how to gain honorable ends by any other than honorable means, and felt contempt for the royal sagacity. James was a coward—Raleigh was brave. James was ready to purchase peace of Spain even on inglorious terms—Raleigh thought of England's glory, and looked on Spain as a proud enemy that ought to be crushed. James had no English feeling, and looked with no pride to England's ships and sailors—Raleigh looked far ahead, and saw, what facts have since proved, that the strength of England must be in ships and sailors. James professed to be a man of letters, and Raleigh was so. The difference was between one who reads and one who thinks as well as reads. James might, perhaps, tell readily what he had read in Duns Scotus or Thomas Aquinas; and Raleigh could tell whether Duns Scotus and the seraphic doctor had written sense or nonsense. With the one, learning was the end of thought—with the other, learning was the material with which thought began. Raleigh had a mind strikingly original—the mind of James was but the lumber-garret in which confusedly to stow away other men's thoughts.

As soon as the wily Cecil had found that his efforts to excite the royal prejudice against Raleigh were successful, his next step was to ensnare his victim in toils which his own hand had long be n secretly preparing, and by an accusation of treason, which he knew to be without foundation, to bring his dreaded rival to the block. With the full light that modern historical research has shed on this subject, it is impossible not to abhor the character of Robert Cecil. It was he who, at the very moment when he professed to be the friend of Raleigh—at the very time when his own son was sheltered under the roof of Raleigh, and was receiving at his hands not hospitality merely, but the exhibition of an affectionate interest little short of parental—it was he who under such circumstances was deliberately plotting the future murder of the man on whom he fawned, and who stood in the way of his unholy ambition. A poor, weak fool, Lord Cobham, was involved in transactions to which Cecil well knew he could give the aspect of a traitorous intercourse with foreign powers, and, relying on the fears and stupidity of Cobham, he hoped by his testimony to implicate and convict Raleigh. This was the outline of his plan, and it needed for its successful accomplishment nothing but the proper selection of a court and jury sufficiently compliant, a vindictive prosecuting attorney, and a total perversion of the established laws of evidence. Most men bent on the perpetration of judicial murder would have paused in the contemplation of these difficult prerequisites to the conviction of an innocent man ; but Robert Cecil was not one to be deterred from his object by difficulties. He moulded the court (of which he himself was a member) to suit his ends. He knew that Coke, the king's attorney, could be vindictive enough, if it were but whispered to him that royalty expected it; his jury it was easy to select, and as for the law, the court was its proper expounder.

When villainy had made all things ready, Raleigh, most unexpectedly to himself, was arrested to answer to the charge of being a traitor to his country by entering into secret engagements with Spain, the nation of all others which he had most uniformly opposed in its attempts, and to which he had probably done more injury by his wisdom and prowess than any other man then living in England.

From the moment of his arrest the very consciousness of his innocence convinced him that he was a doomed man; and he had too much sagacity not to see who it was that was thirsting for his blood, and had prepared the machinery for his condemnation.

But in this new and appalling position, in which the providence of heaven had placed him, he was true to his lofty character. There is something to command more than respect: we feel reverence as we look upon the calm dignity and self-possession with which he rose above the feelings of ordinary men, and girded himself in his moral and intellectual strength to meet the emergency. We hear from him no clamors about the persecution which was dragging him to the scaffold; no cry against the premeditated injustice which he knew to be in store for him. These were subjects to be treated of in another place than a prison— these were themes for the hall of justice. It was not the custom of that day to allow to the accused the benefit of professional aid on his trial. He was aware, therefore, that he was called on to meet (without having made law his study) all the skill and astuteness of Coke (the ablest lawyer of his day), whetted to keenness by personal hatred, and all the inclination in an unfriendly bench to pervert and wrest the law to his ruin. The unfortunate prisoner too knew full well that he had not the sympathy of the people. To his honor be it said, that he had never stooped by unworthy means to make himself a favorite with the populace. Like a great judge of modern times, the only popularity he valued was "that which follows not that which is run after." Those who knew him, and were in immediate employment about him, loved him to the last with a fidelity that death only could destroy; but he was too noble to court indiscriminate professions of love by hypocritical pretences.

With the loftiness of his soul unabated, he came to stand before his accusers, and offer to the world that most sublime of earthly spectacles, a great man struggling with the tempests of adversity, and never forgetting that he is a great man. Impartial posterity has long since recorded its righteous verdict on this most unrighteous trial. History has indelibly stamped its mark of reprobation on the actors in this judicial murder. The lustre which, in the eye of the jurist, gathers around the name of Coke, as one of the fathers in his profession, is tarnished when memory recalls his brutal ferocity in the trial of Raleigh. No biographer has yet attempted to palliate the infamy of his conduct, and his warmest eulogists have been constrained to pass by this transaction of his life in silence, or briefly to hint at it with expressions of regret.

A few extracts from the trial will be sufficient to show the treatment of Raleigh, first premising that the only testimony against him consisted of the statements of Lord Cobham, who, by the way, had given statements and counter-statements no less than *five* times. After Coke had made his charges, Raleigh remarked, "Your words cannot condemn me : my innocency is my defence. Prove one of those things wherewith you have charged me, and I will confess the whole indictment, and that I am the horriblest traitor that ever lived—that I am worthy to be crucified with a thousand torments."

Coke answered, "Nay, I will prove all. Thou art a monster—thou hast an English face, but a Spanish heart."

" Let me answer for myself," exclaimed the insulted prisoner.

" Thou shalt not," cries the attorney.

" It concerneth my *life*," said Raleigh.

" Oh, do I touch you ?" cried Coke, and then proceeded with a repetition of the charges in the indictment. When he had finished, the prisoner quietly remarked, "I do not hear yet that you have spoken one word against me. If my Lord Cobham be a traitor, what is that to me ?"

Coke's answer was so remarkable, that Shakespeare, Raleigh's companion and friend, did not fail by his satire to keep alive its memory. In answer to Raleigh's question, how Cobham's treason could affect him, Coke bawled out, "All that he did was by thy instigation, thou viper, for I *thou* thee, thou traitor."   It was in allusion to this that the poet puts into the mouth of Sir Toby Belch, in "Twelfth Night," his advice to Sir Andrew Aguecheek, touching the proper mode of penning a challenge: "Go write it in a martial hand : be crust and brief—it is no matter how witty, so it be eloquent and full of invention ; taunt him with the licence of ink : if thou *thoust* him some thrice, it shall not be amiss ; and as many lies as will lie in thy sheet of paper, although the sheet were big enough for the bed of Ware in England, set 'em down."

Raleigh's reply to this impertinence was, "It becometh not a man of quality and virtue to call me so ; but I take comfort in it —it is all you can do."   Coke, with a despicable little spirit of triumph, asks, "Have I angered you ?"   "I am in no case to be angry," was the dignified reply.   No, truly, he was too immeasurably Coke's superior on this occasion, and indeed on every other involving aught else but a mere knowledge of law, to be made angry by the scurrility of such a creature.

The only instance in the whole trial in which Raleigh's indignation appears for a moment to have been roused was when the attorney alleged that Cobham had declared that he and Raleigh meant to destroy the king and his issue.   It was afterwards conclusively shown that no such speech had ever been uttered. Raleigh on this allegation exclaimed, "I beseech you, my Lords, let it be proved that Cobham so expressed himself.   You try me by the Spanish inquisition if you proceed only by the circumstances without witnesses.   If by the statute law, by the civil law, and by God's word, it be required that there must be two witnesses at the least, bear with me if I desire one.   Let Cobham be here—let him speak it.   Call my accuser before my face, and I have done.   All is but his accusation.   No other thing hath been brought against me, and yet this accusation he never subscribed.   I beseech you, my Lords, let this Lord be sent for— charge him on his soul—on his allegiance to the king.   If he affirm it, I am content to be found guilty."

And why was not this reasonable request granted ?   Cobham

was then in the very building in which the court sat. King James himself (the despicable fool who sanctioned all this mockery of justice) shall answer. "If," said he, afterward, "Cobham could have spoken one word against Raleigh, his enemies would have brought him from Constantinople." What, then, shall we say of the man who, knowing this, yet permitted the murderous iniquity to be carried to its consummation?

At length the attorney having failed more than once in his proofs, broke forth into abuse, and, on being requested by the court to restrain his anger, took his seat in a passion, refusing to proceed with the cause. The bench, forgetful of its dignity, supplicated him to proceed, and at length yielding to persuasion, he arose again, but only to be more abusive still. Turning to Raleigh, whom he had before called a Spider of Hell, he thus broke out, "Thou art the most vile and execrable traitor that ever lived!" Sir Walter calmly replied, "You speak indiscreetly, barbarously and uncivilly." "I want words," roared Coke, "sufficient to express thy viperous treasons." "I think you want words indeed," was the reply, "for you have spoken one thing half a dozen times." "Thou art an odious fellow," said Coke; "thy name is hateful to all the realm of England for thy pride." "It will go near," answered Raleigh, "to prove a measuring cast between you and me, Mr. Attorney."

These specimens suffice to show us what prospect the prisoner had before him, and prepare us to hear without surprise that he was pronounced guilty.

He doubtless expected this verdict—his dignity and self-possession never forsook him. When asked in the usual form why judgment and execution of death should not pass against him, he rose, and without the least perturbation, said, "My Lords, the jury have found me guilty. They must do as they are directed. I can say nothing why judgment should not proceed. You see whereof Cobham hath accused me. You remember his protestations that I was never guilty. I only desire the king should know of the wrongs done me since I came hither, by Mr. Attorney." Then, after a solemn denial of the charges, he added, "I recommend my wife and son, of tender years, unbrought up, to the king's compassion." Sentence of death was then pronounced, and he was taken to prison. "And thus," says an old writer, "was he tried out of his life by the bawling of the king's counsel on one side, and the bench's insisting on a confession extorted from the Lord Cobham out of fear on the other. And thus did his adversaries reap dishonor and reproach in their victory, while he received triumphant applauses in his overthrow, like some flowers which are sweeter in their fall than others in their bloom. He stood with them at bay from morning till night to the great admiration of the hearers, who all thought that a man of such understanding and experience would hardly be drawn into a plot so foul and foolish. Divers who went thither his enemies, went away with commiseration of his injuries and misfortunes, thinking never man spake better for himself." One of his auditors says "he behaved himself so worthily, so wisely, so temperately, that in half a day the mind of all the company was changed from the extremest hate to the extremest pity."

One of his enemies, who hastened to carry the news of his conviction to the king, was constrained to say that whereas when he saw him first, he was so led with the common hatred, that he would have gone a hundred miles to see him hanged; he would, ere he parted, have gone a thousand to save his life.

We are not ignorant that a modern writer, Napier, has expressed the opinion, founded on the dispatches of Beaumont, the French ambassador, that Raleigh "must have been aware of Cobham's treason." He may have been so without being a participator in it; though we confess the evidence of knowledge even is less satisfactory to us than it appears to have been to Mr. Napier. The purpose of Raleigh he supposes to have been, to make himself master of the plot, get Cobham into his power in Jersey, where Raleigh was governor, and then by disclosing it, to make terms with the king and gain his favor. The witness for this is, after all, but Aubrey, on whom Mr. Napier himself places but little reliance. Raleigh was probably too sagacious ever to have risked everything on such a clumsy contrivance, where premature discovery of his knowledge might implicate him in the treason. Beside, if he had the knowledge supposed, and received it, as Mr. Napier thinks he did, an immediate revelation would have helped his cause with the king quite as much as the clumsy Jersey contrivance.

And now we must look upon this great man in prison awaiting, though innocent, a traitor's death. Protesting his innocence, he wrote once to the king, but in vain. There is, however, one letter preserved of his which it would be unpardonable to omit. It was addressed to his wife, and presents a picture of the man far more vivid than any we can offer by description. It is hard to find within the range of our literature a more touching, appropriate or beautiful composition:

"You shall now receive, my dear wife, my last words in these my last lines. My love I send you, that you may keep it when I am dead; and my counsel that you may remember it when I am no more. I would not, by my will, present you with sorrows, dear Bess—let them go into the grave with me, and be buried in the dust. And, seeing it is not the will of God that ever I shall see you more in this life, bear it patiently and with a heart like thyself. First, I send you all the thanks which my heart can conceive, or my words can express, for your many travails and care taken for me; which, though they have not taken effect as you wished, yet my debt to you is not the less. But pay it I never shall in this world. Secondly, I beseech you for the love you bear me living, do not hide yourself many days after my death. But, by your travails, seek to help your miserable fortunes, and the right of your poor child. Thy mournings cannot avail me— I am but dust. Thirdly, you shall understand that my land was conveyed *bona fide* to my child. I trust my blood will quench their malice that have thus cruelly murdered me, and that they will not seek also to kill thee and thine with extreme poverty. To what friend to direct thee I know not, for all mine have left me in the true time of trial, and I plainly perceive that my death was determined from the first day. Most sorry I am, God knows, that, being thus surprised with death, I can leave you in no better estate. But God hath prevented all my resolutions—even that great God that ruleth all in all. But if you can live free from want, care for no more; the rest is but vanity. Love God, and begin betimes to repose yourself on Him, and therein shall you find true and lasting riches and endless comfort. For the rest, when you have travailed, and wearied your thoughts over all sorts of worldly cogitation, you shall but sit down by sorrow in the end. Teach your son also to love and fear God while he is yet young, that the fear of God may grow up with him. And then God will be a husband to you and a father to him—a husband and a father which cannot be taken from you. When I am gone, no doubt you shall be sought to by many, for the world thinks that I was very rich. But take heed of the pretences of men and their affections. For they last not but in honest and worthy men; and no greater misery can befall you in this life than to become a prey and afterward to be despised. I speak not this, God knows, to dissuade you from marriage, for it will be best for you both in respect of the world and of God. As for me, I am no more yours, nor you mine. Death has cut us asunder, and God hath divided me from the world, and you from me. Remember your poor child for his father's sake, who chose you and loved you in his happiness. Get those letters, if it be possible, which I writ to the Lords, wherein I sued for my life. God is my witness it was for you and yours that I desired life. But it is true that I disdain myself for begging it; for know it, dear wife, that your son is the son of a true man, and one who, in his own respect, despiseth death and all his misshapen and ugly forms. I cannot write much. God he knoweth how hardly I steal this time while others sleep. And it is also high time that I should separate my thoughts from the world. Beg my dead body which, living, was denied thee, and either lay it at Sherborne, if the land continue, or in Exeter church by my father and mother. I can say no more—time and death call me away. The everlasting, powerful, infinite, and omnipotent God, who is goodness itself, the true life and true light, keep thee and thine, have mercy on me, and teach me to forgive my persecutors and accusers, and send us to meet in his glorious kingdom. My dear wife, farewell! Bless my poor boy—pray for me, and let my good God hold you both in his arms! Written with the dying hand of, sometime thy husband, but now, alas! overthrown.

     " Yours that was, but now not my own,

                 " WALTER RALEIGH."

When the day of execution arrived, James, by a display of childish mummery so ridiculous that he contrived to render ludicrous even the horrid solemnities of a public execution, was pleased to reprieve first Cobham, next Lord Grey, and finally Raleigh, who was in momentary expectation of being brought to the block, and anticipated no postponement. Let it not, however, be hence too hastily supposed that the royal pedant had a heart to appreciate the manly virtues of his unhappy prisoner, or a conscience to scourge him for his cruel persecution of the innocent. It was no kingly benevolence that led to the reprieve; it was, as subsequent events proved, but the refinement of a cruelty that loved to protract misery, and that suspended the blow, not with the benevolent intention of sparing the victim, but only that the sword might fall the heavier when it did descend. And now let us look once more on Raleigh in captivity—a grievous captivity of more than twelve weary years.

Consigned to the tower, the first act of his noble, true-hearted wife, was to solicit the privilege of sharing a prison with her persecuted husband. She clung the closer because fortune frowned, and proved the holy deathlessness of her devoted love. She was worthy of the high-souled being who called her wife. Every act proved it. When the despicable thing who occupied the throne, not content with conniving at a murder, stooped next to the meanness of a robbery and deprived Raleigh of his lands, to confer them on one of the swarm of his needy countrymen, who flocked around him to swear that he was a second Solomon, what was the conduct of this faithful woman? She sought the royal presence, and with all the affection and earnestness of a sorrowing, broken-hearted wife and mother, implored the king to have compassion on her and hers, and not to consign them to utter beggary. The courtiers, moved by sympathy, looked on in silence, and in pity for her woes hoped that her sorrows might find some alleviation in the grant of her prayer. The only answer she could obtain from the royal brute was that he must have the lands for Car, one of his favorites. Lady Raleigh, remembering her noble birth and breeding, and, with a lofty burst of indignant feeling, worthy of her husband's wife, scorned to repeat her request; but, falling on her knees before the amazed courtiers and the affrighted king, lifted her hands to heaven, and in the bitterness of her spirit, appealing to the King of kings, besought the God of Heaven to remember her wrongs, to look upon the justice of her cause, and in his own good time to visit those who had so unrighteously brought her and hers to beggary and ruin. It was a fearful malediction from an oppressed and injured woman. While the imprecation yet rung in the ears of the alarmed and astonished king, she rose, took her child by the hand, and with an air of queenly majesty, retired. History would almost lead us to think, as we recall the fate of the infatuated house of Stuart, that her imprecation was heard and answered in heaven.*

But poor as she was, she yet felt herself rich in the possession of her captive husband, to whom she hastened, and whose privations she felt it a privilege to share. And now what was to become of him? We have seen that his life had been one of enterprise and activity. Immured within the gloomy walls of the tower, what shall now relieve the wearisome hours of an unusual and unnatural state of quietude? Books—God be thanked for them—books. We have seen that the prisoner had ever been a student. Were no resources then left to him with his wonderful versatility of talent? The oppressor "held his body bound, but knew not what a range his spirit took." He could sit and sing, "My mind to me a kingdom is." And so sweet was the note, that Prince Henry, the heir apparent to the throne, as rich in intellect and virtue as his father was deficient in both, ex-

---

* It is curious to follow the history of Raleigh's persecutors and enemies and mark their respective fates. The *Stuarts* were hurled from the throne in disgrace. *Robert Cecil* died the miserable victim of remorse, "pushed," as he said, "from the shore of comfort."

"*Cobham*," says Osborn, "died in a room, ascended by a ladder, at a poor woman's house in the Minories, formerly his laundress, rather of hunger than of any more natural disease."

Lewis Stukeley, who acted as a spy on him after his return from Guiana, was commonly known as "Sir Judas," and was finally arraigned at the bar of the King's Bench for clipping the gold coin of the realm, and the miserable Frenchman, Manourie, the other spy, fled the kingdom, because he was involved in Stukeley's guilt, acknowledging that he had falsely accused Raleigh, and was therefore overtaken by God's judgment upon him.

Coke lost favor at court, but died rich, after a life of miserable domestic unhappiness.

claimed, "No monarch in christendom but my father would keep such a bird as this in a cage."

With this noble youth, who had qualities that befit a king, Raleigh became an especial favorite. All the collected stores of the wisdom and experience of many years were freely taxed by the poor prisoner for the amusement and instruction of the prince. Henry thirsted after knowledge, and could appreciate (youth though he was) the genius and attainments of Raleigh. He therefore sought his society and learned to love him. Many an hour of confinement in that sad abode passed by on rapid wings, while Raleigh was spreading the exuberant riches of his own well-stored and ever fertile mind before his affectionate and attentive prince.

It was for him that, amid the gloom of a prison, and with but imperfect aids for reference, Raleigh produced that most astonishing work—his History of the World. Well has it been described as "an extraordinary monument of human labor and genius." Vast in subject, profound in learning and research, wise in its reflections, and beautiful in style, it was composed, as has been well said, "not in the luxury of lettered and philosophic ease, surrounded by books and friends, but in imprisonment, solitude and sorrow—not in the enthusiastic consciousness of unimpaired powers, but with a mind which had been harassed by a cruel persecution, and sickened by hope deferred." * But this was not all: various essays, and on various subjects, were written for the prince by Raleigh, and they were not less wise than various. He taught Henry that ships and seamen were to be England's true strength, and instructing him in naval architecture and navigation the prince had but just commenced build-

* There are but few incidents in English literary history more absurdly ludicrous than the pretended "discovery," as he calls it, of the elder D'Israeli, that Sir Walter Raleigh did not write the "History of the World," which appeared under his name. The "discoverer" drew upon himself the ridicule and chastisement he deserved. Mr. Napier thus speaks of D'Israeli's pretended discovery: "This piece of secret history, alike revolting and preposterous, was well rebutted by Mr. Tytler; but it has been more recently examined, and with signal chastisement, given to the winds, in a small publication, little known, we suspect, though forming one of the most learned and acute contributions to literary history that has appeared in our day." The work alluded to is "Curiosities of Literature, by J. D'Israeli, Esq., Illustrated by Bolton Corney, Esq."

ing a ship when, at the age of eighteen, he was cut down by death. It was a dreadful blow to Raleigh, for he had learned to love him, and he lost a friend who was determined to persevere until he procured the liberation of the poor captive. But if friends fell, enemies too were gathered in by the mighty reaper, death. The time came for Robert Cecil to go to a world where no tricks of statesmen ever turn the current of justice. Life had become to him a weary load. "Ease and pleasure," said the dying man, "quake to hear of death; but my life, full of cares and miseries, desireth to be dissolved." Well might he say "full of cares and miseries," and not the least among them was the misery of remorse. He had climbed the ladder of ambition to its very top, and what had he gained by his toilsome labor? One of his own letters, written soon after he had succeeded in convicting poor Raleigh, answers the question. "Rest content," says he, to Sir John Harrington, "and give heed to one that hath sorrowed in the bright lustre of a court, and gone heavily even on the best seeming fair ground. 'Tis a great task to prove one's honesty, and yet not spoil one's fortune. I wish I waited now in your presence-chamber, with ease at my food and rest in my bed. I am pushed from the shore of comfort, and know not where the winds and waves of a court will bear me. I know it bringeth little comfort on earth, and he is, I reckon, no wise man that looketh that way to heaven." And thus went to his last account the great Robert Cecil. His death, doubtless, accelerated the release of Raleigh, but had it been longer delayed, the prisoner's resources would still have made confinement tolerable. It is wonderful to remark the variety and extent of his intellectual pursuits. Fitting up a small building within the walls as a laboratory, he prosecuted his chemical studies, and when tired of his retorts and alembics, he turned with facility to history or politics, or philosophy. Not even his muse was suffered to slumber. Age, indeed, had brought a change of subjects, but age could not kill his imagination. His numbers flowed as sweetly as before, though more solemnly than when he sang of love to Cecil's son. He now invoked the muse for consolation in the dreariness and gloom of a prison. His lyre was tuned to holier music :

' Rise, O my soul, with thy desires to heaven,
And with divinest contemplation use
Thy time, when time's eternity is given,
And let vain thoughts no more thy mind abuse ;
But down in darkness let them lie ;
So live thy better—let thy worse thoughts die.

" And thou, my soul, inspired with holy flame,
View and review with most regardful eye,
That holy cross, whence thy salvation came,
On which thy Saviour and thy sin did die ;
For in that sacred object is much pleasure,
And in that Saviour is my life—my treasure.

" To thee, O Jesus, I direct my eyes,
To thee my hands, to thee my humble knees,
To thee my heart shall offer sacrifice,
To thee my thoughts, who my thoughts only sees,
To thee myself—myself and all I give,
To thee I die—to thee I only live !"

Another of his productions will serve to show how he who had seen the world in every variety of aspect, had learned to estimate its true worth, and, though it may not prove very complimentary to human nature, it will at least serve to show that

" He was a deep observer, and he looked
Quite through the thoughts of men."

The man of candor and experience will probably think that the absence of compliment is less the fault of Raleigh than of human nature.

" Go, soul ! the body's guest,
Upon a thankless errand,
Fear not to touch the best,
The *truth* shall be thy warrant.
Go, since I needs must die,
And give the world the *lie.*

" Go, tell the Court it glows
And shines like rotten wood—
Go, tell the Church it shows
What's good and doth no good.
If Church and Court reply,
Then give them both the lie.

" Tell potentates they live
  Acting by others' actions,
  Not loved unless they give,
  Not strong, but by their factions.
  If potentates reply,
  Give potentates the lie.

" Tell men of high condition,
  That rule affairs of state,
  Their purpose is ambition,
  Their practice only hate.
  And if they once reply,
  Then give them all the lie.

" Tell zeal it lacks devotion,
  Tell love it is but lust,
  Tell time it is but motion,
  Tell flesh it is but dust.
  And wish them not reply,
  For thou must give the lie.

" Tell physic of her boldness,
  Tell skill it is pretension,
  Tell charity of coldness,
  Tell law it is contention.
  And as they do reply,
  So give them still the lie.

" Tell fortune of her blindness,
  Tell nature of decay,
  Tell friendship of unkindness,
  Tell justice of delay.
  And if they will reply,
  Then give them all the lie."

One more extract, and we will proceed with our story. It consists of the lines found written by Raleigh in his bible:

" E'en such is time, which takes in trust
  Our youth, our joys, and all we have !
  And pays us naught but age and dust,
  Which in the dark and silent grave,
  When we have wandered all our ways,
  Shuts up the story of our days,
  And from which grave and earth and dust,
  The Lord shall raise me up, I trust."

Is it not strange that the charge of impiety should have been brought against the man who thus expresses himself? We can understand, in some degree, how his enemies, while he was yet alive, sought by every species of defamation to blacken his character: but what shall be said of a modern writer and historian of celebrity who claimed the possession of a more than ordinary philosophic spirit, and yet lends himself to the repetition of this and other most unfounded accusations? This will we say, that David Hume was not a philosophic historian, for many of his inaccuracies might have been avoided, had he been willing to sacrifice indolence to duty, and encounter the labor of research; he was not a philosophic historian, because his prejudices sometimes made him an eulogist, when he should have been an impartial judge. No man will ever form a correct opinion of any monarch of the house of Stuart from his pages. Hume has no sympathy with the deep-seated love of liberty and sense of justice that glowed in the bosoms of those who opposed the arbitrary claim of prerogative in his favorite kings. Poorer stuff than the Stuarts to make kings of, never lived in England, and yet no one would learn it from Hume. James the pedant was one of his favorites, and therefore has he done injustice to Raleigh, in more than one particular. If he ever read Raleigh's History of the World, then was he guilty of wilful misrepresentation in accusing him of want of Christian faith: throughout the work there runs an uniform strain of Christian faith and doctrine, sustained by constant reference to the Scriptures as being the word of God:—if he never read it, what right had he to pronounce on Raleigh's opinions until he did read it? Some of the passages in that book would not be misplaced in a theological treatise, and remind one of the gorgeous richness of that "Shakespeare of divinity" as he has been called, Bishop Jeremy Taylor. Take as a specimen a noble strain of Christian philosophy in commenting on the folly of preferring the perishing body to the immortal part. "And though our own eyes do everywhere behold the sudden and resistless assaults of death, and nature assureth us by never-failing experience, and reason by infallible demonstration, that our times upon the earth have neither certainty nor durability; that our bodies are but the anvils of pain and diseases, and our minds the

hives of unnumbered cares, sorrows and passions; yet such is
the blindness and true unhappiness of our condition, and the dark
ignorance which covereth the eyes of our understanding, that we
only prize, pamper and exalt this vassal and slave of death, and
forget altogether, or only remember at our cast away leisure, the
imprisoned, immortal soul, which can neither die with the repro-
bate, nor perish with the mortal parts of virtuous men. But
when is it we examine this great account? Never while we have
our vanity left us to spend. We plead for titles till our breath
fails us; dig for riches while our strength enableth us; exercise
malice while we can revenge; and then, when time hath beaten
from us youth, pleasure and health, and nature itself hateth the
hour of old age, we remember, with Job, that we must go the
way whence we shall not return, and that our bed is made ready
for us in the dark;—and then I say, looking, over-late, into the
bottom of our conscience, which pleasure and ambition had locked
up from us all our lives, we behold therein the fearful images of
our actions past, and withal this terrible inscription, that God
will bring every work into judgment that man hath done under
the sun. But let us not flatter our immortal souls herein; for to
neglect God all our lives, and know that we neglect him—to
offend God voluntarily, and know that we offend him, (casting
our hopes on the peace which we trust to make at parting,) is no
other than a rebellious presumption, and that which is worst of
all, a contemptuous laughing to scorn and deriding of God, his
laws and precepts. They hope in vain, who in this sort flatter
themselves with God's mercy."

Surely this is not the language of a man chargeable with impiety. At length he obtained his release, and humiliating enough
is it to be obliged to add, that he paid for it with money given to
two of the relatives of the favorite Buckingham.

The moment he was free, his thoughts turned once more to
Guiana. He had never forgotten it during the twelve sad years
of his confinement. What little he could save from the wreck of
his once splendid fortune was employed in sending agents at least
once in every two years to keep up his communication with this
land of his hopes. Some of the natives had visited England in
his ships, and had interviews with him in the tower. And now,

when not much of worldly wealth remained, his generous wife
parted with the little she had left of her patrimony, and with a
better treasure still in her son, Walter, just grown up to manhood,
who, greatly resembling his father in the noble traits of his character, embarked with him for Guiana. And now the infamous
treachery of James was soon made apparent. Gondomar, an
exceedingly able and artful man, was then the Spanish Minister
in England, and perfectly understanding the miserable fool who
disgraced the English throne, acquired over him a complete
ascendancy. James was, in truth, afraid of Spain, and the
wretched coward was endeavoring to guard against the possibility
of a rupture with that country, by promoting an alliance between
his son Charles and the Infanta. Sir Walter Raleigh, as an English subject, duly commissioned by James himself as chief commander, was about to embark on an expedition to a country from
which Spain, without any just title, sought to exclude all Englishmen. The object of the expedition was to add to the territory
and increase the wealth of England, and by the royal order, all
the plans of the commander, even to the minutest detail, were
laid before the king. Will it be believed, that the sole object of
the pusillanimous monarch was to lay these very plans before
Gondomar, that he might communicate them to the Spanish
Court, and thus enable Philip to prepare opposition to the expedition, in every step of its progress? Such was literally the fact.
Raleigh found in Guiana copies of his own drawings, and plans
and documents, that left no doubt of the treachery of the royal
villain whom he was seeking to enrich. Of course, his difficulties,
rendered sufficiently distressing by sickness and many other
untoward events, were increased in a tenfold ratio when he found
Spaniards in arms awaiting his arrival, and encouraged to resistance by the perfidy of his own monarch. And here we cannot
withhold an expression of surprise, that Mr. Napier should state
that it does not appear to him "James acted dishonorably, or
otherwise than in consistency with the usages of civilized nations"
in making this communication to Spain. It is readily conceded,
that James conferred no power on Raleigh to commit piratical
depredations on the possessions of the King of Spain. Piracy in
Guiana was the crime of which he was accused on his return. It

is obvious that the prime question was, whether Guiana was a part of the Spanish king's possessions. Spain claimed it under a grant from the Pope; but did England ever recognize such claim? In 1609, seven years before Raleigh's last expedition, the Crown of England granted nearly the whole of Guiana to Mr. Robert Harcourt, and rested the right to do so on Raleigh's previous discovery. If it was England's then, what claim had Spain, founded in the comity of nations, to minute information of an intended expedition of English subjects to English territory, with the approbation of their own sovereign?

Yet would he not be deterred: a party of which his son was one, landed and marched to take possession of a mine, the locality of which was known to Raleigh. The Spaniards, from a small town called St. Thomas, which they had recently built, attacked the English; the violation of peace commenced not with Raleigh or his men: they of course resisted the attack, and put the enemy completely to flight : in the skirmish, however, young Raleigh fell at the head of his men, mortally wounded. The English then burned St. Thomas and returned to the ships, where Raleigh himself had remained expecting the arrival of a Spanish fleet, designed to defeat his plans. Every thing conspired against him. His men had not reached the mine, and he knew that his enemies at home would be but too ready to accuse him of having undertaken the expedition for purposes of plunder only. When he reached the island of St. Christopher's he thus wrote to his wife:

" I was loath to write, because I know not how to comfort you; and God knows I never knew what sorrow meant till now. All that I can say to you is, that you must obey the will and providence of God. Comfort your heart, dearest Bess, I shall sorrow for us both. And I shall sorrow the less, because I have not long to sorrow, because not long to live. The Lord bless and comfort you, that you may bear patiently the death of your most valiant son !"

In another communication, addressed to a friend on the subject of this unfortunate expedition, he thus concludes:

"This is all that I can say, other than that I have spent my poor estate, lost my son and my health, and endured as many sorts of miseries, as ever man did, in hope to do his majesty acceptable service; and have not, to my understanding, committed any hostile act, other than entrance upon a territory belonging rightly to the crown of England when the English were first set upon and slain by the usurping Spaniards."

There were not wanting those who had said when Raleigh sailed that he never meant to return. The news of his failure reached England before he did, and the confidence of his enemies that they should never see him more was greatly increased. Yet he returned to meet on his arrival a royal proclamation, issued at the instance of Gondomar, denouncing the whole expedition. In truth, Raleigh was so dangerous an enemy to Spain, that there lived not in England a man whose death was more desirable to Philip, and Gondomar had instructions to accomplish it. The anxiety of James for an alliance with the Spanish Court furnished him all the opportunity he desired, and the weak King of England was given to understand that the accomplishment of his wishes depended upon the sacrifice of Raleigh.

By the most despicable treachery, in which Sir Lewis Stukely, his kinsman, and a Frenchman named Manourie were the agents, he was once more delivered to the keeper of his old prison, the tower, and instead now of the society of his wife, he was afflicted with the perpetual presence of one selected by the king himself, whose business it was by cunning duplicity to aim at procuring evidence against the unhappy prisoner. It would be incredible of any other king but James, that he could stoop to the despicable artifices by which the life of the unhappy prisoner was sought. Humanity sickens and honor revolts in the recollection of this portion of the life of James. Lady Raleigh was confined a prisoner in her own house and Sir Walter was closely watched in the tower. With an affectation of sympathy, James permitted a correspondence between the parties. But for what purpose? To alleviate the sorrows of either or both? Oh no: but to read their letters in the hope of finding proof of something which could be tortured into evidence of guilt, and then resealing them, to send them according to their directions. This was but one particular of his baseness. All his artifices were unavailing: not a tittle of testimony could he procure. As a last resort he determined to execute him on his former sentence passed fifteen years before. He had never granted poor Raleigh a full formal pardon under the first conviction; he never would, and recent documents show that in the exercise of his vindictive, unforgiving spirit, he purposely withheld it, that he might at any time when he pleased reach the life of his victim. But Raleigh supposed that in the eye of the law he was pardoned. He had consulted the Lord Chancellor Bacon, and he said to him, when he was commissioned to command his last expedition to Guiana—"upon my life, you have a sufficient pardon for all that is past already, the king having under his broad seal made you admiral of your fleet, and given you power over your officers and soldiers."

At the same time when James had resolved upon resorting to the old sentence, he wrote to the Spanish court expressing his willingness either to have the tragedy finished in England or to send Raleigh to suffer death in Spain. Philip as soon as possible transmitted what Mr. Tytler terms his "orders" to James under his own hand, stating "that it would be more agreeable to him that the punishment of Raleigh should take place in England; and as the offence was notorious, that its chastisement should be exemplary and immediate." Intimation was given to the prisoner without delay to prepare for death. "My age" (said he) "is fit for the grave. What have I to do with life? My reputation is lost, my body weak and full of pain. Nothing can be more welcome to me than death." It was necessary, however, that some semblance, at least of legal solemnity, should precede the murder. Bacon, Coke, and Abbot, archbishop of Canterbury, were named commissioners to devise the mode of proceeding. They decided that the prisoner having been convicted of treason, could not be called to answer judicially for any subsequent crime; and recommended that the king should issue a warrant for his execution and publish a narrative of his offences; and a writ of privy seal was dispatched to the Judges, directing them to order execution. The Judges said, no writ of privy seal, nor warrant under the great seal, would entitle them to pass sentence after fifteen years, without allowing the prisoner a hearing. A writ of habeas corpus was therefore recommended, and all this apparatus was provided in a case where the death of the victim was determined, in order that he might be murdered with becoming attention to the technical and scientific proprieties of judicial homicides. His majesty was pleased to approve of the wisdom of this mode of proceeding, and having ordered the Judges to sentence him, and signed the warrant for his execution, then directed the habeas corpus to issue.

It was on the 28th of October. Raleigh was sick of fever in his bed. At eight in the morning, with an ague fit then on him, he was conveyed before the Judges, and sentence was passed. All he asked was that he might have a few days to arrange his affairs, and then took leave of the court with great solemnity, in these words—"I take God to be my judge, before whom I shall shortly appear, that I was never disloyal to his majesty, which I shall justify when I shall not fear the face of any king on earth; and so I beseech you all to pray for me."

The request for a little time between sentence and execution was inhumanly refused, and on his return to prison he was informed that he must die the next morning. On the evening before he died, he was permitted to have his last interview with his wife, and she left not the prison until midnight. The parting scene we will not attempt to describe, but only say that on his side all was cheerful submission to heaven, and a studied effort to comfort her who had so long and so faithfully loved him. When in a flood of tears she informed him that she had obtained the favor of disposing of his body, he replied with a smile: "it is well, Bess, that thou mayest dispose of that dead, thou hadst not always the disposing of when alive."

He was not permitted to select his own clergyman; the divine who was sent, however, was worthy of his calling, and has left on record his conviction of the deep and real christianity of the prisoner. He partook of the sacrament early in the morning, and his cheerfulness increased as he approached eternity. On the scaffold his deportment was all dignity. He answered in his address all the charges that had been brought against him, appealing most solemnly to heaven for the truth of his declarations, and having pronounced his forgiveness of all his enemies, he bade all farewell. He was asked in what faith he died: his reply was: "in the faith professed by the Church of England, adding that he hoped to be saved and to have his sins washed away by the precious blood and merits of our Saviour Christ." And then, says an old writer, who was a spectator of the sad scene, he made a most divine and admirable prayer, after which, rising up and clasping his hands together, he exclaimed: *" Now I am going to God."* The scaffold was cleared and he bid the executioner show him the axe; it was not done immediately, when he became more urgent —"I prithee (said he) let me see it. Dost thou think I am afraid of it?" He took it in his hand, and kissing the blade he passed his finger along the edge, remarking to the sheriff—"'tis a sharp medicine, but a sound cure for all diseases."—He then approached the edge of the scaffold, and kneeling down requested the people to pray for him, continuing himself for some time in this position, occupied in silent devotion. When he arose, he examined the block and fitted himself to it. Finding it as he would have it, he stood up once more and said he was ready. The executioner came forward, and falling on his knees, begged his forgiveness. Raleigh with a smile laid his hand on his shoulder and bade him be satisfied, assuring him that he most cheerfully forgave him, and asked of him only not to strike until he gave the signal and then to strike home. He then laid his neck on the block, and on being desired to make some change in the position of his head, he said, "it mattered little how the head lay, provided the heart was right."—The motion of his lips and hands then indicated that he was occupied in prayer, and in a short time he gave the signal. The executioner, probably from agitation, delayed to strike. Raleigh partially lifted his head and said in a loud voice—"What dost thou fear? Strike, man!"—At two blows his head was severed from his body, and thus at the age of sixty-six was murdered a man who, take him for all in all, knew in his day few equals and no superiors.

His body was privately buried in St. Margaret's Church, Westminster. His head was embalmed and preserved in a case by his devoted wife, who with pious solicitude kept it through a widowhood of twenty-nine years. When she died, the only surviving son of Sir Walter preserved it during his life, and it was finally at his death laid in the same grave with him. One fact alone is quite sufficient to indicate the true character of this bloody transaction. The conviction of Raleigh purported to be for treasonable intercourse with Spain: his execution under this conviction was caused by the injuries done to the town and forces of this very Spain, for which it had been alleged, he entertained a traitorous affection. Had he loved Spain more and England less, he had never died on the scaffold. The true cause of his execution was the desire on the part of James to gratify Spain. But Spain deluded him, the Spanish match never took place, and James caused one of his ministers to write to his agent in Spain, directing him to represent to the Spanish court, that it should act with sincerity toward the English king, since he had given so many proofs of his sincerity, and now lately, "by causing Sir Walter Raleigh to be put to death, CHIEFLY *for the giving them satisfaction*,"—" to *give them content*, he had not spared him, when, by preserving him, he might have given great satisfaction to his subjects, and had at command, upon all occasions, as useful a man as served any prince in Christendom."

No further evidence is necessary. Raleigh was murdered and James was his murderer.

We cannot better conclude our sketch than in the glowing language of Tytler, who thus closes his labors, in delineating the chequered career of Raleigh.

" It is by a frequent contemplation of such lofty and splendid specimens of humanity as Sir Walter Raleigh, that the modern character may be elevated and invigorated. There was indeed in him such a grasp of thought, such an energy of spirit, and such a majesty of expression, that the mind cannot dwell upon either his character or his works without feeling itself exalted, expanded and informed. We see in him a combination of the most various and opposite ingredients in our nature—the coolest and most calculating sagacity, joined with a flowing and gorgeous imagination—the most irrepressible energy of will with the subtlest motions of intellect—the most sanguine and unsubdued spirit, with the most patient resignation to irresistible circumstances. We have also a most improving exhibition of the gradual obscuration of the gay and trusting faith which inexperience fondly reposes in human kind, which a long commerce with mankind, in the course of a perilous life, slowly but amply supplies. Surely there is something to be learned from a man like this—admiral, philosopher, statesman, historian and poet, all in one—first in

5

some, distinguished in all—who, bold and adventurous in discovery, whether moral or geographical, untamed in war, and indefatigable in literature, as inexhaustible in ideas as in exploits, after having brought a new world to light, wrote the history of the old in a prison."

No. 2.

THE FIRST VOYAGE

MADE TO THE COASTS OF AMERICA, WITH TWO BARKS, WHEREIN
WERE CAPTAINS

M. PHILIP AMADAS

AND

M. ARTHUR BARLOWE,

WHO DISCOVERED PART OF THE COUNTRY NOW CALLED

VIRGINIA.

ANNO 1584.

WRITTEN BY ONE OF THE SAID CAPTAINS, AND SENT TO SIR WALTER RALEIGH, KNIGHT,
AT WHOSE CHARGE AND DIRECTION THE SAID VOYAGE WAS SET FORTH.

[This is a reprint from *Hakluyt*, vol. 3, page 246, and, as far as we are informed, the narrative is not to be found in any other publication, except in the form of a reprint, in Pinkerton. Barlowe was the author of it, as we learn from the story itself. He thus writes, " Then the master and the pilot of the admiral, *Simon Fernando*, and the captain, *Philip Amadas*, myself, and others, rowed to the land," &c. As the title shows it to have been " written by *one* of the captains," and this passage proves that it was not *Amadas*, Barlowe must have been the writer].

THE 27th day of April, in the year of our redemption, 1584, we departed from the west of England, with two barks well furnished with men and victuals, having received our last and perfect directions by your letters, confirming the former instructions and commandments delivered by yourself at our leaving the river of Thames. And I think it a matter both unnecessary for the manifest discovery of the country, as also for tediousness' sake, to remember unto you the diurnal of our course, sailing thither and returning, only I have presumed to present unto you this brief discourse, by which you may judge how profitable this land is likely to succeed, as well as to yourself (by whose direction and charge and by whose servants this our discourse hath been performed), as also to her highness, and the commonwealth, in which we hope your wisdom will be satisfied, considering that as much by us hath been brought to light, as by those small means and number of men we had, could any way have been expected or hoped for.

The 10th of May we arrived at the Canaries, and the 10th of June, in this present year, we were fallen into the islands of the West Indies, keeping a more southeastwardly course than was needful, because we doubted that the current of the Bay of Mexico, disemboguing between the Cape of Florida and Havana, had been of greater force than afterward we found it to be. At which islands we found the air very unwholesome, and our men grew for the most part ill-disposed; so that, having refreshed ourselves with sweet water and fresh victuals, we departed the twelfth day of our arrival there. These islands, with the rest adjoining, are so well known to yourself and many others, as I will not trouble you with the remembrance of them.

The second of July we found shoal water, where we smelled so sweet and so strong a smell as if we had been in the midst of some delicate garden abounding with all kinds of odoriferous flowers, by which we were assured that the land could not be far distant; and keeping good watch and bearing but slack sail, the fourth of the same month we arrived upon the coast, which we supposed to be a continent and firm land, and we sailed along the same a hundred and twenty English miles before we could find any entrance or river issuing into the sea.

[Had the computation of time in 1584 been as it now is, it would have been a singular coincidence that the first English colony to America should have made our coast on the anniversary of the day since rendered so memorable by more than one event in our history.. But the fourth of July, 1584, will not correspond with a similar monthly date, since the change of style made by parliament in 1752. The new or Gregorian style makes a difference in date of twelve days. According to our calendar, the arrival on our coast was on the sixteenth of July.]

The first that appeared unto us we entered, though not without some difficulty, and cast anchor about three harquebus-shot within the haven's mouth, on the left hand of the same ; and, after, thanks given to God for our safe arrival thither, we manned our boats and went to view the land next adjoining and to take possession of the same, in the right of the queen's most excellent majesty, as rightful queen and princess of the same, and after delivered the same over to your use, according to her majesty's grant and letters patent, under her highness' great seal.

[The approach of the expedition was from the south, and after making the land, the vessels sailed one hundred and twenty English miles before they found "any entrance or river issuing into the sea." They entered the first that they saw and anchored. The first question that arises is, "What inlet did they enter ?" Certain data are afforded by the narrative itself, from which we may perhaps determine.

1. The ships anchored when they entered "on the left hand" of the inlet, and found, on landing, that they were lying, not alongside of the main land, but of an *island*, which they found to be "twenty miles long, and not above six miles broad." As they approached from the south, and anchored on the *left hand* as they entered, they must have been lying off the *north* end of the island.

2. Barlow subsequently went in his boats, from the place of anchorage, "twenty mile into the river that runneth toward the city of *Skicoak*, which river they call *Occam ;* and the evening following we came to an island, which they call *Roanoke*, distant from the harbor by which we entered *seven leagues.*"

3. Beyond this island was the main land, "and over against this island falleth into this spacious water the great river called *Occam* by the inhabitants."

4. "Into this river (Occam), falleth another great river called *Cipo*, in

which there is found great store of muskles, in which there are pearls ; likewise there descendeth into this Occam another river called *Nomopana*, on the one side whereof standeth a great town called *Chawanook*."

5. "Towards the southwest, *four days' journey*, is situate a town called *Sequotan*," and near to this was "an out island, unhabited, called *Wocokon*."

6. Adjoining to *Sequotan* was a country called *Pomouik*, and next to that, *westward*, was "the country *Newsiok*, situate upon a goodlye river called *Neus*."

7. "Beyond this island, called *Roanoak*, are many maine islands." When the adventurers arrived they supposed the land they first saw to be the continent; "but after we entered into the haven," (thus they say), "we saw before us another mighty long sea; for there lyeth along the coast a tracte of islands, two hundreth miles in length, adjoining to the ocean sea, *and between the islands two or three entrances :* when you are entred between them (these islands being very narrow for the most part, as in most places sixe miles broad, in some places lesse, in fewe more), then there appeareth another great sea, containing in bredth in some places forty, and in some fifty, in some twenty miles over, before you come unto the continent; and in this inclosed sea there are about an hundreth islands of divers bignesses."

These are all the portions of the narrative which have reference to localities, and it is by the aid of these chiefly, if at all, we are to discover the inlet by which the vessels entered. Fortunately, some of the places indicated still retain the original native names. Thus, we still have Roanoke island ; in Chawan-ook we readily find our Chowan, and "the goodlye river, called Neus," still bears the same name. But what do we now call the Occam, Cipo, and Nomopana of the natives ?   Where are Sequotan and Wocokon ?

Taking Roanoak island as a point allowing of no dispute, we will first endeavor to ascertain the *inlet* by which the vessels must have entered from the ocean. The general opinion seems to be that it was the present entrance at Ocracoke. This, however, is scarcely reconcilable with the statements of Barlow in the text.

The distance from his anchorage to Roanoak island he expressly states to be about *seven leagues*, and his anchorage was just within the entrance from the ocean, "about three harquebus-shot within the haven's mouth." Now the distance of Ocracoke inlet from the southern end of Roanoak island is more than twice seven leagues.

Again, on the voyage from the vessels to Roanoak island, which was

made in the ship's boat (for Barlow had but *seven* men with him on
the excursion), he went on the first day twenty miles " into the *river,*
which they call *Occam.*" It is difficult to understand how any one
entering Pamlico Sound at Ocracoke would apply the term *"river"*
to the expanse of water before him, which in its narrowest part,
visible from that inlet, is fully twenty miles in breadth. The accu-
racy of Barlow's description of the general aspect of the sound forbids
the idea that he called it a "*river.*" He says it is "a great *sea,* containing in bredth, in some places, forty, and in some fifty, in some
twenty miles over, before you come to the continent."

But further still, he expressly tells us that this river Occam is "over
against this island ;" [Roanoak] and then "falleth into this spacious
water," [the sound]. It could not then have been as far south as Ocracoke. Again, Barlow says, speaking of the islands that border the coast,
that between them were "*two or three* entrances." We are inclined to
think that Ocracoke was not at that day, 1584, recognized as one of them
by this expedition, nor indeed for some time after, because we find the
Lords Proprietors, under a charter as long after as 1663, directing Sir
William Berkeley, one of their number, and then Governor of Virginia,
to procure a vessel of light draught and explore the inlets to the sound,
particularly one *of which they had heard,* near the rivers Neuse and
Pamlico. This, as the map will show, must have been Ocracoke. The
first *published* account of Ocracoke as an inlet was by Lawson in 1714,
though it probably had been examined some years before that time.

We are for these reasons induced to doubt whether the received
opinion of the entry of the first expedition at Ocracoke is correct.

Where, then, did the vessels enter? We cannot with certainty say,
but the probabilities all point to some inlet more north than Ocracoke.
It may have been Hatteras inlet, or there may have been an entrance
where our modern maps show "New inlet" at the northern end of
Chickomicomico banks. This point is just about seven leagues from
Roanoak island. And here, too, lies a body of water between the outer
banks, and a long island parallel to them, which might very well be
taken for a "river;" and this water extends up to Roanoak island, and
may be the "*Occam*" spoken of. At any rate, all along the eastern
side of the island, and thence down to New inlet, is a narrow strip of
water separated from the rest of the sound by the islands there, which
strangers might suppose to be a river ; and *no where else* is there anything resembling a river which would take the voyager to Roanoak
island. We incline, therefore, to think that this strip of water must
be the "*Occam*" of the natives.

We know not that we can identify the *Cipo* of the aborigines. It may have been Currituck sound ; but more probably was one of the rivers emptying into Albermarle sound, between it and the Chowan.

As to *Nomopana*, it is said to have emptied into the *Occam*, and to have had on its banks a great town called Chawan-ook. How far Barlow may have supposed the Occam to extend to the west, we do not know, as he made no explorations in that direction ; indeed, he does not appear to have gone much beyond Roanoak island, and possibly supposed Albermarle sound to terminate much nearer to Roanoak island than it does. It is hard to resist the conviction that the name of the town is retained in the county we now call Chowan ; and if so, the locality of Chawan-ook was in that district of country. In such case, Nomopana would be the Chowan river, and the ancient native town may have been but the predecessor of our Edenton, or at any rate not far from its site.

As to *Secotan*, it was southwest from Roanoak island, "four days' journey," and near it, on the coast, was an island called "Wocokon." The "four days' journey" here spoken of, we learn from future narratives, was about eighty miles, and fortunately our older maps still retain Wocokon. We have before us no less than four such, one of which, published in 1666, is appended to "a brief description of the province of Carolina," and is pronounced on the title page of the pamphlet of some twenty-five pages, to be "a most accurate map of the whole province." On this Wocokon appears to be our Ocracoke, and the same is true of all the maps alluded to. *Secotan*, therefore, was on the coast somewhere not far from Ocracoke, and Martin says, though we know not his authority, it was "equi-distant from Neuse and Tar rivers and Pamplico sound." This would place Secotan on the borders of Craven and Beaufort counties, somewhere near the head waters of Bay river.

It only remains to ask where was *Pomouik ?* It adjoined Sequotan, and Martin says was the chief town of the king of the Newsioks, whose country was on the Neuse. Barlow calls it a "country," not a town, and says that Newsiok was immediately west of it. It was probably in the tract lying between the head of Bay river and Newbern.

The map at the close of this narrative furnishes the nearest approximation we can make to Indian localities discovered on the first visit to North Carolina by Amadas and Barlow, and is a copy from that which was made on the expedition by the adventurers themselves, and was published by De Bry. Of this map certain particulars are worthy of note.

First. *Ocracoke inlet does not appear on it at all.* The delineation of the coast does not extend to a point so far south. This would seem to be conclusive proof that they did not enter at Ocracoke. They surely never would have omitted in their map so important a locality.

Secondly. *Five* inlets are marked, of which *two* only have names—*Hatorask* and *Trinity Harbor*.* Does this imply that they named those only of which they had some experimental knowledge? Does the use of the word "harbor" imply that here was their usual anchorage outside?

Thirdly. At *every inlet*, without exception, is the representation of a vessel foundering. Does not this mean that *all* were equally dangerous, and negative the idea suggested by some that they designed to picture the comparative excellency of the several inlets? The most northern wreck is that of a sloop, the other four represent two masted vessels. This may indicate the comparative depths of water at the inlets, but clearly intimates also that vessels were likely to be lost at *all*. As confirmatory of the idea that the entrance was made at New inlet, we may remark that on one of our old maps, made in Germany, and, for the date, remarkably correct as to the coast, "Trinity Harbor" is placed at "New Inlet." Here, we think, the larger vessels rode outside, as is pictured in the map, and never entered the sound at all. One of the small craft, in which *oars* are represented, it will be observed appears to be returning from Roanoak island toward the inlet near "Trinity Harbor," and this, according to the Nuremberg map, is "New Inlet." We must not omit to call attention to the uplifted cross in the hand of one in the stern of the boat, as it seems to intimate that the adventurers (like all the rovers of that day) professed at least to desire the propagation of christianity as much as the profits of discovery. Most of the old charters are uncommonly pious in avowing as a motive holy zeal for the spread of the gospel.

We return to the narrative] :

Which being performed [i. e. possession taken], according to the ceremonies used in such enterprises, we viewed the land about us, being, whereas [where] we first landed very sandy and low toward the water side, but so full of grapes, as the very beating and surge of the sea overflowed them, of which we found such plenty as well there as in all places else, both on the sand and on the green soil, on the hills as in the plains, as well on every little shrub, as also climbing towards the tops of high cedars that I think in all the world the like abundance is not to be found; and myself having seen those parts of Europe that most abound, find such difference as were incredible to be written.

[One familiar with North Carolina will not be surprised at this abundance of grapes. The state might unquestionably be made the greatest
vine-growing country on the eastern side of the continent. In the time
of Lawson (1714), there were six varieties of native grape known to
him, which he particularly describes : we believe there were more than
six varieties. Those which he knew, however, were two kinds of black
bunch grapes, one yielding a crimson and the other a white juice ; and
four varieties of the fox-grape, two being a summer, and two a winter
grape. Beside these, Lawson says he once saw a spontaneous *white*
bunch grape in North Carolina. We of this day *know* there is such
a grape, though some modern writers have said that no native white
grape was ever found on this continent. Mr. Wiley, we believe, is the
first who has called attention to the fact, that the three finest native grapes
of our country all spread from North Carolina. These are the Scuppernong, the Catawba, and the Isabella. The Scuppernong derives its name
from Scuppernong creek or river, at the mouth of Albermarle sound.
The first vine was found in Tyrrel county by some of the first explorers
under Amadas and Barlow, and tradition relates that they transplanted
a small vine with its roots, to Roanoak island. That vine is yet alive, and
covers an immense extent of ground. The true Scuppernong is a *white*
grape, round, very sweet and large, and furnishes a wine like Malmsey.
But there are no less than five varieties of grape about Albermarle
sound, which, from the contiguity of the Scuppernong creek, are called
by its name. That which we have described, however, is the true
Scuppernong, and no grape is more luscious.

The banks of the Catawba furnish the native home of the grape known
by the name of the river. It is now celebrated at the north as a table
grape, and in Ohio as a wine grape. It is still found wild in North
Carolina.

The Isabella is now more generally cultivated for table use than any grape
on the continent. It is supposed to be a hybrid between the Burgundy,
introduced into South Carolina by the Huguenots, and the native fox
grape of the Carolinas. The tradition is, that it first showed itself at
Dorchester, South Carolina. There Governor Benjamin Smith, of
North Carolina, obtained cuttings which he planted at Smithville near
Wilmington. From this stock Mrs. Isabella Gibbs transported a vine
to Long Island, where the grape, which is one of our hardiest, flourished
and attracted attention. It was called the Isabella, in compliment to
Mrs. Gibbs, who introduced it at the north. It is certain that the
Long Island stock came from North Carolina : it is not equally certain

whether Smithville obtained it from Dorchester.   This grape will
stand the northern climate better than any other].

We passed from the sea-side towards the tops of those hills next
adjoining, being but of mean height, and from thence we beheld
the sea on both sides to the north and to the south, finding no end
any of both ways.   This land lay stretching itself to the west,
which after we found to be but an island of twenty miles long,
and not above six miles broad.   Under the bank or hill whereon
we stood, we beheld the valleys replenished with goodly cedar
trees, and having discharged our harquebus-shot, such a flock of
cranes (the most part white) arose under us, with such a cry,
redoubled by many echoes, as if an army of men had shouted
altogether.

This island had many goodly woods full of deer, conies, hares
and fowl, even in the midst of summer, in incredible abundance.
The woods are not such as you find in Bohemia, Moscovia, or
Hercynia, barren and fruitless, but the highest and reddest cedars
of the world, far bettering the cedars of the Azores, of the Indies,
or Lybanus; pines, cypress, sassaphras, the lentish, or the tree
that bears the mastick, the tree that bears the rind of black cinnamon, of which Master Winter brought from the Streights of
Magellan, and many other of excellent smell and quality.

We remained by the side of this island two whole days before
we saw any people of the country : the third day we espied one
small boat rowing towards us, having in it three persons ; this
boat came to the island-side, four harquebus-shot from our ships,
and there two of the people remaining, the third came along the
shore-side towards us, and we being then all within board, he
walked up and down upon the point of the land next unto us ;
then the master and the pilot of the Admiral, Simon Fernando,
and the captain, Philip Amadas, myself and others, rowed to the
land, whose coming this fellow attended, never making any show
of fear or doubt.   And after he had spoken of many things not
understood by us, we brought him, with his own good liking,
aboard the ships, and gave him a shirt, a hat and some other
things, and made him taste of our wine, and our meat, which he
liked very well ; and after having viewed both barks, he departed,
and went to his own boat again, which he had left in a little cove

or creek adjoining; as soon as he was two bow-shot into the water, he fell to fishing, and in less than half an hour, he had laden his boat as deep as it could swim, with which he came again to the point of the land, and there he divided his fish into two parts, pointing one part to the ship and the other to the pinnace; which, after he had, as much as he might, requited the former benefits received, departed out of our sight.

The next day there came unto us divers boats, and in one of them the king's brother, accompanied with forty or fifty men, very handsome and goodly people, and in their behavior as mannerly and civil as any of Europe. His name was *Granganimeo*, and the king is called *Wingina*, the country *Wingandacoa*, and now by her majesty Virginia. The manner of his coming was in this sort, he left his boats altogether as the first man did, a little from the ships by the shore, and came along to the place over against the ships, followed with forty men. When he came to the place, his servants spread a long mat upon the ground, on which he sat down, and at the other end of the mat four others of his company did the like, the rest of his men stood round about him, somewhat afar off; when we came to the shore to him with our weapons, he never moved from his place, nor any of the other four, nor never mistrusted any harm to be offered from us, but sitting still he beckoned us to come and sit by him, which we performed, and being set, he made all signs of joy and welcome, striking on his head and his breast, and afterwards on ours, to show we were all one, smiling and making show the best he could of all love, and familiarity. After he had made a long speech unto us, we presented him with divers things, which he received very joyfully and thankfully. None of the company durst speak one word all the time; only the four which were at the other end spake one in the other's ear very softly.

[As to this name, *Wingandacoa*, it never was the Indian name of the country, but was misapplied to it by a mistake of the English. Sir Walter himself, in his History of the World, tells us so. In speaking of Peru, Yucatan, and Paria, after showing that these names were but words of the native language, which the Spaniards mistook for names of the places, he thus proceeds: "The same happened among the English, which I sent under Sir Richard Grenville to inhabit Virginia. For

when some of my people asked the name of that country, one of the
savages " [who, of course, did not understand the query of the Eng-
lish] " answered ' *Win-gan-da-coa*,' which is as much as to say,
' You wear good clothes,' or '.gay clothes.' "]

The king is greatly obeyed, and his brothers and children rever-
enced ; the king himself in person was, at our being there, sore
wounded in a fight which he had with the king of the next country, called Wingina, and was shot in two places through the body,
and once clean through the thigh, but yet he recovered ; by reason whereof, and for that he lay at the chief town of the country,
being five days' journey off, we saw him not at all.
• After we had presented this his brother with such things as we
thought he liked, we likewise gave somewhat to the other that
sat with him on the mat, but presently he arose and took all from
them, and put it into his own basket, making signs and tokens,
that all things ought to be delivered unto him, and the rest were
but his servants and followers. A day or two after this, we fell
to trading with them, exchanging some things that we had, for
chamoys, buff and deer skins ; when we showed him all our
packet of merchandise, of all things that he saw, a bright tin dish
most pleased him, which he presently took up and clapt it before
his breast, and after made a hole in the brim thereof and hung it
about his neck, making signs that it would defend him against his
enemies' arrows ; for those people maintain a deadly and terrible
war with the people and king adjoining. We exchanged our tin
dish for twenty skins, worth twenty crowns, or twenty nobles ;
and a copper kettle for fifty skins, worth fifty crowns. They
offered us good exchange for our hatchets and axes, and for knives,
and would have given any thing for swords, but we would not
depart with any. After two or three days, the king's brother
came aboard the ships and drank wine, and ate of our meat and
of our bread, and liked exceedingly thereof ; and after a few days
overpassed, he brought his wife with him to the ships, his daughter and two or three children ; his wife was very well favored, of
mean stature, and very bashful ; she had on her back a long cloak
of leather, with the fur side next to her body, and before her a
piece of the same ; about her forehead she had a band of white
coral, and so had her husband, many times ; in her ears she had

bracelets of pearls, hanging down to her middle, (whereof we delivered your worship a little bracelet,) and those were of the bigness of good pease. The rest of her women, of the better sort, had pendants of copper hanging in either ear, and some of the children of the king's brother, and other noblemen, have five or six in either ear; he himself had upon his head a broad plate of gold, or copper, for, being unpolished, we knew not what metal it should be, neither would he by any means suffer us to take it off his head, but feeling it, it would bow [bend] very easily. His apparel was as his wives, only the women wear their hair long on both sides, and the men but on one. They are of colour yellowish, and their hair black for the most part; and yet we saw children that had very fine auburn, and chestnut-coloured hair.

[The white "coral" here spoken of, as worn by the wife of Granganimeo, was probably the nacre of conch shells, of which the *wampum* or *peak* of the natives was made. The *pearls* also, represented as hanging from her ears, may have been real; but if so, they were probably but coarse specimens, as we have no reason to believe that the pearl-oyster was abundant in our waters, or that the Indians were pearl-divers: indeed the pearls are said elsewhere to be derived from *muscles* taken in the "great river" they called *Cipo*, which may have been Currituck sound. We know not whether muscles are particularly abundant now in its waters, but we know that in 1714, when Lawson wrote, they were very numerous throughout the whole sea coast region of the state.

A more interesting fact is here recorded, inasmuch as it shows the presence of *copper*, which we now know to abound in some parts of North Carolina; and further that the natives had either found out how to reduce the ore, or had discovered the metal in its native state. We are inclined to think they may have done the first, for experience has shown, in the case of other savages, that it is not beyond their attainment.

But a fact yet remains more interesting and mysterious still. Europeans had been among these aborigines *before* Amadas and Barlow. Who they were and whence they came, we never shall know; but children were seen by our voyagers with *auburn and chestnut colored hair*. Our native tribes in the United States were all Mongolidæ, and marked by the straight, coarse black hair of the Northern Asiatic. Auburn hair might well therefore excite surprise, and call for explanation. The explanation the natives gave was that twenty-six years before. (in 1558) a ship was cast away near Secotan, manned by *white* people; that some of the crew were saved, and preserved by the natives; that after remaining some few weeks at Wocokon (Ocracoke) they attempted to leave in the frail craft of the country, which they had endeavored to fit for the purpose, and probably perished, as their boats were subsequently found stranded on the shores of another island not far from Wocokon; the natives added that these were the only whites that had ever appeared among them, and that they were seen by the dwellers around Secotan only.]

After that these women had been there, there came down from all parts great store of people, bringing with them leather, coral, divers kinds of dyes very excellent, and exchanged with us; but when Granganimeo, the king's brother, was present, none durst trade but himself, except such as wear red pieces of copper on their heads like himself; for that is the difference between the nobleman, and the governors of countrys, and the meaner sort. And we both noted there, and you have understood since by these men which we brought home, that no people in the world carry more respect to their king, nobility and governors, than these do. The king's brother's wife, when she came to us (as she did many times) was followed with forty or fifty women always, and when she came into the ship, she left them all on land, saving her two daughters, her nurse, or one or two more. The king's brother always kept this order, as many boats as he would come withall to the ships, so many fires would he make on the shore afar off, to the end that we might understand with what strength and company he approached. Their boats are made of one tree, either of pine, or of pitch-trees, a wood not commonly known to our people, nor found growing in England. They have no edge-tools to make them withall, if they have any they are very few, and those it seems they had twenty years since, which, as those two men declared, was out of a wreck, which happened upon their coast of some christian ship, being beaten that way by some storm and outrageous weather, whereof none of the people were saved; but only the ship, or some part of her being cast upon the land, out of whose sides they drew the nails and the spikes, and with those they made their best instruments. The manner of making their boats is thus; they burn down some great tree, or take such as are wind-fallen, and putting gum and rosin upon one side thereof, they set fire into it, and when it has burnt it hollow, they cut out the coal with their shells, and ever where they would burn it deeper or wider they lay on gums, which burn away the timber, and by this means they fashion very fine boats, and such as will transport twenty men. Their oars are like scoops, and many times they set with long poles as the depth serves.

[These *"men which we brought home,"* were two of the natives named *Manteo* and *Wanchese,* both of whom returned on a subsequent expedition to Carolina. From their story it would seem that there had been another wreck on the coast, about six years after that mentioned in the previous note; which would be in 1564. In this no lives were saved, but the Indians obtained from the wreck nails and spikes out of which they made edge tools. But for the explanation by Manteo and his companion of the source whence this iron was derived, its presence would have much perplexed the archæologist; for the absence of *iron* tools or weapons, among our natives (before their introduction by Europeans) is a fact, at once uniform and remarkable.]

The king's brother had great liking of our armours, a sword, and divers other things which we had, and offered a great box of pearl in gage for them; but we refused it for this time, because we would not make them know, that we esteemed thereof, until we had understood in what places of the country the pearl grew, which now your worship does very well understand.

He was very just of his promise; for many times we delivered him merchandise upon his word, but ever he came within the day and performed his promise. He sent us every day a brace or two of fat bucks, conies, hares, fish, the best in the world. He sent us divers kinds of fruits, melons, walnuts, cucumbers, gourds, pease, and divers roots, and fruits very excellent good, and of their country corn, which is very white, fair and well tasted, and grows three times in five months; in May they sow, in July they reap; in June they sow, in August they reap; in July they sow, in September they reap; only they cast the corn into the ground, breaking a little of the soft turf with a wooden mattock, or pick-axe; our selves proved the soil, and put some of our pease in the ground, and in ten days they were of fourteen inches high, they have also beans very fair, of divers colors and wonderful plenty; some growing naturally, and some in their gardens, and so have they both wheat and oats.

[It is not at all improbable that oats were found growing wild in North Carolina by the first European visitors; they still are found wild on other parts of the continent. As to the wheat, however, some doubts may be entertained, whether it was what is ordinarily now known as wheat. The adventurers, however, were Englishmen and should have known the grain perfectly. It was probably some variety of the *Triticum* (of which there are many) which is divided into two families, *Cerealia* yielding edible seeds, and the *Agropyra* which are but grasses. Of the former there are many varieties, and some of them grow wild in temperate climates. Barlowe may have seen one of these, and, without minute examination, may, from its general resemblance, have pronounced it to be wheat. The wheats cultivated in England are mostly varieties of the *Triticum hybernum* or winter wheat, and the *T. turgidum*, or common bearded wheat, and these, we apprehend, were introduced into this country by Europeans.]

The soil is the most plentiful, sweet, fruitful, and wholesome of all the world; there are alone fourteen sweet smelling timber trees, and for the most part their underwood are bays and such like; they have those oaks that we have, but far greater and better. After they had been divers times aboard the ships, myself, with seven more, went twenty miles into the river, that runs towards the city of Skicoak, which river they call *Occam;* and the evening following we came to an island, which they call Roanoak, distant from the harbor by which we entered, seven leagues; and at the north end thereof was a village of nine houses, built of cedar, and fortified round about with sharp trees, to keep out their enemies, and the entrance into it made like a turn-pike, very artificially; when we came towards it, standing near unto the water's side, the wife of Granganimeo, the king's brother came running out to meet us very cheerfully and friendly, her husband was not then in the village; some of her people she commanded to draw our boat on shore for the beating of the billow; others she appointed to carry us on their backs to the dry ground, and others to bring our oars into the house for fear of stealing. When we were come to the outer room, having five rooms in her house,

she caused us to sit down by a great fire, and after took off our
clothes and washed them, and dried them again, some of the
women plucked off our stockings and washed them, some washed
our feet in warm water, and she herself took great pains to see all
things ordered in the best manner she could, making great haste to
dress some meat for us to eat.

After we had thus dried ourselves, she brought us into the inner
room, where she set on the board standing along the house, some
wheat like furmentee, [furmety] sodden venison and roasted, fish
sodden, boiled and roasted, melons raw and sodden, roots of
divers kinds, and divers fruits; their drink is commonly water,
but while the grape lasteth, they drink wine; and for the want of
corks to keep it, all the year after they drink water; but it is
sodden with ginger in it, and black cinnamon, and sometimes
sassaphras, and divers other wholesome, and medicinable herbs
and trees. We were entertained with all love and kindness, and
with as much bounty (after their manner) as they could possibly
devise. We found the people most gentle, loving, and faithful,
void of all guile and treason, and such as live after the manner of
the golden age. The people only care how to defend themselves
from the cold in their short winter, and to feed themselves with
such meat as the soil affords; their meat is very well sodden, and
they make broth very sweet and savory; their vessels are earthen
pots, very large, white and sweet, their dishes are wooden plates
of sweet timber; within the place where they feed was their
lodging, and within that their Idol, which they worship, of whom
they speak incredible things. While we were at meal, there came
in at the gates two or three men with their bows and arrows from
hunting, whom when we espied, we began to look one towards
another, and offered to reach our weapons; but as soon as she
espied our mistrust, she was very much moved, and caused some
of her men to run out, and take away their bows and arrows, and
break them, and withal, beat the poor fellows out of the gate
again. When we departed in the evening, and would not tarry
the whole night, she was very sorry, and gave us into our boat
our supper half dressed, pots and all, and brought us to our boat
side, in which we lay all night, removing the same a pretty distance from the shore; she perceiving our jealousy, was much

grieved, and sent divers men and thirty women, to sit all night on the bank side by us, and sent us into our boats five mats to cover us from the rain, using very many words to entreat us to rest in their houses ; but because we were few men, and if we had miscarried, the voyage had been in very great danger, we durst not adventure any thing, although there was no cause of doubt; for a more kind and loving people there can not be found in the world, as far as we have hitherto had trial.

[As to the *wine* made by the natives, it was probably no more than the juice of the grape, drunk as soon as it was expressed.]

Beyond this island there is the main land, and over against this island, falls into this spacious water, the great river called *Occam* by the inhabitants, on which stands a town called Pomeiock, and six days journey from the same is situate their greatest city, called Skicoak, which this people affirm to be very great; but the savages were never at it, only they speak of it by the report of their fathers and other men, whom they have heard affirm it to be above one hour's journey about.

[Unless we are careful, a similarity of names may here lead us into error. We have already spoken of a *district* or country, called *Pomouik*, which had for its western boundary the country *Newsiok*, " situate upon a goodly river called the *Neus*." This was a tract lying, as we think, between the head of Bay River and Newbern.

We here read of a *town*, not a district, called *Pomeiok*, standing on the river *Occam*, which was far distant from the Neuse, or any of its tributaries. This town was on the main land immediately west of Roanoak island, in what is now Hyde county. It is marked on Smith's map as not far from *Dasamonguepeuc*. The *district* of *Pomouik* must therefore not be confounded with the *town* of *Pomeiock*.

Of their " greatest city, called *Skicoak*," it is on With's map, but placed conjecturally, as it was not visited by the English.]

Into this river falls another great river, called *Cipo*, in which there is found great store of muscles, in which there are pearls; likewise there descendeth into this Occam another river called *Nomopana*, on the one side whereof stands a great town called *Chawanook*, and the lord of that town and country is called Poonens; this Poonens is not subject to the king of *Wingandacoa*, but is a free lord; beyond this country is there another king, whom they call *Menatonon*, and these three kings are in league with each other. Towards the southwest, four days journey, is situate a town called *Sequotan*, which is the southernmost town of *Wingandacoa*, near into which, six and twenty years past, there was a ship cast away, whereof some of the people were saved, and those were white people, whom the country people preserved.

And after ten days remaining in an out island uninhabited, called *Wocokon*, they with the help of some of the dwellers of Sequotan, fastened two boats of the country together, and made masts unto them, and sails of their shirts, and having taken into them such victuals as the country yielded, they departed, after they had remained in this out island three weeks; but shortly after, it seemed they were cast away, for the boats were found upon the coast, cast a land in another island adjoining; other than these, there was never any people apparelled, or white of colour, either seen or heard of amongst these people; and these aforesaid were seen only of the inhabitants of Secotan, which appeared to be very true, for they wondered marvellously when we were amongst them at the whiteness of our skins, ever coveting to touch our breasts, and to view the same. Besides, they had our ships in marvellous admiration, and all things else were so strange unto them, as it appeared that none of them had ever seen the like. When we discharged any piece, were it but a harquebus, they would tremble thereat for very fear, and for the strangeness of the same; for the weapons which themselves use are bows and arrows; the arrows are but of small canes, headed with a sharp shell or tooth of a fish, sufficient enough to kill a naked man. Their swords be of wood hardened; likewise they use wooden breast-plates for their defence. They have beside a kind of club, in the end whereof they fasten the sharp horns of a stagg, or other beast. When they go to war they carry about with them their idol, of whom they ask counsel, as the Romans were wont of the oracle of Apollo. They sing songs as they march towards the battle, instead of drums and trumpets, their wars are very cruel and bloody, by reason whereof, and of their civil dissensions, which have happened of late years amongst them, the people are marvellously wasted, and in some places the country left desolate.

Adjoining to this country aforesaid, called Secotan, begins a country called Pomouik, belonging to another king whom they call Piamacum, and this king is in league with the next king adjoining towards the setting of the sun, and the country New-siok, situate upon a goodly river called Neus; these kings have mortal war with Wingina, king of Wingandacoa; but about two years past there was a peace made between the king Piamacum and the lord of Secotan, as these men which we have brought with us to England, have given us to understand; but there remained a mortal malice in the Secotans, for many injuries and slaughters done upon them by this Piamacum. They invited divers men, and thirty women of the best of his country to their town to a feast, and when they were altogether merry, and praying before their idol, (which is nothing else but a mere illusion of the devil,) the captain and lord of the town came suddenly upon them and slew them every one, reserving the women and children; and these two have oftentimes since persuaded us to surprise Piamacum, his town, having promised and assured us that there will be found in it a great store of commodities. But whether their persuasion be to the end they may be revenged of their enemies, or for the love they bear to us, we leave that to the trial hereafter.

Beyond this island called Roanoak, are main islands, very plentiful of fruits and other natural increases, together with many towns, and villages, along the side of the continent, some bounding upon the islands, and some stretching up further into the land.

When we first had sight of this country, some thought the first land we saw to be the continent, but after we entered into the haven, we saw before us another mighty long sea; for there lieth along the coast a tract of islands, two hundred miles in length, adjoining to the ocean sea, and between the islands, two or three entrances; when you are entered between them (these islands being very narrow for the most part, as in most places six miles broad, in some places less, in few more) then there appeared another great sea, containing in breadth, in some places, forty, and in some fifty, in some twenty miles over, before you come unto the continent, and in this enclosed sea there are above a hundred islands of divers bignesses, whereof one is sixteen miles long, at which we were, finding it a most pleasant and fertile ground, replenished with goodly cedars and divers other sweet woods, full of currants, of flax, and many other notable commodities, which we at that time had no leisure to view. Besides this island, there are many, as I have said, some of two, of three, of four, of five miles, some more, some less, most beautiful and pleasant to behold, replenished with deer, conies, horses, and divers beasts, and also at them the goodliest and best fish in the world, and in great abundance.

Thus, sir, we have acquainted you with the particulars of our discovery made this present voyage, as far forth as the shortness of the time we there continued would afford us to take view of; and so contenting ourselves with this service at this time, which we hope hereafter to enlarge, as occasion and assistance shall be given, we resolved to leave the country and to apply ourselves to return for England, which we did accordingly, and arrived safely in the west of England about the middle of September.

And whereas we have above certified you of the country taken in possession by us, to her majesty's use, and so to yours by her majesty's grant, we thought good for the better assurance thereof, to record some of the particular gentlemen and men of account, who then were present as witnesses of the same, that thereby all occasion of cavil to the title of the country, in her majesty's behalf may be prevented, which otherwise, such as like not the action may use and pretend, whose names are—

Master PHILIP AMADAS, " ARTHUR BARLOW,	} *Captains.*
WM. GREENEVILE, JOHN WOOD, JAS. BROWEWICH, HENRY GREENE, BENJAMIN WOOD, SIMON FERDINANDO, NICHOLAS PETMAN, JOHN HEWES,	} *Of the Company.*

We brought home also two of the savages, being lusty men, whose names were *Wanchese* and *Manteo.*

[The whole period of the stay of this expedition in our waters was but about two months].

Arrival of the Englishemen in Virginia 1584

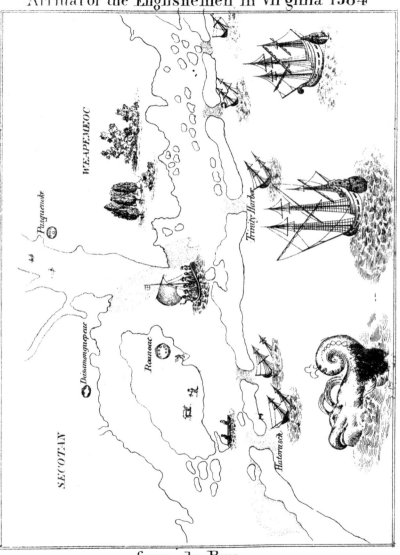

WEAPEMEOC

Pasquenoke

SECOTAN

Dasamonquepeuc

Roanoac

Trinity Harbor

Hatorask

from de Bry

No. 3.

THE VOYAGE

MADE BY

SIR RICHARD GREENVILLE,

FOR

SIR WALTER RALEIGH,

TO

VIRGINIA.

IN THE YEAR 1585.

[*Reprinted from* HAKLUYT, *Vol. III., page* 251].

[The southern part of what is now the United States had received from the Spaniards the general name of *Florida*. We have seen that the portion next north of it received from Elizabeth the name of *Virginia*, which at first included a large extent of country, embracing, in fact, our northern and north-eastern coast states. The more northern part received from the French the name of *Canada*. Subsequently, the name of *New England* was applied to a part of our country, which still retains it. The first three great divisions were at this time known to Europeans by the names here mentioned.

Sir Richard Greenville (or, as it is sometimes written Grenville, or Granville,) was the cousin of Sir Walter Raleigh. "This officer," says Tytler, "whose life was as enterprising as his death was heroic, had, in his early years, served against the Turks; and after sharing in the glory of the battle of Lepanto, returned to England with the reputation of an experienced soldier, which he increased by his conduct during the Irish rebellion. The queen promoted him to be sheriff of Cork; and on his coming to England, he was chosen to represent the county of Cornwall in parliament, in which he exhibited uncommon talents and energy." The "heroic death" here alluded to presents one of the most extraordinary records of naval warfare to be found in history. Indeed, were not the story well attested, one might be pardoned for some incredulity of circumstances so remarkable. Of its authenticity, however, no room is left for reasonable doubt, and Sir Walter himself was among those who, because it was so remarkable, employed his pen in preserving the facts it embodied.

In the times of Greenville, the hostility between England and Spain was of the most embittered character. England had commenced her naval career, and Spain was her only dangerous rival on the seas. About the year 1591, Admiral Lord Thomas Howard sailed to intercept the Plate fleet of Spain, at the Azores. His squadron consisted of six of the queen's ships, six victuallers of London (supply ships), and two or three pinnaces. Sir Richard Greenville was Vice-Admiral, and commanded the "Revenge." The squadron reached Flores (one of the Azores), and there awaited the arrival of the Spanish treasure ships. The king of Spain, having intelligence of this, dispatched a fleet of *fifty-three* sail to the Azores, to protect his vessels from America and convoy them home. The Spanish squadron was in sight before the English knew it was on the seas. It took them by surprise: a part of many of the crews of the English ships were on shore procuring water and other necessaries when the Spaniards hove in sight; and of those on board more than half were on the sick list, and unfit for service. The English had scarcely time to weigh anchor, and Greenville was the last to do so, because he was unwilling to leave his crew on shore, of whom ninety were at the time lying *sick* upon the island ; and after all were on board, he could muster but one hundred men fit for service. The Spaniards were on his weather-bow in large numbers, and his only chance was to trust to the sailing of his ship. But he indignantly rejected the thought of such a resort, and protested that he would rather die than run from an enemy. He then addressed his men, and told them that he would fight his way through the Spanish ships, which now formed two squadrons. He accordingly bore down on the nearest, and forced them to "spring their luff" and fall under his lee ; but while thus occupied, the San Philip (a very large ship) had succeeded in getting the wind of him, and so becalmed him that his ship could neither make way nor answer her helm. The San Philip was a ship of three tiers of guns. While the Revenge was thus entangled, four others of the enemy came up, two on the larboard, and two on the starboard side. This was the state of things about three o'clock in the afternoon, when the fight began. The San Philip was soon crippled and obliged to withdraw, and some said she foundered. The fight was continued with great fury, and as often as the Spaniards attempted to board, they were beaten back into their own ships or knocked into the sea. At last night came, but the fight still continued until a late hour, when there was a pause. Some of the Spanish ships were sunk, in others immense numbers were slain, and the brave handful on board the Revenge was sadly diminished. Greenville himself had been slightly wounded in the commencement of the fight, but never left the deck for eight hours ; at the expiration of that time a musket ball entered his body, and while the surgeon was dressing the wound, another shot struck him in the head, and the surgeon was killed by his side. Still he fought on, and as fast as one Spanish vessel was disabled and hauled off, another took her place ; so that when morning dawned, the Revenge had actually been engaged, at close quarters, for fifteen consecutive hours with fifteen different ships of the enemy, and repulsed them all. When daylight came, all that remained of her was a naked hull, riddled with shot, for she had received eight hundred discharges of artillery, and some of her wounds were under water. She had six feet of water in her hold ; her deck was covered with the limbs and carcases of forty of her brave crew ; not a living man on board was without a wound, and some, unable to move, were stretched upon the bloody deck; every spar was gone, every strand of her tackle cut, her upper works razeed to the water's edge, and the whole mass lying on the waters like a log, and incapable of any motion but that communicated by the swell of the sea. Greenville now commanded that she should be sunk with all on board, that the Spaniards might not carry home a splinter even as a trophy. He had such satisfaction as he could derive from knowing that he had completely destroyed four of the largest ships of the enemy; and he told his crew that for a few short hours or days more of life, it was not worth while to lessen the honor of their country. Many of them joined in this opinion; but a majority thought that there were some brave men on board who might yet live to serve their country, and that the Spaniard could take no honor, for that the Revenge could never be removed from the place where she was, being literally cut to pieces.

The Spanish Admiral, Don Alphonso Bacan was glad to take their surrender, and consented that all their lives should be saved and that they should be sent to England. The survivors were then removed by the Spanish boats, Greenville and the master gunner, to the very last, desiring to destroy the vessel.

When Greenville was carried on board of the Spanish Admiral, he was treated with the greatest respect, as was due to his indomitable courage, and every effort was made for his recovery; but the heroic old sailor would not probably have enjoyed life if saved by a Spaniard: he told them they might do with his body what they pleased, for it was now of no use to him; and as he neared his end (two or three days after he was taken on board the Admiral) he uttered in Spanish these his last words:—" here die I, Richard Greenville, with a joyful and quiet mind, having ended my life like a true soldier, that has fought for his country, queen, religion and honor."—Such was the man who led the second colony of Raleigh to North Carolina.]

The ninth day of April, in the year above said, [1585] we departed from Plymouth, our fleet consisting of the number of seven sails, to wit, the Tiger, of the burden of seven score tons, a Flyboat, called the Roe-Buck, of the like burden, the Lion, of a hundred tons or thereabouts, the Elizabeth, of fifty tons, and the Dorothy, a small bark, whereunto were also adjoined, for speedy services, two small pinnaces. The principal Gentlemen of our company were these: M. Ralph Lane; M. Thomas Candish; M. John Arundell; M. Raymund; M. Stukeley; M. Bremige; M.

Vincent, and M. John Clarke, and divers others, whereof some were captains, and other some assistants for counsel and good discretion in the voyage.

[The splendid ships of the merchant marine of our day renders it strange to us that voyages should have been made across the Atlantic in such small craft as we have here named. The largest vessel was but of one hundred and forty tons, and some were of less size than a modern pilot boat. But even the "Caraval," in which Columbus discovered the Continent, was of some *thirty* tons only ; and the luxurious accommodations, the skill and the safety of an Atlantic voyage now, furnish no proper picture of the risk and privations of the first European voyages to America. The humblest passenger and most common seaman probably have more comforts now, than the Admiral, Sir Richard Greenville, had in 1585.

Among the names of the "principal gentlemen" will be seen that of *Stukeley*. He also was a cousin of Raleigh, and of the admiral also ; and was the father of Sir Lewis Stukeley, who was employed by the government of King James, to act as a spy on Raleigh, and under the guise of friendship to entrap him into unguarded speech that might afford evidence of treason. He had a large and infamous share in producing Raleigh's execution.

The name of *Candish* is also in the list. This is a contraction of Cavendish, and the individual here alluded to made some noise in the course of his short and turbulent life. Thomas Cavendish was the son of a gentleman of fortune, and upon his father's death came into the possession of ample means, a considerable part of which he employed in fitting out a vessel of one hundred and twenty tons, in which he sailed on this expedition with Greenville. He was extravagant and wasteful, and ere long found himself with finances considerably reduced. After the fashion of his day he resolved to go into the business of honorable stealing, and to plunder the Spaniard on the high seas, as a gentleman corsair.

During the reign of Elizabeth, when the contest was obstinate and constant between England and Spain for naval supremacy, this practice was by no means uncommon even among men of fortune. Cavendish obtained a commission from the queen and cruised on the western coast of South America. He had three vessels, which he had fitted out, of one hundred and twenty, sixty, and forty tons respectively ; and one hundred and twenty-three men in all. He sold or mortgaged all that remained of

his property to make this preparation.   He was thus a desperate
adventurer who "periled all upon the cast of a single die."—With
these vessels he circumnavigated the globe in about twenty-five months,
and made really important surveys and observations in the straits of
Magellan and elsewhere.   He burned and plundered a considerable
number of Spanish towns on the coast of South America, and finally,
off the shores of California, captured the great annual treasure-ship of
Spain, filled with merchandise, and $122,000 in silver.   He arrived
safely in England, " rich enough to purchase a fair earldom," and was
knighted by the queen.   In three years he squandered the fruits of his
piratical maraudings, and then became partner in a joint stock company
that was started for similar plunders on a much larger scale.   This
combination of land and sea thieves, soon quarreled among themselves,
and the company was unsuccessful.   He died at sea while on the
return from a bootless expedition in 1593, when he was but twenty-
nine years old.   It is said vexation and fatigue caused his early death.
A full account of this unfortunate expedition, up to nearly the time of
his death, written by himself, may be found in the fourth volume of
Purchas, page 1192.   His voyage round the world is contained in the
third volume of Hakluyt, page 803.]

The 14th day of April we fell in with Lancerota and Forteventura,
isles of the Canaries, and from thence we continued our course
for Dominica, one of the Antilles of the West Indies, wherewith
we fell in the 7th day of May, and the 10th day following we came
to an anchor at Cotesa, a little island situate near to the island of
St. John, where we landed, and refreshed ourselves all that day.

The 12th day of May we came to an anchor in the bay of Mos-
kito, in the island of St. John, within a falcon-shot of the shore,
where our general, Sir Richard Greenvil, and the most part of
our company landed, and began to fortify very near to the sea-
side ; the river run by the one side of our fort, and the other two
sides were environed with woods.

The 13th day we began to build a new pinnace within the fort,
with the timber that we then felled in the country, some part
whereof we cut three miles up in the land, and brought it to our
fort upon trucks, the Spaniards not daring to make or offer resistance.

The 16th day there appeared unto us, out of the woods, eight horsemen of the Spaniards, about a quarter of a mile from our fort, staying about half an hour in viewing our forces, but as soon as they saw ten of our shot marching towards them, they presently retired into the woods.

The 19th day, Master Candish, who had been separated from our fleet in a storm in the Bay of Portugal, arrived at Cotesa, within the sight of the Tiger, we thinking him, afar off, to have been either a Spaniard, or Frenchman of war, thought it good to weigh achor, and to go room [*sic*] with him, which the Tiger did, and discerned him at last to be one of our consorts, for joy of whose coming our ships discharged their ordinance, and saluted him according to the manner of the seas.

The 22d day, twenty other Spanish horsemen shewed themselves to us upon the other side of the river, who being seen, our general dispatched twenty footmen towards them and two horsemen of ours, mounted upon Spanish horses, which we before had taken in the time of our being on the island: they showed to our men a flag of truce, and made signs to have a parley with us, whereupon two of our men went half of the way upon the sands, and two of theirs came and met them; the two Spaniards offered very great salutations to our men, but began according to their Spanish proud humors, to expostulate with them about their arrival and fortifying in their country, who notwithstanding by our men's discreet answers were so cooled, that (whereas they were told, that our principal intention was only to furnish ourselves with water and victuals, and other necessaries, whereof we stood in need, which we craved might be yielded us with fair and friendly means, otherwise our resolution was to practice force, and to relieve ourselves by the sword) the Spaniards, in conclusion, seeing our men so resolute, yielded to our requests with large promises of all courtesy, and great favor, and so our men and theirs departed.

The 23d day our pinnace was finished, and launched, which being done, our general with his captains and gentlemen, marched up into the country about the space of four miles, where in a plain marsh they stayed, expecting the coming of the Spaniards according to their promise, to furnish us with victuals, who keeping their old custom for perjury and breach of promise, came not; whereupon our general fired the woods thereabout, and so retired to our fort, which the same day was fired also, and each man came aboard to be ready to set sail the next morning.

The 29th day we set sail from St. John, being many of us stung before upon shore with the muskitos, but the same night we took a Spanish frigate, which was forsaken by the Spaniards upon the sight of us, and the next day, in the morning very early, we took another frigate, with good and rich freight, and divers Spaniards of account in her, which afterwards we ransomed for good round sums, and landed them in St. John's.

The 26th day our lieutenant, Master Ralph Lane, went in one of the frigates which we had taken, to Roxo bay, upon the south-west side of St. John, to fetch salt, being thither conducted by a Spanish pilot: as soon as he arrived there, he landed with his men to the number of twenty, and intrenched himself upon the sands immediately, compassing one of their salt hills within the trench; who being seen of the Spaniards, there came down towards him two or three troops of horsemen and footmen, who gave him the looking and gazing on, but durst not come near him to offer any resistance, so that Master Lane, maugre their troops, carried their salt aboard and laded his frigate, and so returned again to our fleet the 29th day, which rode at St. German's Bay. The same day we all departed, and the next day arrived in the island of Hispaniola.

JUNE.

The 1st day of June we anchored at Isabella, on the north side of Hispaniola.

The 3d day of June the governor of Isabella, and captain of the Port de Plata, being certified by the reports of sundry Spaniards, who had been well entertained aboard our ships by our general, that in our fleet were many brave and gallant gentlemen, who greatly desired to see the governor aforesaid, he thereupon sent gentle commendations to our general, promising within few days to come to him in person, which he performed accordingly.

The 5th day the aforesaid governor accompanied with a lusty friar and twenty other Spaniards, with their servants and negroes, came down to the seaside where our ships rode at anchor; who being seen, our general manned immediately the most parts of his boats with the chief men of our fleet, every man appointed and furnished in the best sort: at the landing of our general the Spanish governor received him very courteously, and the Spanish gentlemen saluted our English gentlemen, and their inferior sort did also salute our soldiers and seamen, liking our men, and likewise their qualities; although at the first they seemed to stand in fear of us, and of so many of our boats, whereof they desired that all might not land their men; yet, in the end, the courtesies that passed on both sides were so great, that all fear and mistrust on the Spaniards' part was abandoned.

In the meantime, while our English general and the Spanish governor discoursed betwixt them of divers matters, as of the state of the country, the multitude of the towns and people, and the commodities of the island, our men provided two banqueting houses covered with green boughs, the one for the gentlemen, the other for the servants, and a sumptuous banquet was brought in served by us all in plate, with the sound of trumpets, and concert of music, wherewith the Spaniards were more than delighted. Which banquet being ended, the Spaniards in recompense of our courtesy, caused a great herd of white bulls and kine to be brought together from the mountains, and appointed for every gentleman and captain that would ride, a horse ready saddled, and then singled out three of the best of them to be hunted by horsemen after their manner; so that the pastime grew very pleasant for the space of three hours, wherein all three of the beasts were killed, whereof one took the sea, and there was slain with a musket. After this sport, many rare presents and gifts were given and bestowed on both parts, and the next day we played the merchants in bargaining with them by way of truck and exchange of divers of their commodities, as horses, mares, kine, bulls, goats, swine, sheep, bull-hides, sugar, ginger, pearl, tobacco, and such like commodities of the island.

The 7th day we departed with great good will from the Spaniards from the island of Hispaniola, but the wiser sort do impute this great show of friendship and courtesy used towards us by the Spaniards, rather to the force that we were of, and the vigilance and watchfulness that was amongst us, than to any hearty good will, or sure friendship entertained; for, doubtless, if they had

been stronger than we, we might have looked for no better courtesy at their hands than Master John Hawkins received at St.
John de Ulloa, or John Oxnam, near the Streights of Darien, and
divers others of our countrymen in other places.

[The reference here is to two acts of singular treachery and cruelty practiced by the Spaniards toward the English. That, in the case of Sir
John Hawkins, is recorded in Hakluyt, vol. 3. page 523 ; and that in
the case of Oxnam or Oxenham in the same volume, page 526].

The 8th day we anchored at a small island to take seals, which
in that place were understood to have been in great quantity,
where the general and certain others with him in the pinnace
were in very great danger to have been all cast away, but by the
help of God they escaped the hazard, and returned aboard the
admiral in safety.

The 9th day we arrived and landed in the Isle of Caycos, in
which island we searched for salt-ponds upon the advertisement
and information of a Portuguese, who indeed abused our general
and us, deserving a halter for his hire, if it has so pleased us.

The 12th we anchored at Guanima, and landed.

The 15th and 16th we anchored and landed at Cyguates.

The 20th we fell with the main of Florida.

The 23d we were in great danger of a wreck on a breach called
the Cape of Fear.

The 24th we came to anchor in a harbor, where we caught in
one tide so much fish as would have yielded us twenty pounds in
London. This was our first landing in Florida.

[At this early period, and on an unknown coast, it is not probable that
the boundary between Florida and Virginia was very well defined,
and hence we are not surprised that the coast is spoken of as that of
Florida. This name, however, was properly applied only to the regions discovered, possessed and claimed by the Spaniards ; and though
they probably had coasted as far north as Wocokon (Ocracoke), and
even beyond, yet they never made settlements there. The names
here mentioned leave no doubt of the locality intended. Cape Fear
and Ocracoke still retain their names : we have here also evidence of
the very early period (1585) in which the name of *Fear* was applied
to the cape ; this we believe, however, is the first historical record of

the name.   The earliest authentic chart containing the name is believed to be Smith's, bearing date 1607.   At least we have seen none earlier. On the same chart, Cape Hatteras is called Cape Amadas.   According to the map of 1666, as well as various others, Wococon is our Ocracoke].

The 26th we came to anchor at Wocokon.

The 29th we weighed anchor to bring the Tiger into the harbor, where, through the unskilfulness of the master, whose name was Fernando, the Admiral struck on ground and sunk.

[Theodore de Bry translated into Latin the history of this expedition, as furnished by Lane and Hariot, and published it in his great work.   It may be found in his " *Perigrationes in Americam, Part I*, 1590."   Hakluyt, in his account, has omitted some few passages, as he wished to condense and relate, not the perils, but the discoveries of his countrymen.   From the Latin of De Bry we translate the following :
"The sea-coast of Virginia abounds in islands, which cause the entrance into that country to be very difficult: for, although there are breaches at frequent intervals, which seem to promise commodious entrance, nevertheless we found them, to our great loss, to be shallow, and troubled with breakers ; nor were we able ever to penetrate into the interior, until we had made trial at various places with our smaller craft. At length, we found an entrance at a certain place, well known to our Englishmen : [he means those who had been on the first voyage].   Entering, therefore, and pursuing our navigation a little way, we observed a great river making its way out from this region of islands, which, however, we could not ascend, because of its narrowness, and the heaps of sand which obstructed its mouth.   Therefore, prosecuting our navigation further, we came to a large island, and then to a town called Roanoak."   The original of this is from the account of Hariot, which will be presented to the reader hereafter.   The original English, in its perfect form, probably, is not in existence ; but nearly the whole of it was printed by Hakluyt.]

JULY.   .

The 3d day of July we sent word of our arriving at Wococon, to Wingina at Roanoak.

The 6th, Master John Arundell was sent to the main, and *Manteo* with him, and Captain Aubry and Captain Boniton, the same day, were sent to Croatoan, where they found two of our men left there, with thirty others, by Captain Raymond some twenty days before.

[The precise locality of Croatan, or, as it is here written, Croatoan, is perhaps best settled by the ancient maps of North Carolina. According to the old chart of 1666, on which the name first appears, as well as on an old German map of Nuremburg, Croatoan seems to have been some portion of the banks lying between Cape Lookout and Cape Hatteras; perhaps the part now known as Borden's Banks, lying between old Topsail inlet and Bogue inlet, on the modern maps, having Bogue sound immediately north of it, and was in what is now the county of Carteret. On one of the later maps, however, another Croatoan, or rather Croatan, appears. Lawson, in his map, marks the present county of Tyrrel, opposite Roanoak island, by that name. The date of this, however, is 1709, and we have seen it on no other map among a dozen now before us. The Croatoan of the first adventurers was undoubtedly an *island* on the coast, and no part of the main land : for the first news of the arrival of Drake's fleet came to Lane from the man whom he had placed there to keep a lookout *seaward* for the expected supply ships. The approach of vessels could not have been seen from Tyrrel county. The paragraph of the narrative immediately preceding this note would also seem to imply that it was an island. A party with *Manteo* is sent "to the main," and another party sent the same day " to Croatoan," as if it were *not* on " the main." Beside, men were found on it who had been left by one of the ships that certainly never was on the shores of Tyrrel county. We shall, however, advert to this subject hereafter.

The 8th, Captain Aubry and Captain Boniton returned with two of our men found by them, to us at Wococon.

The 11th day, the general, accompanied in his tilt boat with Master John Arundell, Master Stukely, and divers other gentlemen, Master Lane, Master Candish, Master Hariot, and twenty others in the new pinnace, Captain Amadas, Captain Clarke with ten others in a ship-boat; Francis Brook and John White in another ship-boat, passed over the water from Wococon to the main land, victualled for eight days : in which voyage we first discovered the towns of *Pomeiok*, *Aquascogoc*, and *Secotan*, and also the great lake called by the savages *Paquipe*, with divers other places, and so returned with that discovery to our fleet.

The 12th, we came to the town of *Pomeiok*.

The 13th, we passed by water to *Aquascogoc*.

The 15th, we came to *Secotan*, and were well entertained there of the savages.

The 16th, we returned thence, and one of our boats, with the admiral, was sent to Aquascogoc, to demand a silver cup which one of the savages had stolen from us, and not receiving it according to his promise, we burned and spoiled their corn, all the people being fled.

The 18th, we returned from the discovery of Secotan, and the same day came aboard our fleet, riding at Wococon.

[From this paragraph we learn that Amadas was on this second voyage, as he had been on the first. Of Master Hariot, Master Lane, and John White, we shall hear again in the history of North Carolina colonization. At present we pass them by ; each, hereafter, will tell his own story. Of the localities here mentioned, Pomeiok and Secotan were not unknown to Amadas, for they are mentioned in the narrative of his voyage. The first named was probably, as we have already said, the country lying between the head of Bay River and Newbern ; and Secotan was, we think, on the head waters of Bay River, near or upon the boundary between Beaufort and Craven counties. Where was *Aquascogoc*, and where the "lake *Paquipe ?*" As to the latter, it is here said to be "great." Martin says it was Matamuskeet, in Hyde county, and as no other lake in this region but that can be called "great" with any propriety, he is probably correct.

It is more difficult, from our limited data, to form an opinion as to the situation of Aquascogoc. On the 12th of July, the party was in the town of Pomeiok : they were then in the country lying between the head waters of Bay River and Newbern. On the 13th, (the next day,) they were at Aquascogoc, to which place they went *by water*. On the 15th, (two days after,) they were at Secotan ; that is, on the borders of Beaufort and Craven, somewhere about the sources of Bay River.

Aquascogoc, consequently, was some place to which they could go by water in one day from the country lying just southeast of Newbern. The only water by which they could then travel was the Neuse river, and this would make Aquascogoc the country lying nearer the mouth of the river, possibly somewhere about Broad creek, perhaps not so low down ; two days after, we find them at the head of Bay river, and as they traveled by boat, two days, or part thereof, would be about the time they required to pull down to the mouth of the Neuse, and

up Bay river to the head of it.   What confirms this is, that on the day
after, (July 16,) we find them leaving Secotan, descending Bay river,
and ascending, we think, the Neuse, to revisit Aquascogoc, which they
reached on the 18th, (i. e. in two days,) and then took vengeance for
the theft of a silver cup, by burning the town and destroying the growing corn.   In one day after this destruction, they reached their ships,
and this they might readily do from the locality we suppose to be
Aquascogoc, by crossing the southern end of Pamlico sound.]

The 21st, our fleet anchoring at Wococon, we weighed anchor
for Hatorask.

The 27th, our fleet anchored at Hatorask, and there we rested.

The 29th, *Granganimeo*, brother to *Wingina*, came aboard the
Admiral, and *Manteo* with him.

AUGUST.

The 2d, the Admiral was sent to *Weapomeiok*.

[Where was this place ?   The map of Barlowe, made on the first voyage,
and published by De Bry, makes Weapomeiok the country lying immediately on the north side of Albermarle sound.   The "Admiral" was
"Master Philip Amadas."   On the 25th of August, Greenville sailed
for England, leaving, as we shall see, a colony behind him; his whole stay
in North Carolina was about two months, from the 24th of June to
the 25th of August.

The map subjoined was originally made by John Wyth, who was a member of the second expedition, and has been preserved by De Bry, from
whom we derived our copy.   On it we have endeavored to indicate all
the Indian localities that have been named, according to the best opinion
we can form from the data within our reach.

The 5th, Master Arundell was sent for England.

The 25th, our general weighed anchor and set sail for England.

No. 4.

AN ACCOUNT

OF THE PARTICULARITIES OF THE EMPLOYMENTS OF

THE ENGLISHMEN

LEFT IN VIRGINIA BY

RICHARD GRANVILLE,

UNDER THE CHARGE OF

MASTER RALPH LANE,

GENERAL OF THE SAME;

FROM THE 17TH OF AUGUST, 1585, UNTIL THE 18TH OF JUNE, 1586,

AT WHICH TIME THEY DEPARTED THE COUNTRY.

———

SENT AND DIRECTED TO

SIR WALTER RALEIGH.

[*From* HAKLUYT's VOYAGES, *Vol. III., page* 255.]

[This we suppose to be from the pen of Ralph Lane, and infer that it was
sent by him "from the new fort in Virginia" to his friend Hakluyt,
who has preserved it for us.]

The names of those, as well gentlemen as others, that remained one whole year in *Virginia*, under the government of Master Ralph Lane:—

MASTER PHILIP AMADAS, *Admiral of the Country.*

Master Hariot,
Master Acton,
Master Edward Stafford,
Thomas Luddington,
Master Marvyn,
Master Gardiner,
Captain Vaughan,
Master Kendall,
Master Prideox,
Robert Holecroft,
Rice Courtney,
Master Hugh Rogers,
Master Thomas Harvy,
Master Snelling,
Master Anthony Russe,
Master Allyne,
Master Michael Polison,
John Cage,
Thomas Parre,
William Randes,
Gefferey Churchman,
William Farthow,
John Taylor,
Philip Robins,
Thomas Philips,
Valentine Beale,
Thomas Fox,
Darby Glande,
Edward Nugen,
Edward Kelley,
John Gostigo,
Erasmus Clefs,

Edward Ketcheman,
John Linsey,
Thomas Rottenbury,
Roger Deane,
John Harris,
Francis Norris,
Matthew Lyne,
Edward Kettell,
Thomas Wisse,
Robert Biscombe,
William Backhouse,
William White,
Henry Potkin,
Dennis Barnes,
Joseph Borges,
Dougham Gannes,
William Tenche,
Randall Latham,
Thomas Hulme,
Walter Mill,
Richard Gilbert,
Stephen Pomarie,
John Brocke,
Bennett Harrie,
James Stevenson,
Charles Stevenson,
Christopher Lowde,
Jeremie Man,
James Mason,
David Salter,
Richard Ireland,
Thomas Bookener,

William Philips,	Thomas Smart,
Randall Mayne,	Robert ——,
James Skinner,	John Evans,
George Eseven,	Roger Large,
John Chandeler,	Humfrey Garden,
Philip Blunt,	Francis Whitton,
Richard Poor,	Rowland Griffyn,
Robert Yong,	William Millard,
Marmaduke Constable,	John Twit,
Thomas Hesket,	Edward Seclemore,
William Wasse,	John Anwike,
John Fever,	Christopher Marshall,
Daniel ——,	David Williams,
Thomas Taylor,	Nicholas Swabber,
Richard Humfrey,	Edward Chipping,
John Wright,	Silvester Beching,
Gabriel North,	Vincent Cheyne,
Bennett Chappell,	Hance Walters,
Richard Sare,	Edward Barecombe,
James Lacie,	Thomas Skevelabs,
—— Smolkin,	William Walters.

[This list of one hundred and seven names comprises what may be called
the first *colony* proper, in North Carolina. Of Amadas we know but
little more than may be inferred from the fact that he was one of the
captains of the first expedition in the previous year; and possessed so
much of character that he held the office of "Admiral of the Country"
on this his return to it. The second name on the list, " Master Hariot,"
is that of one who will hereafter be noticed. " Master Stafford" would
seem, from the narratives yet to come, to have been a man of energy,
intelligence and worth, who clung to the fortunes of the colony, not
only on this expedition, but in the subsequent one, conducted by John
White. Of the others here named, we can discover nothing.]

*An extract of Master Ralph Lane's letter to M. Richard Hakluyt,
Esq., and another gentleman of the Middle Temple, from
Virginia.*

In the meanwhile, you shall understand, that since Sir Richard
Greenvil's departure from us, as also before, we have discovered
the main to be the goodliest soil under the cope of heaven, so

abounding with sweet trees, that bring such sundry rich and
pleasant gums, grapes of such greatness, yet wild, as France,
Spain nor Italy have no greater, so many sorts of apothecary
drugs, such several kinds of flax, and one kind like silk, the same
gathered of a grass, as common there, as grass here. And now
within these few days we have found here maize, or Guinea wheat,
whose ear yielded corn for bread four hundred upon one ear, and
the cane makes very good and perfect sugar, also terra samia,
otherwise terra sigillata. Besides that, it is the goodliest and
most pleasing territory of the world; for the continent is of a
huge and unknown greatness, and very well peopled and towned,
though savagely, and the climate so wholesome, that we had not
one sick since we touched the land here. To conclude, if Virginia had but horses and kine in some reasonable proportion, I
dare assure myself, being inhabited with English, no realm in
Christendom were comparable to it. For this already we find,
that what commodities soever Spain, France, Italy, or the East
parts do yield unto us, in wines of all sorts, in oil, in flax, in rai-
sins, pitch, frankincense, currants, sugars, and such like, these
parts do abound with the growth of them all, but being savages
that possess the land, they know no use of the same. And sundry other rich commodities, that no parts of the world, be they
West or East Indies, have, here we find great abundance of. The
people naturally are most courteous, and very desirous to have
cloths, but especially of coarse cloth rather than silk, coarse can-
vas they also like well of, but copper carries the price of all, so it
be made red. Thus good M. Hakluyt and M. H., I have joined
you both in one letter of remembrance, as two that I love dearly
well, and commending me most heartily to you both, I commit
you to the tuition of the Almighty.

From the new fort in Virginia, this third of Sept., 1585.

Your most assured friend,

(Signed)   RALPH LANE.

[Two individuals worthy of remark are here brought to our notice.
Ralph Lane was appointed governor of those who were to be left to
form the colony. Of his early life we know nothing. Bancroft says,
he was " a man of considerable distinction," and we learn from Oldys

that after this expedition he was knighted by the queen; he was also of the council of war formed on the approach of the Spanish Armada. The narrative given by himself of his doings shows him to have been energetic, active and decided; though perhaps not always discreet. Bancroft affirms that he "did not possess the qualities suited to his station;" and alludes to the fact that he was imposed on by the falsehoods of the natives, and had no sagacity to detect their cunning. We are not prepared to concur entirely in this opinion. It is an easy matter for us, at this day, with far more knowledge both of the savage and his country than Lane possessed, to imagine that we can see gross errors in his mode of proceeding; but should we ask ourselves to define in detail, what we ourselves would have done in precisely his situation, we should perhaps find that we could not devise plans very different from those he adopted.

He had the rough courage of a soldier of his day, he endured hardships with his men, he had judgment to see that Roanoke island was not a proper site for the colony, and to devise a plan by which two parties, one on the land and the other on the water, should attempt to meet and find on the Chesapeake bay, a better locality, of which he had but heard from an Indian prince, his prisoner. He had wit and prudence enough to secure the fidelity of that prisoner by keeping his only son as a hostage; he pursued the wise policy of attaching that son to him by great personal kindness: he exhibited a provident forethought for the supply of his men with food, when disappointed in his expectation of an arrival from England with supplies. The personal attachment he had created in his young hostage was the means of his discovering a wide spread plot for the destruction of the colony by the natives; he nipped it in the bud by promptitude and courage, and exhibited therein, precisely those qualities, which he knew then, as we know now, are just those and those only which can overawe savages. Whether sagacious or not he reminds us forcibly, in a review of his measures and a survey of his conduct, of Captain John Smith's proceedings in circumstances not unlike his own. We must not therefore too hastily conclude that Lane was not fitted for his station. It is probable that in that day, no man that could have been sent would have been better qualified. Sir Walter Raleigh was one of the wisest men of his age, and one too that understood human nature well, and "looked quite through the thoughts of men." He was not likely to choose an unfit agent in an enterprise on which he had expended so much, and in which he felt so deep a personal interest.

"His discoveries were inconsiderable," says the historian. We dissent
from this statement entirely. Lane and his men were in Carolina one
year. The country was all unknown to them, and they were surrounded
by savages. Their whole number (including Lane) was one hundred
and eight. They had no means of exploration but by water in small
boats. Now let us see what portions of the state they visited during
that year. Beginning at the south, "Croatoan," they will be found to
have visited of our present counties, Carteret, Craven, a part of Jones,
Beaufort, Hyde, and all the five counties north of Albermarle sound,
from Currituck sound to Chowan river. They ascended Chowan river,
and thus coasted at least Bertie, Hertford and Gates, for they went up
to the junction of the Meherrin and Nottoway rivers. They ascended
the Roanoke until they were " one hundred and sixty miles from home "
(Roanoke island) and as the distance from that spot to the mouth of
the Roanoke is some fifty miles, they must have been up the river one
hundred and ten miles ; they then ascended it for two days more, and
if but ten miles per day be allowed, they must have ascended the
Roanoke one hundred and thirty miles from its mouth. This would
have taken them along the borders of Martin, Bertie, Halifax, North-
ampton and Warren counties. To the northward, they went one
hundred and thirty miles from Roanoke island ; here their voyage must
have been up Currituck sound which took them into Virginia.
Leaving the water, they traveled into the country of the " Chesapeans"
which was " distant fifteen miles from the shoare " : so that they almost
reached the Chesapeake bay below Norfolk. In short, toward the
south they journeyed from eighty to one hundred miles ; northward they
went one hundred and thirty miles ; northwestward (toward Chowan)
they traveled one hundred and thirty miles, and westward, up the
Roanoke nearly if not quite as far as its waters are in North Carolina ;
and visited or coasted no less than eighteen of our present counties. In fact
they *crossed the entire state* from the sea shore at Croatan into Virginia.
We submit that this amount of discovery made in one year, by a little
handful of men, in a perfectly wild and unknown country, peopled by
hostile savages, hardly deserves to be called " inconsiderable."

As to " M. Richard Hakluyt *Esquire*," the suffix of honor to his name
would appear to us of this day somewhat misplaced, as he was entitled
to the prefix of " *Reverend*," and, let us add, did it no discredit. The
obligations of North Carolina to him are not small. But for him it
may be doubted, whether we ever should have known the particulars
of the early efforts made by Raleigh to colonize the state. Hakluyt

was born at Eyton in Herefordshire in 1553. He commenced his education at Westminster school, and while there, even in his boyhood, acquired the taste for maritime history and geography which distinguished him through life. He had a cousin of the same name, who was a student at the temple, and was fond of geographical studies, and he it was who probably implanted in our Westminster school boy the fondness for voyages, and discoveries.

From Westminster, Hakluyt went to Christ Church, Oxford, and there became so eminent for his studies in cosmography that he was appointed public lecturer on that subject. He was one of the earliest English collectors of voyages and maritime journals, and in 1582 published a small volume of " Voyages and Discoveries," which formed the basis of his subsequent larger work. In 1548, he went to Paris as chaplain to the English embassy, and remaining there for five years, added to his collections. Here among other documents he became possessed of the specimens of Mexican picture writing, published by Purchas in his third volume. It seems that the Spanish governor of Mexico obtained (not without difficulty) the book of the Indians with their own interpretations of the pictures, and caused the latter to be translated from Mexican into Spanish. He then sent the book thus translated, together with the original, to the Emperor Charles V. The ship was taken by a French war vessel, and brought into some port of France. Andrew Thevet, the French king's geographer, became possessed of the manuscripts, and upon his death, Hakluyt bought them for *twenty French crowns*, and acting for Sir Walter Raleigh, employed Michael Locke to translate them from the Spanish into English. The cost of the engravings, however, prevented their publication then ; and after Hakluyt's death, all his papers went, by his direction, into the hands of his brother clergyman, Samuel Purchas, whose tastes harmonized with his own. Purchas subsequently published them, and thus gave to Europe its *first* fac-simile of Mexican picture writing. These have been largely added to since by Humboldt and others, and particularly by Lord Kingsborough in his great work.

While Hakluyt was in Paris, he was appointed a prebendary in Bristol Cathedral ; and on his return home, he was chosen by Sir Walter Raleigh a member of " the corporation of counsellors, assistants, and adventurers," to whom he assigned his patent. It was in consequence of this appointment that he prepared his great work—a collection of " the principal navigations, voyages, and discoveries of the English nation, made by sea or overland, within the compass of these **1500** years." The first volume was published, in folio, in 1589, and the third and last in 1600. The work is very valuable, and a perfect edition is hardly to be procured. Beside the narratives of between two and three hundred voyages, related commonly by those who performed them, or by contemporaries, the work comprises patents, letters, instructions, and other documents, all rare, and some not to be found anywhere else. Without a study of this, and the similar work by Purchas in four volumes, it is impossible to obtain an accurate knowledge of the early settlements and colonization of the United States. In 1605, Hakluyt was promoted to a prebend in Westminster, which, with the rectory of Wetheringsel in Suffolk, was all the ecclesiastical preferment he ever had. Enthusiasts in their favorite pursuit, as both he and Purchas were, they yet were diligent as preachers, and men of irreproachable lives. Hakluyt died in 1616, and was buried in Westminster Abbey. His name has been perpetuated by his contemporary, the celebrated navigator, Henry Hudson, who bestowed on one of the promontories on the coast of Greenland the name of "Hakluyt's Headland."]

That I may proceed with order in this discourse, I think it requisite to divide it into two parts. The first shall declare the particulars of such parts of the country within the main as our weak number and supply of things necessary did enable us to enter into the discovery of.

The second part shall set down the reasons generally moving us to resolve on our departure at the instant with the General Sir Francis Drake, and our common request for passage with him, when the barks, pinnaces, and boats, with the masters and mariners meant by him to be left in the country for the supply of such as for a further time meant to have stayed there, were carried away with tempest and foul weather. In the beginning whereof shall be declared the conspiracy of Pemisapan with the savages of the main to have cut us off, &c.

THE FIRST PART:

DECLARING THE PARTICULARS OF THE COUNTRY OF

VIRGINIA.

First, therefore, touching the particularities of the country, you shall understand that our discovery of the same has been extended from the island of Roanoak (the same having been the place of our settlement or inhabitation) into the South, into the North, into the Northwest, and into the West.

The uttermost place to the southward of any, Secotan, being by estimation fourscore miles distant from Roanoak. The passage from thence was through a broad sound within the main, the same being without kenning land, and yet full of flats and shoals. We had but one boat with four oars to pass through the same, which boat could not carry above fifteen men with their furniture, baggage, and victual, for seven days at most; and as for our pinnace, besides that she drew too deep water for that shallow sound, she would not stir for an oar: for these and other reasons (winter also being at hand), we thought good wholly to leave the discovery of those parts until our stronger supply.

To the northward our furthest discovery was to the Chesipeans, distant from Roanoak about one hundred and thirty miles; the passage to it was very shallow and most dangerous, by reason of the breadth of the sound, and the little succor that, upon flaw, was there to be had.

But the territory and soil of the Chesipeans (being distant fifteen miles from the shore), for pleasantness of seat, for temperature of climate, for fertility of soil, and for the commodity of the sea, besides multitudes of bears (being an excellent good victual), and great woods of sassafras and walnut-trees, is not to be excelled by any other whatsoever.

There be sundry kings, whom they call *Weroances*, and countries of great fertility adjoining to the same, as the *Mandoags*, *Tripanieks*, and *Opossians*, which all came to visit the colony of the English, which I had for a time appointed to be resident there.

To the northwest, the farthest place of our discovery was to

Chawanook, distant from Roanoak about one hundred and thirty miles. Our passage thither layed through a broad sound, but all fresh water, and the channel of great depth, navigable for good shipping, but out of the channel full of shoals.

The towns about the water's side, situated by the way, are these following : *Passaquenoke*, "the woman's town," *Chepanoc*, *Weapomeiok*, *Muscamunge*, and *Metackwem :* all these being under the jurisdiction of the king of *Weapomeiok*, called *Okisco ;* from *Muscamunge* we enter into the river and jurisdiction of *Chawanook*, there the river begins to straighten until it comes to *Chawanook*, and then groweth to be as narrow as the Thames between Westminster and Lambeth.

Between *Muscamunge* and *Chawanook*, upon the left hand as we pass thither, is a goodly high land, and there is a town which we called The Blind Town, but the savages called it *Ohanoak*, and has a very goodly corn-field belonging into it : it is subject to *Chawanook*.

Chawanook itself is the greatest province and seignory lying upon that river, and the very town itself is able to put seven hundred fighting men into the field, besides the forces of the province itself.

[These towns, we infer from the text, were all on the north side of Albermarle sound, between its head and that part of the shore opposite to Roanoak island. The locality of *Weapomeiok* is furnished by the early maps. From that in De Bry, it would seem to have been a *general* name for the country north of Albermarle, including probably Camden, Pasquotank, Perquimons, and it may be, part of Gates. But there was also a *town* named Weapomeiok, the chief town, it is likely, of the district alluded to. At any rate, every town named, except Chawanook, is said to be subject to the jurisdiction of Weapomeiok.

We have no difficulty in fixing the locality of *Passaquenoke*, or "the Woman's Towne," for that also is on De Bry's map. It was in the southwest corner of the present county of Pasquotank, not far from the sound. And here we would remark, in passing, that we find on some maps the name of Pasquotank written in *two* words, *Passo-Tanck*. The meaning is at present beyond our discovery.

Chawanook also tells its locality in its name : it was on the Chowan river. The map of 1666 gives us the name, and places it on the eastern

side of Chowan, below the junction of the Meherrin and Black, and below the point at which Bennet's Creek enters the Chowan. It was in
the northern part of Chowan county. This, as the text informs us, was
a large town, capable of mustering seven hundred warriors, and had
beside at least one tributary. Vestiges of it, therefore, would be
likely to remain, after smaller places had been entirely obliterated ;
and it is observable that as late as 1738, when Wimble made his map,
at the locality indicated above, he marks an "Indian town." Possibly
the spot thus noted by Wimble marks the site of Chawanook.

Muscamunge, we are told, is left behind as we enter the river and jurisdiction of Chawanook, which was on the *upper* waters of the Chowan.
This town, therefore, was on the lower waters of the river on their
eastern side, somewhere between the mouth or sound proper, and the
point above, where it "groweth to be as narrow as the Thames between
Westminster and Lambeth." This would place it on the waters which
bound Chowan county on its western side, above the sound proper ;
and here accordingly it is found on Smith's map of 1629. On the
opposite side, on "the left hand," says the text, "as we pass between
Muscamunge and *Chawanook*," is "a goodly high land," which had a
town on it. The English called it "the blinde town." Its Indian name
was *Ohanoak*. This was in Bertie, on its eastern side, somewhere on
the waters of the Chowan. It is found on Smith's map. And here,
we would suggest, we have probably the origin of the name now applied to the river, which, bordering Bertie on the west and south, empties into Albermarle. We call it Roanoke, an easy corruption from
Ohanoak. Its Indian name was *Moratoc*.

As to *Chepanock* and *Metackwem*, Smith's map enables us to fix their
respective localities. Chepanock was in the lower part of Perquimons
county, near the sound, and Metackwem (called by Smith Metocaum)
was in Bertie, on the Chowan river a few miles north of Walnut
Point].

The king of the said province is called *Menatonon*, a man im-
potent in his limbs, but otherwise for a savage a very grave and
wise man, and of a very singular good discourse in matters concerning the state, not only in his own country, and the disposition
of his own men, but also of his neighbors round about him, as
well far as near, and of the commodities that each country
yielded. When I had him prisoner with me, for two days that
we were together, he gave me more understanding and light of

the country than I have received by all the searches and savages
that before I or any of my company had had conference with:
it was in March last past, 1586. Amongst other things he told
me, that going three days' journey in a canoe by his river of
Chawanook, and then descending to the land, you are within four
days' journey to pass over land northeast to a certain king's
country, whose province lays upon the sea, but his place of
greatest strength is an island situate, as he described unto me, in
a bay, the water round about the island very deep.

[There is a remarkable degree of accurate knowledge of the country
 shown in this statement of the king of Chawanook. Ascend the Chowan
 three days' journey, paddling in a canoe, leave the river, and proceed
 on foot north-eastwardly, imagine the land travel to be through a wilderness, and about four days' of such journeying, will bring one to the
 country around Norfolk : the " island in a bay " is probably Craney
 Island].

Out of this bay, he signified unto me, that this king had so
great a quantity of pearl, and does so ordinarily take the same,
as that not only his own skins that he wears, and the better sort
of his gentlemen and followers are full set with the said pearl,
but also his beds and houses are garnished with them, and that
he has such quantities of them that it is a wonder to see.

He showed me that the said king was with him at Chawanook
two years before and brought him certain pearl, but the same of
the worst sort, yet was he fain to buy them of him for copper at
a dear rate, as he thought. He gave me a rope of the same pearl,
but they were black, and naught, yet many of them were very
great, and a few amongst a number very orient and round, all
which I lost, with other things of mine, coming aboard Sir Francis Drake, his fleet, yet he told me that the said king had great
store of pearl that were white, great and round, and that his
black pearl his men did take out of shallow water, but the white
pearl his men fished for in very deep water.

It seemed to me by his speech, that the said king had traffic
with white men that had clothes as we have, for these white
pearl ; and that was the reason that he would not depart with
other than with black pearl to those of the same country.

[As to the pearls here spoken of, allusion was made to the existence of
pearls in the voyage of Amadas and Barlowe.   The pearl-oyster *may*
once have abounded in the waters of Carolina and south-eastern Virginia, but we know of no evidence for such a fact save that contained
in the story of this and the previous voyage.   As to the *white* persons
who (according to Lane's conjecture) were in the habit of coming to
trade for the white pearl : if any such came, they were probably Spaniards, who belonged to the settlements of that nation made on the
Atlantic coast further south.   There were Spanish colonies in what is
now Florida, before the first visit of the English to Roanoak island ;
and that their vessels sometimes came on the coast of North Carolina,
is rendered very probable from the fact of the wreck of two European
vessels near Secotan, mentioned in the narrative of Amadas and
Barlowe].

The king of Chawanook promised to give me guides to go overland into that king's country whensoever I would, but he advised
me to take good store of men with me, and good store of victuals,
for he said, that king would be loth to suffer any strangers to
enter into his country, and especially to meddle with the fishing
for any pearl there, and that he was able to take a great many
men into the field, which he said would fight very well.

Hereupon I resolved with myself, that if your supply had come
before the end of April, and that you had sent any store of boats,
or men to have had them made in any reasonable time, with a
sufficient number of men and victuals to have found us until the
new corn were come in, I would have sent a small bark with two
pinnaces about the sea to the northward to have found out the
bay he spoke of, and have sounded the bar, if there were any,
which should have ridden there in the said bay about that island,
while I with all the small boats I could make, and with two hundred men, would have gone up to the head of the river of Chawanook, with the guides that Menatonon would have given me,
which I would have been assured should have been of his best
men (for I had his best beloved son prisoner with me) who also
should have kept me company in a handlock with the rest, foot by
foot, all the voyage overland.

[We have here proof of the judgment and good sense of Lane.   Had he carried out this plan of a double expedition by water and land, he would undoubtedly have found the bay of Chesapeake and Craney island, and his explorers, of both parties, would have met there, thus anticipating the settlement of Jamestown by some twenty years. And although Lane was unable to carry out his scheme of exploration, yet there can be no doubt that this statement of his influenced Sir Walter Raleigh in directing the course of his future adventures. For John White, who commanded the colony of the next expedition, was ordered merely to *stop* at Roanoke island for a time, and then proceed further north to this great bay, and find on it a better site for the colony than that on Roanoke island. So also Captain John Smith, at a subsequent period, made at once with his companions for the Chesapeake, and did not touch in North Carolina at all. And Sir Walter thus directed because of this information brought home to him by Lane. If we take into consideration what the latter *saw* and what he *heard*, that subsequently proved true, his discoveries and correct information were too valuable to be called " inconsiderable." Raleigh was sagacious enough to deem them far otherwise.]

My meaning was further, at the head of the river, in the place of my descent where I would have left my boats, to have raised a sconse with a small trench, and a pallisado upon the top of it ; in the which, and in the guard of my boats I would have left five and twenty, or thirty men, with the rest would I have marched with as much victual as every man could have carried with their furniture, mattocks, spades and axes, two days' journey. In the end of my march, upon some convenient plot, would I have raised another sconse, according to the former, where I would have left fifteen or twenty. And if it would have fallen out conveniently, in the way I would have raised my said sconse upon some corn-field, that my company might have lived upon it.

And so I would have holden this course of insconsing every two days' march, until I had been arrived at the bay or port he spake of, which finding to be worth the possession, I would there have raised a main fort, both for the defence of the harbor, and our shipping also, and would have reduced our whole habitation from Roanoak and from the harbor and port there (which by proof is very naught) unto this other before mentioned ; from whence, in the four days' march before specified, could I at all

times return with my company back unto my boats, riding under
my sconse ; very near whereunto, directly from the west, runs a
most notable river, and in all those parts most famous, called the
river of *Moratoc*. This river opens into the broad sound of Weapomeiok. And whereas the river of Chawanook, and all the other
sounds and bays, salt and fresh, shew no current in the world in
calm weather, but are moved altogether with the wind ; this river
of Moratoc has so violent a current from the west and southwest,
that it made me almost of opinion that with oars it would scarce
be navigable ; it passes with many creeks and turnings, and for
the space of thirty miles' rowing and more, it is as broad as the
Thames betwixt Greenwich and the Isle of Dogs, in some place
more, and in some less ; the current runs as strong, being entered
so high into the river, as at London bridge, upon a vale water.

And for that not only Menatonon, but also the savages of Moratoc themselves do report strange things of the head of the river,
and that from Moratoc itself, which is a principal town upon the
river, it is thirty days, as some of them say, and some say forty
days' voyage to the head thereof, which head, they say, springs
out of a main rock, in that abundance, that forthwith makes a
most violent stream ; and further, that this huge rock stands so
near unto the sea, that many times in storms, (the wind coming
outwardly from the sea,) the waves thereof are beaten into the
said fresh stream, so that the fresh water, for a certain space,
groweth salt and brackish ;—I took a resolution with myself,
having dismissed Menatonon upon a ransom agreed for, and sent
his son into the pinnace to Roanoak, to enter presently so far into
that river with two double wherries, and forty persons one or
other, as I could have victual to carry us, until we could meet
with more either of the Moratocs, or of the Mangoaks, which is
another kind of savages, dwelling more to the westward of the
said river ; but the hope of recovering more victual from the savages made me and my company as narrowly to escape starving in
that discovery before our return, as ever men did, that missed the
same.

[Here we learn that Lane had found the harbor and port at Roanoke to
be, what we, on geological considerations, feel very sure it always has
been, " very naught." And we think we may add, on scientific con-

siderations, that no efforts at reopening closed inlets will ever make either inlet or harbor at Roanoke otherwise than " very naught." We fear that *no inlet on the coast of North Carolina, north of Cape Hatteras, can ever be made permanently good for vessels of any size.* One fact seems indisputable, that all the inlets between the Capes of the Chesapeake and Cape Hatteras have been growing *worse*, ever since Europeans settled the country, and some, once open, are now *entirely obliterated.* The natural causes which have produced such results are and must be still operative ; and, however energetically scientific skill may be brought to bear in combating them, the enormous outlay required to insure and perpetuate even partial success, will be such as to render the enterprise hopelessly unremunerative. It will be literally a casting of money into the sea. The very existence of the long banks through which inlets once existed, *formed as they are from action on the seaward side alone,* tell the whole story. They point out their origin, and the consequent perpetuity of the obstacles they *must* create, and indicate, to science at least, the immense difficulty, not to say impossibility of their permanent removal.

Lane here gives us also the original Indian name of what we now call the Roanoke river, *Moratoc.* His description leaves us in no doubt as to the stream he means; but if there were doubt, it would be removed by the old map of 1666 which marks the river with the name, Moratoc. We learn here too the original Indian name of Albermarle sound ; he calls it, " the broad sound of *Weapomeiok.*" We wish we knew its meaning.

As to the great length of the river, and its origin in a rock near a sea, we must not too hastily condemn Lane for an easy credulity in believing such marvellous stories. He relates them but *as stories,* told him by " Menatonon, and the savages of Moratoc," he calls them " strange things," and above all, he resolves to test the truth of the Indian's account of the river by personal exploration. Bancroft says, " he had not the sagacity which could rightly interpret the stories or the designs of the natives ;" if he could not interpret their story (and we really see not what there was in it to *interpret ;* for it was a plain statement of facts simply), he at least did all a man of sense could do in determining to find out for himself whether they stated facts truly. But he could not interpret their *designs.*" This is no reproach; very wise men have been deceived by the cunning of the North American Indian ; but Lane was watchful enough, very soon to detect their plans, and by promptitude and courage, he *defeated them.* But he was weak enough to believe the Roanoke rose near the sea. There is no proof that he did so believe : but suppose he did, it would not prove weakness of mind. It might prove deplorable ignorance and weakness in a writer of the present day so to believe, because the geography of the country is now very well known : but Lane must not be judged by our modern knowledge ; all west of him was a perfect wilderness. How was he instinctively to discover that there was no sea, west of him ? "The keenest observer was Hariot," says Mr. Bancroft. He is named by the historian as one of the " men of merit whom the world remembers," and he certainly was familiar with much of the scientific knowledge the world then had. Now what was his opinion as to the head of the Roanoke ? A very inaccurate one as we all can testify, but here it is, agreeing with that which is imputed to Lane. "For this river of Moratoc promiseth great things, and by the opinion of M. Hariot, the head of it, by the description of the country " (and what else had any of them to go by) " either riseth from—*the Bay of Mexico* [!], or else from very near unto the same that openeth out into the South Sea." Hariot merely supposed the northern shore of the Gulf of Mexico to be several degrees further north than it is ; but he knew that the Gulf made far into the continent toward the Pacific. He had learned that from the early Spanish expeditions, which by the way touched not its northern shores. But, alas for poor Lane ! " the hope of gold attracted Lane to make a short excursion up the Roanoke : " short we have seen it was not ; but short or long, the motive was *gold*. If every man who seeks gold on some excursion or other, is therefore to be condemned as inefficient, silly, and imbecile, I know not what will be the fate of most men. There are living men who have sought and are still eagerly seeking gold, by other means than that of ascending the Moratoc. They may not indeed find the gold any more than Lane did ; but when they return, will they be able to tell the world any thing as important to its interests as the discovery of a noble river ? Perhaps not. If Lane had *found* the gold, would the historian have ever sneered at him for *seeking* it ? Probably not. It is an easy thing to sit down in the comforts of a man's study, with the surroundings of maps and books and all modern appliances for gaining knowledge, and for the sake of making a point antithetical, or polishing a period, or euphoniously rounding off a sentence, to send a man down to posterity, historically damned by a dash of the pen : but to quiet thinkers and readers, who are just men, the question will come up, " is this *right*."]

For Pemisapan, who had changed his name of Wingina upon the death of his brother Granganimeo, had given both the Choanists, and Mangoaks word of my purpose touching them, I having been forced to make him privy to the same, to be served by him of a guide to the Mangoaks; and yet he did never rest to solicit continually my going upon them, certifying me of a general assembly even at that time made by Menatonon at Chawanook of all his Weroances, and allies to the number of three thousand bows, preparing to come upon us at Roanoak, and that the Mangoaks also were joined in the same confederacy, who were able of themselves to bring as many more to the enterprise: And true it was that at that time the assembly was holden at Chawanook about us, as I found at my coming thither, which being unlooked for did so dismay them, as it made us have the better hand at them. But this confederacy against us of the Choanists and Mangoaks was altogether and wholly procured by Pemisapan himself, as Menatonon confessed unto me, who sent them continual word, that our purpose was fully to destroy them; on the other side he told me, that they had the like meaning towards us.

He in like sort having sent word to the Mangoaks of mine intentions to pass up into their river, and to kill them (as he said) both they and the Moratocs, with whom before we were entered into a league; and they had ever dealt kindly with us, abandoned their towns along the river, and retired themselves with their *Crenepos,** and their corn, within the main, in so much, as having passed three days' voyage up the river, we could not meet a man, nor find a grain of corn in any of their towns; whereupon considering with myself that we had but two days' victual left, and that we were then one hundred and sixty miles from home, besides casualty of contrary winds or storms, and suspecting treason of our own savages in the discovery of our voyage intended, though we had no intention to be hurtful to any of them, otherwise than, for our copper, to have had corn of them, I at night upon the corps of guard, before the putting forth of sentinels, advertised the whole company of the case we stood in for victual, and of my opinion we were betrayed by our own savages, and of

---

* " Their women."

purpose drawn forth by them, upon vain hope to be in the end starved, seeing all the country fled before us; and therefore while we had those two days' victual left, I thought it good for us to make our return homeward, and that it were necessary for us to get the other side of the sound of Weopomeiok in time, where we might be relieved upon the weirs of Chypanum, and the women's town, although the people were fled.

[He means by the fish they might find in the weirs.]

Thus much I signified unto them, as the safest way; nevertheless, I did refer it to the greatest number of voices, whether we should adventure the spending of our whole victual in some further view of that most goodly river in hope to meet with some better pass, or otherwise to retire ourselves back again. And for that they might be the better advised, I willed them to deliberate all night upon the matter, and in the morning at our going aboard to set our course according to the desires of the greatest part. Their resolutions fully and wholly was (and not three found to be of the contrary opinion) that while there was left one-half pint of corn for a man, we should not leave the search of that river, and that there were in the company two mastiffs, upon the pottage of which, with sassafras leaves, (if the worst fell out) the company would made shift to live two days, which time would bring them down the current to the mouth of the river, and to the entry of the sound, and in two days more, at the farthest, they hoped to cross the sound and to be relieved by the weirs; which two days they would fast rather than to draw back a foot till they had seen the Mangoaks, either as friends or foes. This resolution of theirs did not a little please me, since it came of themselves, although for mistrust of that which afterward did happen, I pretended to have been rather of the contrary opinion.

And that which made me most desirous to have some doings with the Mangoaks, either in friendship or otherwise to have had one or two of them prisoners, was, for that it is a thing most notorious to all the country, that there is a province to the which the said Mangoaks have recourse and traffic up that river of Moratoe, which has a marvellous and most strange mineral. This

mine is so notorious amongst them, as not only to the savages
dwelling up the said river, and also to the savages of Chawanook,
and all them to the westward, but also to all them of the main,
the country's name is of fame, and is called *Chaunis Temoatan*.

The mineral, they say, is *Wassador*, which is copper, but they
call by the name of Wassador every metal whatsoever : they say
it is of the color of our copper, but our copper is better than
theirs, and the reason is for that it is redder and harder, whereas
that of Chaunis Temoatan is very soft and pale : they say that
they take the said metal out of a river that falls very swift from
the rocks and hills, and they take it in shallow water. The manner is this : they take a great bowl, by their description as great
as one of our targets, and wrap a skin over the hollow part thereof, leaving one part open to receive in the mineral ; that done,
they watch the coming down of the current, and the change of
the color of the water, and then suddenly chop down the said
bowl with the skin, and receive into the same as much ore as will
come in, which is ever as much as their bowl will hold, which
presently they cast into a fire, and forthwith it melts, and does
yield in fine parts, at the first melting, two parts of metal for
three parts of ore.   Of this metal the Mangoaks have so great
store, by report of all the savages adjoining, that they beautify
their houses with great plates of the same, and this to be true, I
received by report of all the country, and particularly by young
Skiko, the king of Chawanook's son, my prisoner, who also himself had been prisoner with the Mangoaks, and set down all the
particularities to me before mentioned ; but he had not been at
Chaunis Temoatan himself, for he said it was twenty days' journey
overland from the Mangoaks to the said mineral country, and that
they passed through certain other territories between them and
the Mangoaks before they came to the said country.

[Of this famous region, *Chaunis Temoatan*, I can find no other account
   than that which is here written. It was perhaps like the El Dorado
   which lured Raleigh to Guiana. The Indians themselves may, however, have believed the stories they told, and may have seen gold from
   the country west of them, which they deemed a species of inferior soft
   copper. Metal to them was valuable only as it could be utilized to the
   necessary purposes of practical life. They knew nothing of " bullion "

or " specie " or a current " medium of exchange :" their trade was barter
merely.

It is curious enough that if we proceed westward from the country where
the adventurers then were, we shall come presently, at the distance of
some 150 miles or little more, upon the gold-producing region of North
Carolina. So, too, of copper, with which the savages appear to have
been familiar enough, we of this day know localities where they might
have procured it not so far from them as the gold region. We may,
then, (with the information we have) *imagine*, if we please, " Chaunis
Temoatan " to have reached, on the one hand, from Chatham, Moore
and Robinson counties, to the Great Catawba, and on the other, from
our southern boundary up to the middle or beyond, of Randolph, David-
son, Rowan and Iredell counties. The natives did *not* lie when they
said gold was west of them ; and Lane was *not* deceived if he believed
them. Singular is it that we should now be telling the world, as an
indisputable truth, and such it is, the very same story that caused the
poor Indians to be branded as liars—viz., that our good country is surpassingly rich in metallic wealth, deposited in the earth. What if
some future historian should call us liars ! Will it make us so ?]

Upon report of the premises, which I was very inquisitive in
all places where I came to take very particular information of, by
all the savages that dwelt towards those parts, and especially of
Menatonon himself, who in every thing did very particularly
inform me, and promised me guides of his own men, who should
pass over with me, even to the said country of Chaunis Temoatan
(for overland from Chawanook to the Mangoaks is but one day's
journey from sun rising to sun setting, whereas by water it is
seven days with the soonest). These things, I say, made me very
desirous by all means possible to recover the Mangoaks, and to
get some of their copper for an assay, and therefore I willingly
yielded to their resolutions. But it fell out, very contrary to all
expectation and likelihood, for after two days' travel, and our
whole victual spent, lying on shore all night, we could never see
man, only fires we might perceive made along the shore where
we were to pass, and up into the country, until the very last day.
In the evening whereof, about three of the clock, we heard certain
savages call, as we thought, Manteo, who was also at that time
with me in the boat ; whereof we all being very glad, hoping of

some friendly conference with them, and making him to answer
them, they presently began a song, as we thought, in token of our
welcome to them, but Manteo presently betook him to his piece,
and told me that they meant to fight with us, which word was not
so soon spoken by him, and the light-horseman [*sic.*] ready to put to
shore, but there lighted a volley of their arrows amongst them in
the boat, but did no hurt, God be thanked, to any man.

[Here we note two things : 1st. The fidelity of Manteo ; he was always
true to the whites ; and 2dly. The fact that he understood the language
of the natives upon the Roanok, while he was himself a native of *Croatoan,* down near Ocracoke. The fact is important ethnologically ; but
we shall have occasion to speak of the native dialects hereafter.]

Immediately, the other boat lying ready with their shot to scour
the place for our hand weapons to land upon, which was presently
done, although the land was very high and steep, the savages
forthwith quitted the shore, and betook themselves to flight ; we
landed, and having fair and easily followed for a small time after
them, who had wooded themselves we knew not where ; the sun
drawing then towards the setting, and being then assured that
the next day, if we would pursue them, though we might happen
to meet with them, yet we should be assured to meet with none
of their victual, which we then had good cause to think of ; therefore, choosing for the company a convenient ground in safety to
lodge in for the night, making a strong corps of guard, and putting out good sentinels, I determined, the next morning, before
the rising of the sun, to be going back again, if possibly we might
recover the mouth of the river, into the broad sound, which at
my first motion I found my whole company ready to assent unto ;
for they were now come to their dog's porridge, that they had
bespoken for themselves, if that befell them which did, and I
before did mistrust we should hardly escape. The end was, we
came the next day by night to the river's mouth, within four or
five miles of the same, having rowed in one day down the current,
as much as in four days we had done against the same ; we lodged
upon the island, where we had nothing in the world to eat but
pottage of sassafras leaves, the like whereof for a meat was never
used before, as I think. The broad sound we had to pass the next

day all fresh and fasting; that day the wind blew so strongly, and the billow so great, that there was no possibility of passage without sinking of our boats. This was upon Easter eve, which was fasted very truly. Upon Easter day, in the morning, the wind coming very calm, we entered the sound, and by four of the clock we were at Chypanum, whence all the savages that we had left there were fled, but their weirs did yield us some fish, as God was pleased not utterly to suffer us to be lost; for some of our company of the light-horsemen were far spent. The next morning we arrived at our home, Roanoak.

[We are at a loss to explain what Lane means by "the light-horsemen."]

I have set down this voyage somewhat particularly, to the end it may appear unto you, (as true it is,) that there wanted no great good will from the most to the least amongst us, to have perfected this discovery of the mine; for that the discovery of a good mine, by the goodness of God, or passage to the South-Sea, or some way to it, and nothing else, can bring this country in request to be inhabited by our nation. And with the discovery of either of the two above shewed, it will be the most sweet and healthful climate, and therewithal the most fertile soil (being manured) in the world; and then will sassafras, and many other roots and gums there found make good merchandise and lading for shipping, which otherwise of themselves will not be worth the fetching.

[Lane seems here to think the discovery of one of two things indispensable to the prosperity of the country; these are "the discovery of a good mine by the goodness of God," or "a passage to the South Sea, or some way to it;" and naively enough he adds, that if either of them can be found, "it will be the most sweete and healthfullest climate, and therewithall the most fertile soyle (*being manured*) in the world." Being manured enough, we suppose, would make the soil fertile, without mine or South Sea passage; and "the most sweete and healthfullest climate" has not been ordinarily supposed to depend on the presence of a mine, or a way to the Pacific. But is there not a sly touch of quiet humor, not to say irony in the rough sailor's writing? May he not mean that the prospect of gain will make men think *any* climate salubrious. There are men who talk at this day of the salubrity of Batavia, and the delightfully invigorating and wholesome breezes over the Isthmus of Panama. Nay, there are those who, in the eager pursuit of money, cannot be persuaded that even Tophet is in an uncomfortably warm latitude.]

Provided, also, that there be found out a better harbor than yet there is, which must be to the northward, if any there be, which was mine intention to have spent this summer in the search of, and of the mine of Chaunis Temoatan : the one I would have done, if the barks that I should have had of Sir Francis Drake, by his honorable courtesy, had not been driven away by storm, the other if your supply of more men, and some other necessaries had come to us in any conveniency. For this river of Moratoc promised great things, and by the opinion of M. Hariot the head of it, by the description of the country, either rises from the bay of Mexico, or else from very near unto, that opens out into the South Sea.

[Here Lane finds another and much more reasonable prerequisite to the prosperity of the country, "a better harborough" [harbor] than any he then knew. If the harbor of Beaufort with its excellent and deep inlet existed at that day, even as it does now, we can account for its having been then overlooked on but two grounds : 1st, it was nearer the settlements of Spanish enemies, at the south, who sometimes visited the coast; and, 2d, the country immediately around it was so utterly barren as to promise no return to labor. Food could not be made to grow on sand only. But be this as it may, no country lying on the sea can prosper without a harbor; and if there be a good one on her coast, that country is bound by the strong obligation of interest, individual and national, to concentrate her efforts to make that harbor a depôt for her products, and the chief seat of her foreign trade. Even as in Lane's day, so is it now : all that Carolina wants is a good harbor. She has it in her power to make one that few can rival. But all Lane's ideas were of a harbor "to the northward," as we shall see directly].

And touching the mineral, thus does M. Youghan affirm, that though it be but copper, seeing the savages are able to melt it, it is one of the richest minerals in the world.

Wherefore, a good harbor found to the northward, as before is said, and from thence four days overland to the river Choanook, sconses being raised; from whence again overland, through the province of Choanook, one day's voyage to the first town of the Mangoaks up the river of Moratoc by the way, as also upon the said river, for the defence of our boats, like sconses being set, in this course of proceeding you shall clear yourself from all those dangers and broad shallow sounds before mentioned, and gain within four days' travel into the heart of the main, two hundred miles at the least, and so pass your discovery into that most notable country, and the likeliest parts of the main, with far greater felicity than otherwise can be performed.

Thus, sir, I have though simply, yet truly, set down unto you that my labor with the rest of the gentlemen, and poor men of our company (not without both pain and peril, which the Lord in his mercy many ways delivered us from) could yield unto you ; which might have been performed in some more perfection, if the Lord had been pleased that only that which you had provided for us had at the first been left with us, or that he had not in his eternal providence, now at the last, set some other course in these things than the wisdom of man could look into ; which truly the carrying away by a most strange and unlooked-for storm of all our provisions, with barks, master, mariners, and sundry also of mine own company, all having been so courteously supplied by the General Sir Francis Drake, the same having been most sufficient to have performed the greatest part of the premises, must ever make me to think the hand of God only (for some his good purpose to myself yet unknown) to have been in the matter.

THE SECOND PART:

TOUCHING THE CONSPIRACY OF PEMISAPAN, THE DISCOVERY OF THE SAME, AND AT THE LAST, OF OUR REQUEST TO DEPART WITH SIR FRANCIS DRAKE FOR ENGLAND.

[*Pemisapan* was the name assumed by *Wingina*, who, the reader will recollect, was king of *Windangacoa*, as the English erroneously called it, at the time of the arrival of Amadas and Barlowe. He was, however, not seen by them at all, as he was then suffering from wounds received in battle. His brother, *Granganimeo*, was his representative, and manifested particular friendship for the English. Their father was *Ensenore*. Unfortunately for the adventurers, *Granganimeo* died soon after Lane's arrival, and it was upon the happening of that event, that Wingina changed his name. *Ensenore* was then the only friend the whites had near the king, and they needed one, for *Pemisapan* was hostile to them in heart. Unhappily for the English, *Ensenore* died in the spring of 1586, and then *Pemisapan* formed the conspiracy which Lane here relates. Among the chief conspirators was *Wanchese*, who, with *Manteo*, had visited England on the return of Amadas and Barlowe, and had come back with Lane. The particular cause of the ill-will of *Wanchese* toward the English, we know not: it was, however, in strong contrast to the feelings of *Manteo*, who to the last continued one of the most faithful friends the colonists had. Of the fate of *Wanchese* we are ignorant.]

Ensenore, a savage, father to Pemisapan, being the only friend to our nation that we had amongst them, and about the king, died the 20th of April, 1586. He alone had before opposed himself in their consultations against all matters proposed against us, which both the king and all the rest of them after Granganganimeo's death were very willing to have preferred. And he was not only by the mere providence of God during his life, a means to save us from hurt, as poisoning and such like, but also to do us very great good, and singularly in this.

The king was advised and of himself disposed, as a ready means, to have assuredly brought us to ruin in the month of March, 1586, himself also with all his savages to have run away from us, and to have left his ground in the island unsowed; which if he had done, there had been no possibility in common reason (but by the immediate hand of God) that we could have been preserved from starving out of hand. For at that time we had no weirs for fish, neither could our men skill of the making of them, neither had we one grain of corn for seed to put into the ground.

In mine absence on my voyage that I had made against the Chaonists, and Mangoaks, they had raised a bruit among themselves, that I and my company were part slain, and part starved by the Chaonists, and Mongoaks. One part of this tale was too true, that I and mine were like to be starved, but the other false.

Nevertheless until my return, it took such effect in Pemisapan's heart, and in those against us, that they grew not only into contempt of us, but also, (contrary to their former reverend opinion in shew, of the Almighty God of Heaven, and Jesus Christ whom we serve and worship, whom before they would acknowledge and confess the only God) now they began to blaspheme, and flatly to say, that our Lord God, was not God, since he suffered us to sustain much hunger and also to be killed of the Renapoaks, for so they call by that general name all the inhabitants of the whole main, of what province soever. In so much as old Ensenore, neither any of his fellows, could for his sake have no more credit for us, and it came so far that the king was resolved to have presently gone away as is aforesaid.

But even in the beginning of this bruit I returned, which when he saw, contrary to his expectation, and the advertisement that he had received; that not only myself, and my company were all safe, but also, by report of his own three savages which had been with me besides Manteo in that voyage, that is to say, *Tetepano*, his sister's husband *Eracno*, and *Cossine*, that the Chaonists and Mangoaks (whose name and multitude besides their valor is terrible to all the rest of the provinces) durst not for the most part of them abide us, and that those that did abide us were killed, and that we had taken Menatonon prisoner, and brought his son that he best loved to Roanoak with me, it did not a little assuage all devices against us: on the other side, it made Ensenore's opinions to be received again with greater respect, for he had often before told them, and then renewed those his former speeches, both to the king and rest, that we were the servants of God, and that we were not subject to be destroyed by them, but contrary wise, that they amongst them that sought our destruction, should find their own, and not be able to work ours; and that we, being dead men, were able to do them more hurt, than now we could do being alive, an opinion very confidently at this day holden by the wisest amongst them, and of their old men, as also, that they have been in the night, being a hundred miles from any of us, in the air shot at, and struck by some men of ours, that by sickness had died among them: and many of them hold opinion, that we be dead men returned into the world again, and that we do not remain dead but for a certain time, and that then we return again.

All these speeches then again grew in full credit with them, the king, and all, touching us, when he saw the small troop re turned again, and in that sort from those whose very names were terrible unto them; but that which made up the matter on our side for that time was an accident, yea rather, (as all the rest was) the good providence of the Almighty, for the saving of us, which was this.

Within certain days after my return from the said journey, Menatonon sent a messenger to visit his son the prisoner with me, and sent me certain pearls for a present, or rather, as Pemisapan told me, for the ransom of his son, and therefore I refused them; but the greatest cause of his sending them, was to signify unto me, that he had commanded Okisko, king of Weopemiok, to yield himself servant, and homager, to the great Weroanza of England, and after her, to Sir Walter Raleigh, to perform which command- ment received from Menatonon, the said Okisko, jointly with this Menatonon's messenger, sent four and twenty of his principal men to let me know that from that time forward, he, and his succes- sors were to acknowledge her majesty their only sovereign, and next unto her, as is aforesaid.

All which being done, and acknowledged by them all, in the presence of Pemisapan his father, and all his savages in council then with him, it did for the time thoroughly (as it seemed) change him in disposition toward us, insomuch as forthwith Ensenore won his resolution of him, that out of hand he should go about, and withal, to cause his men to set up weirs forthwith for us; both which he at that present went in hand withal, and did so labor the expedition of it, that in the end of April he had sown a good quantity of ground, so much as had been sufficient to have fed our whole company (God blessing the growth) and that by the belly, for a whole year; besides that he gave us a certain plot of ground for ourselves to sow. All which put us in marvellous comfort, if we could pass from April until the beginning of July, (which was to have been the beginning of their harvest) that then a new supply out of England, or else our own store would well enough maintain us. All our fear was of the two months betwixt, in which mean space, if the savages should not help us with Cassava, and Chyna, and that our weirs should fail us (as often they did), we might very well starve, notwithstanding the growing corn, like the starving horse in the stable, with the growing grass, as the proverb is ; which we very hardly had escaped but only by the hand of God, as it pleased him to try us. For within few days after, as before is said, Ensenore our friend died, who was no sooner dead, but certain of our great enemies about Penisapan, as Osacan, a Weroance, Tanaquiny and Wanchese most principally, were in hand again to put their old practices in use against us, which were readily embraced, and all their former devices against us renewed, and now brought in question. But that of starving us, by their forbearing to sow, was broken by Ensenore in his life, by having made the king all at one instant to sow his ground, not only in the island, but also at Dasamonguepeuc in the main, within two leagues over against us. Nevertheless there wanted no store of mischievous practices among them, and of all they resolved principally of this following.

First, that Okisko, king of Weopomeiok, with the Mandoags, should be moved, and with great quantity of copper entertained to the number of seven or eight hundred bows, to enterprise the matter thus to be ordered. They of Weopomeiok should be invited to a certain kind of month's mind, which they do use to solemnize, in their savage manner, for any great personage dead, and should have been for Ensenore. At this instant, also, should the Mandoags, who were a great people, with the Chesipeans and their friends, to the number of seven hundred of them, be armed at a day appointed to the main of Dasamonguepeuc, and there lying close at the sign of fires, which should interchangeably be made on both sides, when Pemisapan with his troop above named should have executed me, and some of our Weroances, (as they called all our principal officers,) the main forces of the rest should have come over into the island, where they meant to have dispatched the rest of the company, whom they did imagine to find both dismayed and dispersed abroad in the island, seeking of crabs and fish to live withal. The manner of their enterprise was this :—

Tarraquine and Andacon, two principal men about Pemisapan,

and very lusty fellows, with twenty more appointed to them, had the charge of my person, to see an order taken for the same, which they meant should in this sort have been executed. In the dead time of the night they would have beset my house, and set fire in the reeds that the same was covered with; meaning, as it was likely, that myself would have come running out of a sudden amazed in my shirt without arms, upon the instant whereof they would have knocked out my brains.

The same order was given to certain of his fellows, for M. Hariot, so for all the rest of our better sort, as for us at the town. Now, to the end that we might be the fewer in number together, and so be the more easily dealt withal, (for, indeed, ten of us, with our arms prepared, were a terror to a hundred of the best sort of them,) they agreed, and did immediately put it in practice, that they should not for any copper sell us any victuals whatever; besides, that in the night they should send to have our weirs robbed, and also to cause them to be broken, and once being broken, never to be repaired again by them. By this means the king stood assured, that I must be enforced, for lack of sustenance there, to disband my company into sundry places, to live upon shell fish, for the savages themselves do, going to Hatorask, Croatoan, and other places, fishing and hunting, while their grounds be in sowing, and their corn growing, which failed not his expectation. For the famine grew so extreme among us, our weirs failing us of fish, that I was enforced to send Captain Stafford with twenty with him to Croatoan, my lord admiral's island, to serve two turns in one; that is to say, to feed himself and his company, and also to keep watch if any shipping came upon the coast to warn us of the same. I sent M. Pridiox with the pinnace to Hatorask, and ten with him, with the Provost Marshal, to live there, and also to wait for shipping; also I sent every week, sixteen or twenty of the rest of the company to the main over against us, to live of casada and oysters.

In the meanwhile, Pemisapan went of purpose to Dasamonguepeuc, for three causes: The one to see his grounds there broken up, and sowed for a second crop: the other to withdraw himself from my daily sending to him for supply of victual for my company; for he was afraid to deny me anything, neither durst he in my presence, but by color and with excuses, which I was content to accept for the time, meaning in the end, as I had reason, to give him the jump once for all; but in the meanwhile, as I had ever done before, I and mine bore all wrongs, and accepted of all excuses.

My purpose was to have relieved myself with Menatonon, and the Chaonists, who in truth, as they are more valiant and in greater number than the rest, so are they more faithful in their promises, and since my late being there had given many tokens of earnest desire they had to join in perfect league with us, and therefore were greatly offended with Pemisapan and Weopomeiok for making him believe such tales of us.

The third cause of his going to Dasamonguepeuc was to dispatch his messengers to Weopomeiok and to the Mandoags, as aforesaid, all which he did with great imprest of copper in hand, making large promises to them of greater spoil.

The answer, within few days after, came from Weopomeiok, which was divided into two parts : First, for the king Okisko, who denied to be of the party for himself, or any of his special followers, and therefore did immediately retire himself with his force into the main; the other was concerning the rest of the said province who accepted of it; and in like sort the Mandoags received the imprest.

The day of their assembly aforesaid at Roanoak was appointed the tenth of June, all which the premises were discovered by Skyco, the king Menatonon, his son my prisoner, who, having once attempted to run away, I laid him in the bilboes, threatening to cut off his head, whom I remitted at Pemisapan's request, whereupon, he being persuaded that he was our enemy to the death, he did not only feed him with himself, but also made him acquainted with all his practices. On the other side, the young man finding himself as well used at my hand as I had means to show, and that all my company made much of him, he flatly discovered all unto me, which also afterwards was revealed unto me by one of Pemisapan's own men, that night before he was slain.

These mischiefs being all instantly upon me and upon my company to be put in execution, it stood me in hand to study how to prevent them, and also to save all others, which were at that time as aforesaid so far from me, whereupon I sent to Pemisapan to put suspicion out of his head, that I meant presently to go to Croatoan, for that I had heard of the arrival of our fleet (though I in truth neither heard nor hoped for so good adventure), and that I meant to come by him to borrow of his men to fish for my company, and to hunt for me at Croatoan, as also to buy some four days' provision to serve for my voyage.

He sent me word that he would himself come over to Roanoak, but from day to day he deferred only to bring the Weopomeioks with him and the Mandoags, whose time appointed was within eight days after. It was the last of May, 1586, when all his own savages began to make their assembly at Roanoak, at his commandment sent abroad unto him, and I resolved not to stay longer upon his coming over, since he meant to come with so good company, but thought good to go and visit him with such as I had, which I resolved to do the next day; but that night I meant by the way to give them in the island a canvisado, and at the instant to seize upon all the canoes about the island, to keep him from advertisement.

But the town took the alarm before I meant it to them. The occasion was this : I had sent the master of the light horsemen, with a few with him, to gather up all the canoes in the setting of the sun, and to take as many as were going from us to Dasamonguepeuc, but to suffer any that came from thence to land. He met with a canoe going from the shore, and overthrew the canoe, and cut off two savages' heads ; this was not done so secretly but he was discovered from the shore, whereupon the cry arose ; for in truth they, privy to their own villainous purposes against us, held as good espial upon us, both day and night, as we did upon them.

The alarm given, they took themselves to their bows, and we to our arms, some three or four of them at the first were slain with our shot ; the rest fled to the woods. The next morning, with the light horsemen and one canoe, taking twenty-five with the colonel of the Chesipeans, and the sergeant-major, I went to Dasamonguepeuc, and being landed, sent Pemisapan word by one of his own savages that met me at the shore, that I was going to Croatoan, and meant to take him in the way to complain unto him of Osocon, who the night past was conveying away my prisoner, whom I had there present tied in a handlock. Hereupon the king did abide my coming to him, and finding myself amidst seven or eight of his principal Weroances and followers (not regarding any of the common sort), I gave the watch-word agreed upon (which was, Christ our victory), and immediately those his chief men and himself had by the mercy of God for our deliverance, that which they had purposed for us. The king himself being shot through by the colonel with a pistol, lying on the ground for dead, and I, looking as watchfully for the saving of Manteo's friends, as others were busy that none should escape, suddenly he started up and ran away as though he had not been touched, insomuch as he overran all the company, being by the way shot thwart the buttocks by mine Irish boy with my petronel. In the end an Irishman serving me, one Nugent, and the deputy provost, undertook him; and I, in some doubt lest we had lost both the king and my man by our own negligence to have been intercepted by the savages, we met him returning out of the woods with Pemisapan's head in his hand.

This fell out the first of June, 1586, and, the eighth of the same, came advertisement to me from Captain Stafford, lying at my Lord Admiral's island [Croatoan], that he had discovered a great fleet of three and twenty sails; but whether they were friends or foes he could not yet discern. He advised me to stand upon as good guard as I could.

The ninth of the said month, he himself came unto me, having that night before and that same day traveled by land twenty miles; and I must truly report of him from the first to the last, he was the gentleman that never spared labor or peril, either by land or water, fair weather or foul, to perform any service committed unto him.

[This Captain Stafford, who appears in the list of adventurers as "Master Edward Stafford," and whom Lane here so highly commends, seems not only to have been fitted for the rough work on which he had entered, but to have been sustained by his enthusiasm in perseveringly prosecuting it; for we shall see presently that he was an active and valuable member of the company under John White].

He brought me a letter from the general, Sir Francis Drake, with a most bountiful and honorable offer for the supply of our necessities to the performance of the action we were entered into; and that not only of victuals, munition and clothing, but also of barks, pinnaces and boats; they also by him to be victualed, manned and furnished to my contentation.

The tenth day he arrived in the road of our bad harbor; and coming there to an anchor, the eleventh day I came to him, whom I found indeed, most honorable to perform that which in writing and message, he had most courteously offered, he having aforehand propounded the matter to all the captains of his fleet, and got there liking and consent thereto.

With such thanks unto him and his captains for his care both of us and of our action, not as the matter deserved, but as I could, both for my company and myself, I (being aforehand prepared what I would desire) craved at his hands that it would please him to take with him into England a number of weak and unfit men for my good action, which I would deliver to him; and in place of them to supply me of his company with oar-men, artificers and others.

That he would leave us so much shipping and victual, as about August the next following would carry me and all my company into England, when we have discovered somewhat, that for lack of needful provision in time left with us, as yet remained undone.

That it would please him withal to leave some sufficient masters not only to carry us into England, when time should be, but also to search the coast for some better harbor, if there were any, and especially to help us to some small boats and oar-men.

Also for a supply of calivers, handweapons, match and lead, tools, apparel and such like.

He having received these my requests, according to his usual commendable manner of government (as it was told me) calling his captains to counsel; the resolution was that I should send such of my officers of my company as I used in such matters, with their notes, to go on board with him, which were the master of victuals, the keeper of the store, and the vice treasurer, to whom he appointed forthwith for me the *Francis*, being a very proper bark of seventy tons, and took present order for bringing the victual aboard for a hundred men for four months, with all my other demands whatsoever, to the uttermost.

And further, he appointed for me two pinnaces and four small boats, and that which to perform all his former liberality towards us, was that he had gotten the full assents of two as sufficient experimented Masters as were any in his fleet, by judgment of them that knew them, with very sufficient goings, to carry with me, and to employ themselves most earnestly in the action, as I should appoint them, until the term which I promised of our return into England again. The name of one of those masters was *Abraham Kendall*, the other *Griffith Herne*.

While these things were in hand, the provision aforesaid being brought, and in bringing aboard, my said masters being also gone aboard, my said barks having accepted of their charge, and mine own officers, with others in like sort of my company with them (all which was dispatched by the said general the twelfth of said month) the thirteenth of the same, there arose such an unwonted storm, and continued four days, that had like to have driven all on shore, if the Lord had not held his holy hand over them, and the general very providently foreseeing the worst himself, then about my dispatch putting himself aboard; but in the end having driven sundry of the fleet to put to sea, the *Francis* also with all my provisions, my two masters, and my company aboard, she was seen to be free from the same, and to put clear to sea.

This storm having continued from the thirteenth to the sixteenth of the month, and thus my bark put away as aforesaid, the general coming a shore made a new proffer unto me, which was a ship of one hundred and seventy tons, called the bark *Bonner*, with a sufficient master and guide to tarry with me the time appointed, and victualed sufficiently to carry me and my company into England, with all provisions as before; but he told me that he would not for any thing undertake to have her brought into our harbor, and therefore he was to leave her in the road, and to leave the care of the rest unto myself, and advised me to consider with my company of our case, and to deliver presently unto him in writing what I would require him to do for us; which being within his power, he did assure me, as well for his captains as for himself, should be most willingly performed.

Hereupon calling such captains and gentlemen of my company as then were at hand, who were all as privy as myself to the general's offer, their whole request was to me, that considering the case that we stood in, the weakness of our company, the small number of the same, the carrying away of our first appointed bark, with those two special masters, with our principal provisions in the same, by the very hand of God as it seemed, stretched out to take us from thence; considering also that his second offer, though most honorable on his part, yet of ours not to be taken, insomuch as there was no possibility for her with any safety to be brought into the harbor; seeing furthermore our hope for supply with Sir Richard Greenville, so undoubtedly promised us before Easter, not yet come, neither then likely to come this year, considering the doings in England for Flanders, and also for America, that therefore I would resolve myself with my company to go into England in that fleet, and accordingly to make request to the general, in all our names, that he would be pleased to give us present passage with him. Which request of ours by myself delivered unto him, he most readily assented unto, and so he, sending immediately his pinnaces unto our island for the fetching away of a few that there were left with our baggage, the weather was so boisterous, and the pinnaces so often on ground, that the most of all we had, with all our cards, books and writings were by the sailors cast overboard; the greater number of the fleet being much grieved with their long and dangerous abode in that miserable road.

From whence the general, in the name of the Almighty, weighing his anchors, (having bestowed us among his fleet,) for the relief of whom he had in that storm sustained more peril of wreck than in all his former most honorable actions against the Spaniards, with praises unto God for all, set sail the nineteenth of June, 1586, and arrived in Portsmouth the seven and twentieth of July the same year.

[In "Sir Francis Drake Revived," printed in London in 1653, we have an account of the circumstances here related, which we subjoin for comparison with Lane's account. And we are the more prompted to this, because it shows, from other testimony than Lane's, that he did not wish to abandon the enterprise, and was therefore not quite so unfitted for his place as some have supposed.

" The 9th of June, upon sight of one speciall great fire (which are very ordinary all alongst this coast, even from the Cape of Florida hither,) the general sent his skiffe to the shore, where they found some of our English countrymen (that had been sent thither the year before by *Sir Walter Raleigh*,) and brought one aboard, by whose direction we proceeded along to the place which they make their port." [They found them at Croatoan, near Ocracoke; but proceeded thence to another place " which they make their port." This does not countenance the idea that the colonists entered at Ocracoke inlet.] " But some of our shipps being of great draught unable to enter, we anchored all without the harbour in a wilde road at sea, about two miles from shore.

" From whence the generall wrote letters to Master *Ralph Lane*, being governour of those English in Virginia, and then at his fort, about six leagues from the road, in an island which they call Roanoac :" [This again shows that the inlet they used could not have been Ocracoke, which was more than *six leagues* distant from Roanoak, " wherein in specially he shewed how ready he was to supply his necessities and wants which he understood of, by those he had first talked withall.

" The morrow after, Master Lane himself, and some of his company comming unto him, with the consent of his captains, he gave them the choice of two offers, that is to say : either he would leave a ship, pinnace and certain boates with sufficient masters and marriners, together furnished with a month's victuall, to stay and make farther discovery of the country and coasts, and so much victuall likewise that might be sufficient for the bringing of them all (being an hundred and three persons) into England, if they thought good after such time, with any other thing they would desire, and that he might be able to spare.

" Or else, if they thought they had made sufficient discovery already, and did desire to return into England, he would give them passage. But they, as it seemed, *being desirous to stay*, accepted very thankfully and with great gladness that which was offered first. Whereupon the ship being appointed and received into charge, by some of their owne company, sent into her by Master Lane, before they had received from the rest of the fleet the provision appointed them, there arose a great storm (which they said was extraordinary and very strange) that lasted three days together, and put all our fleet in great danger to be driven from their ankoring upon the coast. For we brake many cables and lost many ankors. And some of our fleet which had lost all, (of which number was the ship appointed for Master Lane and his company) was driven to put to sea in great danger, in avoyding the coast, and could never see us againe untill we met in England. Many also of our small pinnaces and boates were lost in this storm.

" Notwithstanding after all this, the generall offered them, (with consent of his captains,) another ship with some provision, although not such a one for their turnes as might have been spared them before, this being unable to be brought into their harbour. Or else, if they would, to give them passage into England, although he knew he should perform it with greater difficulty than he might have done before.

"But Master Lane, with those of the chiefest of his company he had there with him, considering what should be best for them to doe, made request unto the generall under their hands, that they might have passage for England: the which being granted, and the rest sent for out of the country and shipped, we departed from that coast the 18th of June.

" And so, God be thanked, both they and we in good safety arrived at Portsmouth in July 28, 1586, to the great glory of God, and to no small honour to our prince, our country and ourselves."

And upon this state of facts, the modern historian utters his sentence of condemnation against Lane. He says that " Lane shared the despondency of his men," and requested with them passage to England. And again, " the return of Lane was a precipitate desertion : a little delay would have furnished the colony with ample supplies. A few days after its departure, a ship arrived laden with all stores needed by the infant settlement." And further, " another fortnight had hardly elapsed when Sir Richard Grenville appeared off the coast with three well furnished ships." Ah ! he knows all that *now ;* but did Lane know these vessels were at hand ? He had been expecting these very supplies for months and months, and yet they came not. Is he to be judged on the " *ex post facto* wisdom" of the historian ? But take the facts as stated. What proof is there that Lane desponded with his men ? They all being " desirous to stay" gladly accepted the first offer of Sir Francis Drake to give them a vessel. Does this indicate despondency ? A storm drove that vessel off, and she returned to Carolina no more. Another is offered, tne best Drake could offer, doubtless ; but what was she ? A vessel, that from her size, could not be brought into their harbor. Was she then to remain in the open roadstead, anchored at sea, on the coast of North Carolina ? Of what use would she have been to the colonists, and how long would she have remained unshattered ? Beside, to man and sail her would have probably required half if not more of all Lane's men, for Drake expressly said the sole care of her must be among the colonists. And where was she to sail ? What Lane wanted was small craft, a pinnace and boats, to explore the sounds and rivers. She could not enter the sound. For his purposes, she was useless then ; as the writer just quoted says, "not such a one for their turnes as might have been spared them before."

But even she, unfit as she was, was not rejected without consideration. There was no "precipitate desertion" by Lane. He was directly the opposite of precipitate, for he called into consultation "the chiefest of his company." Hariot was among them, so was Stafford, so was Amadas, "the admiral of the company," who had been on the coast of North Carolina, and in its waters before. They *all* joined in the request to Drake to take them to England ; and Lane, as if he foresaw that at some future day the historian might throw obloquy on *him* for this departure from Carolina, caused his companions to verify its necessity *in writing ;* for they made their request "*under their hands.*"

Indeed, we think that the conduct of Lane, in this very particular of leaving with the colony for England, is one of the strongest evidences that he was fitted for his position as its governor and head. He enumerates very distinctly the reasons which influenced him :—the weakness of his company,—its small number,—the loss of the first vessel with his provision and her officers,—the impossibility of making use of the second vessel, or even safely mooring her in any harbor he knew,—the disappointment in the expected and long-due supplies from England, and the reasonable calculations that they would not come during the year,—all these were weighty considerations for him as the responsible head. And, that he might be sure he estimated them calmly and dispassionately, he took counsel with his chief and best companions, and found that they viewed them precisely as he did, and actually *requested him to take the colony back in Drake's fleet.* And not until he had thus considered the whole subject did he act. Now here was cool deliberation and inquiry such as became a man responsible for the lives and safety of more than a hundred of his fellow-creatures ; and let any one disposed hastily to condemn Lane, just imagine himself to be in precisely similar circumstances, and ask himself if, being so, he would not have acted very much as Lane did, except, perhaps, after much shorter deliberation. There is, in writing history, a considerate justice due even to the minor personages of life's drama. Let them have it].

No. 5.

THE THIRD VOYAGE

MADE

BY A SHIP, SENT IN THE YEAR
1586

TO THE RELIEF OF THE COLONY PLANTED IN

VIRGINIA.

AT THE SOLE CHARGE OF

SIR WALTER RALEIGH.

[Reprinted from HAKLUYT, *Vol. III., page* 265].

[This is the narrative of the voyage made by the vessel that arrived on the coast of Carolina, immediately after Lane and the colonists left in Drake's fleet. From it we learn :

1. That the colonists under Lane had resolutely determined "to spend the residue of their lifetime in that country;" which negatives the idea of that "despondency" of which Bancroft speaks.

2. That they came to this resolution after the "colony half despaired of the coming of any supply" from England, such as had been promised, and as they expected.

3. That, like sensible men, after making such a determination, "they sowed, planted, and set such things as were necessary for their reliefe in so plentifull a maner, as might have sufficed them two yeeres without any further labour."

4. That when Drake arrived, "their corne which they had sowed was within one fortnight of reaping."

5. That when the storm drove off the vessels, their numbers were greatly diminished, because in the ships designed by Drake for them, "at that instant were the chiefest of the English colony."

The writer of this short story (we know not who he was) calls North Carolina "this paradise of the world." The old state is not quite that, but it is a country to which the affections of its children, wherever they may be scattered, cling with wonderful tenacity. We have met North Carolinians in many and widely separated regions of our common country : we have encountered few whose hearts did not dwell with fond affection on their native land. In these exceptions there was a cause. The men were such as their countrymen could neither respect nor esteem. God had made them very little; they thought themselves very great; and their countrymen, with pious reverence, acquiesced in the decree of heaven. The men hated them accordingly.

Sir Richard Greenville's arrival with three ships is also here noted. He left *fifteen* men on Roanoake island, not *fifty*, as Smith, Stith and others have said].

In the year of our Lord 1586, Sir Walter Raleigh, at his own charge, prepared a ship of a hundred tons, freighted with all manner of things, in most plentiful manner, for the supply and relief of his colony then remaining in Virginia; but before they et sail from England it was after Easter, so that our colony half despaired of the coming of any supply, wherefore every man prepared for himself, determining resolutely to spend the residue of their life time in that country. And for the better performance of this their determination, they sowed, planted, and set such things as were necessary for their relief in so plentiful a manner as might have sufficed them two years without any labor. Thus, trusting to their own harvest, they passed the summer till the tenth of June, at which time their corn which they had sowed was within one fortnight of reaping; but then it happened that Sir Francis Drake, in his prosperous return from the sacking of Saint Domingo, Cartagena, and Saint Augustine, determined in his way homeward to visit his countrymen, the English colony then remaining in Virginia. So, passing along the coast of Florida, he fell in with the parts where our English colony inhabited, and having espied some of that company, there he anchored and went aland, where he conferred with them of their state and welfare, and how things had past with them. They assured him that they lived all, but hitherto in some scarcity, and as yet could hear of no supply out of England, therefore they requested him that he would leave with them some two or three ships, that if in some reasonable time they heard not out of England, they might then return themselves. Which he agreed to. Whilst some were then writing their letters to send into England, and some others making reports of the accidents of their travels each to the other, some on land, some on board, a great storm arose, and drove the most of their fleet from their anchors to sea, in which ships, at that instant, were the chiefest of the English colony; the rest on land perceiving this, hasted to those three sails which were appointed to be left there, and for fear they should be left behind, they left all things confusedly, as if they had been chased from thence by a mighty army, and no doubts so they were; for the hand of God came upon them for the cruelty and outrages committed by some of them against the native inhabitants of that country.

Immediately after the departing of our English colony out of this paradise of the world, the ships above mentioned, sent and set forth at the charges of Sir Walter Raleigh, and his discretion, arrived at Hatorask, who after some time spent in seeking our colony up in the country, and not finding them, returned with all the aforesaid provision into England.

About fourteen or fifteen days after the departure of the afore-said ship, Sir Richard Greenvill, General of Virginia, accompanied with three ships well appointed for the same voyage, arrived there, who not finding the aforesaid ships according to his expectation, nor hearing any news of our English colony there seated, and left by him anno 1585, himself traveling up into divers places of the country, as well as to see if he could hear any news of the colony left there by him the year before, under the charge of Master Lane, his deputy, as also to discover some places of the country; but after some time spent therein, not hearing any news of them, and finding the places which they inhabited desolate, yet unwilling to lose the possession of the country which Englishmen had so long held, after good deliberation, he determined to leave some men behind to retain possession of the country, whereupon he landed fifteen men in the isle of Roanoak, furnished plentifully with all manner of provision for two years, and so departed for England.

Not long after, he fell with the isles of Azores, on some of which islands he landed, and spoiled the towns of all such things as were worth carriage, where also he took divers Spaniards. With these and many other exploits done by him in his voyage, as well outward as homeward, he returned into England.

No. 6.

A BRIEF AND TRUE REPORT

OF THE NEW FOUND LAND OF

VIRGINIA:

OF THE COMMODITIES THERE FOUND, AND TO BE RAISED, AS WELL
MERCHANTABLE AS OTHERS:

WRITTEN BY

THOMAS HARIOT,

SERVANT TO

SIR WALTER RALEIGH,

A MEMBER OF THE COLONY,

AND

THOSE EMPLOYED IN DISCOVERING,

A FULL TWELVEMONTH.

———

[*Reprinted from* HAKLUYT, *Vol. III., page* 266.]

RALPH LANE, *one of her Majesty's Esquires, and Governor of the Colony in Virginia, above mentioned, for the time there resident—to the gentle reader, wishes all happiness in the Lord.*

Albeit (gentle reader) the credit of the reports, in this treatise contained, can little be furthered by the testimony of [such an] one as myself, through affection judged partial, though without desert; nevertheless, forsomuch as I have been requested, by some my particular friends, who conceive more rightly of me, to deliver freely my knowledge of the same, not only for the satisfying of them, but also for the true information of any other whosoever, that comes not with a prejudiced mind to the reading thereof; thus much upon my credit I am to affirm, that things universally are so truly set down in this treatise by the author thereof, an actor in the colony, and a man no less for his honesty than learning commendable, as that I dare boldly avouch, it may very well pass with the credit of truth even amongst the most true relations of this age. Which as for mine own part I am ready any way with my word to acknowledge, so also (of the certainty thereof assured by mine own experience) with this my public assertion I do affirm the same. Farewell in the Lord.

[We preface Hariot's tract with the account given of him by Anthony a Wood in his Athenæ Oxonienses; Bliss's Edition Vol. II. p. 299.—He thus writes :

"THOMAS HARIOT or HARRIOT tumbled out of his mother's womb into the lap of the Oxonian muses, anno 1560, but in what parish I cannot yet tell. All the registers that begin before that time (namely that of St. Ebbe, S. Aldate, S. Thomas, which begins that year, S. Michael, all Saints, and S. Peter in the east) I have searched but cannot find his name. That of S. Mary's parish, wherein I suppose this our author was born, hath been lost several years, and there is no register remaining, that goes above the year 1599. After he had been instructed in grammar learning within this city of his birth, he became either a batler or a commoner of S. Mary's Hall, wherein undergoing the severe discipline then and there kept up by Richard Pygot and Thom. Philipson the principals thereof, he took the degree of bac. of arts in 1579, and in the latter end of that year did compleat it by determination in School-street. Soon after, coming to the knowledge of that heroic knight, Sir W. Raleigh, for his admirable skill in the mathematics, he entertain'd him in his family, allow'd him an yearly pension,* and was instructed by him at leisure hours in that art. In 1584 he went with the said knight, and first colony, into Virginia; † when being settled, he was imployed in the discovery and surveying thereof, and to make what knowledge he could of the commodities it yielded, and concerning the inhabitants and their manners and customs. After his return into England, Sir Walter got him into the acquaintance of that noble and generous count, Henry, Earl of Northumberland, who finding him to be a gentleman of an affable and peaceable nature, and well read in the obscure parts of learning, he did allow him an yearly pension of £120. About the same time Rob. Hues and Walter Warner, two other mathematicians, who were known also to the said count, did receive from him yearly pensions also, but of less value, as did afterwards Nich. Torperley whom I shall mention elsewhere. So that when the said Earl was committed prisoner to the Tower of London in 1606, to remain there during life, our author, Hues, and Warner, were his constant companions, and were usually called the Earl of Northumberland's three *magi*. They had a table at the Earl's charge, and the Earl himself did constantly converse with them, either singly or all together, as Sir Walter, then in the Tower, did. Our author Hariot was a great acquaintance with Sir Tho. Aylesbury, knt., a singular lover of learning and of the mathematic arts. To whom Dr. Rich. Corbet sending a poem when the blazing star appeared, dated 9th Dec. 1618, doth by the way, mention our author thus :

> " Now for the peace of God and men advise,
>   (Thou that hast wherewithall to make us wise)
>   Thine own rich studies, and deep Hariot's mine,
>   In which there is no dross, but all refine.‡

" But notwithstanding his great skill in mathematics, he had strange thoughts of the scripture, and always undervalued the old story of the creation of the world, and could never believe that trite position, *Ex nihilo, nihil fit.* He made a *Philosophical Theology*, wherein he cast off the OLD TESTAMENT, so that consequently the NEW would have no foundation. He was a Deist, and his doctrine he did impart to the said count and to Sir Walter Raleigh when he was compiling the

* Pref. R. Hakluyt ad *Orbem Novum*, scriptum per Mart. Angler. Par. 1587.

† [Here are two errors. Sir Walter never went himself to Virginia ; nor was Hariot on the *first* voyage with Amadas and Barlowe in 1584. He went with Greenville in 1585.]—*Editor.*

‡ In his Poems, printed at London 1672, p. 56.

History of the World; * and would controvert the matter with eminent divines of those times; who therefore having no good opinion of him, did look on the manner of his death (which I shall anon mention) as a judgment upon him for those matters and for nullifying the scripture. When he was a young man he was stiled by an author of note, † '*juvenis in illis disciplinis*' (meaning in the mathematics) '*excellens.*' When in his middle age, by another,‡ '*homo natus ad artes illustrandas,*' &c. ; and when dead, by a third of greater note,§ *mathematicus insignis.* His epitaph, which was made or caused to be made by his executors, or those to whom he left his goods, books and writings, viz. Sir J. Aylesbury before mentioned, and Rob. Sidney, viscount Lisle, saith, that '*omnes scientias coluit, et in omnibus excelluit; mathematicis, philosophicis, theologicis, veritatis indagator studiosissimus, Dei Triniunius cultor piissimus,*' &c.   As for his writings, they are these:

" *A brief and true Report of the New-foundland of Virginia ; of the commodities there found to be raised,* &c. Lond. 1588, qu.   Put into Latin by C. C. A. and published and adorned with many admirable cuts, by Theodore de Bry of Liege—Francof. ad Mœnum, 1590, fol. The English copy is mostly, if not all, involved in the third vol. of R. Hakluyt's Voyages, p. 266, &c.

" *Ephemeris Chyrometrica,* MS. in the library at Sion Coll. Lond.

" *Artis analyticæ Praxis, ad Æquationes Algebraicas nova, expedita et generali methodo, resolvendas, Tractatus posthumus,* &c. Lond. 1631, in a thin fol. and dedic. to Henry E. of Northumberland. The sum of this book coming into the hands of Aylesbury before mentioned, Walt. Warner did undertake to perfect and publish it, conditionally, that Algernon, eldest son of the said Henry E. of Northumberland would, after his father's death, continue his pension to him during his natural life. Which being granted at the earnest desires and entreaties of Aylesbury made to that Lord, Warner took a great deal of pains in it, and at length published it in that sort as we see it now extant.   By the

---

* [This statement of Wood's is flatly denied by respectable authority, and Hariot's writings, together with the esteem which he certainly possessed, of distinguished and orthodox men, do not countenance the opinion that he was a Deist. Sir Walter Raleigh was certainly not one, and the very work Wood refers to, the History of the World, conclusively shows it. We will presently show from Hariot's own writings that he is most grossly misrepresented, and that he was a firm believer in Christianity.]

Editor.

† Hakluyt et sup. in præf

‡ Nath. Torperley in præfat. ad *Declides Cælometricas,* &c. anno 1602.

◊ Cambden in *Annal Jac.* I.   MS. sub anno 1621.

way it must be known that this Walt. Warner was a Leicestershire man born, but whether educated in this University, I cannot as yet find ; that he was esteemed a good philosopher as mathematician, &c. As for our author Hariot, who for some time lived in Sion Coll. near to London, he died second July in sixteen hundred twenty and one ; whereupon his body was conveyed to S. Christopher's Ch. in London by the brethren of the mathematical faculty, and by them committed to the earth with solemnity.   Over his grave was soon after erected a comely monument with a large inscription thereon, but destroy'd with the church itself, by the dreadful fire that hapned in that city, in the beginning of Sept. in 1666.   This person tho' he was but little more than sixty years of age when he died, yet had not an unusual and rare disease seized upon him, he might have attain'd, as 'tis thought, to the age of eighty.   The disease was an ulcer in the lip (cancer), and Dr. Alex. Rhead was his physician, who, tho' he had cured many of worser and more malignant diseases, yet he could not save him.—Thus far Anthony a. Wood.

The epitaph on Hariot's tomb was as follows :

SISTE VIATOR, LEVITER PREME,
JACET HIC JUXTA, QUOD MORTALE FUIT.

C. V.

THOMÆ HARRIOTI.

HIC FUIT DOCTISSIMUS ILLE HARRIOTUS DE SYON AD
FLUMEN THAMESIN, PATRIA, ET EDUCATIONE
OXONIENSIS.

QUI OMNES SCIENTIAS COLUIT,
QUI IN OMNIBUS EXCELLUIT,

MATHEMATICIS, PHILOSOPHICIS, THEOLOGICIS,
VERITATIS INDAGATOR STUDIOSISSIMUS,
DEI TRINI-UNIUS CULTOR PIISSIMUS,
SEXAGENARIUS, AUT EO CIRCITER,
MORTALITATI VALEDIXIT, NON VITÆ,
ANNO CHRISTI, M.DC.XXI., JULII 2.

A few words more only remain to be said of Hariot.   After Warner published Hariot's work on Algebra, Des Cartes adopted the improvements suggested in it, and for a considerable time they were imposed upon the French nation as his own. Wallis afterward in his "History of Algebra" detected and exposed the theft, as also did Dr. Zach, astronomer to the Duke of Saxe Gotha, in 1788, as may be seen in the astronomical publications of the Academy of Sciences at Berlin for that year. A very full and satisfactory account of the algebraic notation invented by Hariot may be found in the *Histoire des Mathematiques* by Montucla— Tome 2, page 105—111 ; and also in the *Allgemeine Encyklopâdie*, Von Ersch und Gruber, article HARRIOTSCHER LEHRSATZ. In this latter work (article Harriot), we find a part of the testimony produced by Dr. Zach in support of Hariot's claim against Des Cartes. It is in a curious letter from the Duke of Northumberland to Hariot, which was found in 1784 at Petworth, the seat of the Earl of Egremont, to whom various MSS. of Hariot, together with other papers, had descended from the Earl of Northumberland. The Duke thus writes :

"Doe you not here startle to see every day some of your inventions taken from you, for I remember longe since you told me as much, that the motions of the planets were not perfect circles ? So you taught me in the curious way to observe weight in water, and within a while after Ghetaldi comes out with it in print. A little before Vieta prevented you of the gharland for the great invention of algebra. All these were your dues, and manie others that I could mention ; and yet to [too] great reservednesse had robd you of these glories. But all the inventions be greate, the first and last, I mean, yet when I survei your store house, I see they are the smallest things," &c.]

To the adventurers, favorers and well-willers of the enterprise for the inhabiting and planting in Virginia:

Since the first undertaking by Sir Walter Raleigh to deal in the action of discovering of that country, which is now called and known by the name of Virginia, many voyages having been thither made at sundry times to his great charge, as first in the year 1584, and afterwards in the years 1585, 1586, and now of late this last year 1587: there have been divers and variable reports, with some slanderous and shameful speeches bruited abroad by many that returned from thence, especially of that discovery which was made by the colony transported by Sir Richard Greenvill in the year 1585, being of all others the most principal, and as yet made of most effect ; the time of their abode in the country being a whole year, when as in the other voyage before, they stayed but six weeks, and the others after were only for supply and transportation, nothing more being discovered than had been before. Which reports have done not a little wrong to many that otherwise would have also favored and adventured in the action, to the honor and benefit of our nation, besides the particular profit and credit which would have redounded to themselves the dealers therein ; as I hope by sequel of events, to the shame of those that have avouched the contrary, shall be manifest, if you the adventurers, favorers and well-willers do but either increase in number, or in opinion continue, or having been doubtful, renew your good liking and furtherance to deal therein according to the worthiness thereof already found, and as you shall understand hereafter to be requisite. Touching which worthiness through cause of the diversity of relations and reports, many of your opinions could not be firm, nor the minds of some that are well disposed be settled in any certainty.

I have, therefore, thought it good, being one that have been in the discovery, and in dealing with the natural inhabitants specially employed, and having therefore seen and known more than the ordinary, to impart so much unto you of the fruits of our labors, as that you may know how injuriously the enterprise is slandered, and that in public manner at this present, chiefly for two respects.

First, that some of you which are yet ignorant or doubtful of the state thereof, may see that there is sufficient cause why the chief enterpriser, with the favor of her majesty, notwithstanding such reports, has not only since continued the action by sending into the country again, and replanting this last year a new colony, but is also ready, according as the times and means will afford, to follow and prosecute the same.

Secondly, that you seeing and knowing the continuance of the action, by the view hereof you may generally know and learn what the country is, and thereupon consider how your dealing therein, if it proceed, may return you profit and gain, be it either by inhabiting and planting, or otherwise in furthering thereof.

And lest that the substance of my relation should be doubtful unto you, as of others by reason of their diversity, I will first open the cause in a few words, wherefore they are so different, referring myself to your favorable constructions, and to be adjudged of, as by good consideration you shall find cause.

Of our company that returned, some, for their misdemeanor and ill-dealing in the country, have been there worthily punished, who, by reason of their bad natures, have maliciously not only spoken ill of their governors, but for their sakes, slandered the country itself. The like also have those done which were of their consort.

Some being ignorant of the state thereof, notwithstanding since their return amongst their friends and acquaintances, and also others, especially if they were in company where they might not be gainsaid, would seem to know so much as no men more, and make no men so great travelers as themselves. They stood so much, as it may seem, upon their credit and reputation, that having been a twelve months in the country, it would have been a great disgrace unto them, as they thought, if they could not have said much, whether it were true or false. Of which some have spoken of more than ever they saw, or otherwise knew to be there. Other some have not been ashamed to make absolute denial of what, which although not by them, yet by others is most certainly and there plentifully known, and other some make difficulties of those things they have no skill of.

The cause of their ignorance was, in that they were of that many that were never out of the island where we were seated, or not far, or in the leastwise, in few places else, during the time of our abode in the country; or of that many, that after gold and silver was not so soon found, as it was by them looked for, had little or no care of any other thing but to pamper their bellies, or of that many which had little understanding, less discretion, and more tongue than was needful or requisite.

Some also were of a nice bringing up, only in cities or towns, or such as never (as I may say) had seen the world before. Because there were not to be found any English cities, nor such fair houses, nor at their own wish any of their old, accustomed dainty food, nor any soft beds of down or feathers, the country was to them miserable, and their reports thereof according.

Because my purpose was that, in brief, to open the cause of the variety of such speeches, the particularities of them, and of many envious, malicious, and slanderous reports and devices else, by our own countrymen besides, as trifles that are not worthy of wise men to be thought upon, I mean not to trouble you withal, but will pass to the commodities, the substance of that which I have to make relation of unto you.

The treatise whereof, for your more ready view and easier understanding, I will divide into three special parts.   In the first I will make declaration of such commodities there already found or to be raised, which will not only serve the ordinary turns of you which are and shall be the planters and inhabitants, but such an overplus sufficiently to be yielded, or by men of skill to be provided, as by way of traffic and exchange with our own nation of England, will enrich yourselves the providers, those that shall deal with you, the enterprises in general, and greatly profit our own countrymen, to supply them with most things which heretofore they had been fain to provide either of strangers or of our enemies, which commodities, for distinction sake, I call merchantable.

In the second I will set down all the commodities which we know the country by our experience does yield of itself for victual and sustenance of man's life, such as are usually fed upon by the inhabitants of the country, as also by us during the time we were there.

In the last part I will make mention generally of such other commodities beside, as I am able to remember, and as I shall think behooveful for those that shall inhabit, and plant there, to know of; which specially concern building, as also some other necessary uses, with a brief description of the nature and manners of the people of the country.

THE FIRST PART, OF MERCHANTABLE COMMODITIES.

Silk of grass, or grass-silk. There is a kind of grass in the country, upon the blades whereof there groweth very good silk, in form of a thin glittering skin to be stript off.   It grows two feet and a half high, or better, the blades are about two feet in length, and half an inch broad.   The like grows in Persia, which is in the self same climate as Virginia, of which very many of the silk works that come from thence into Europe are made. Hereof, if it be planted and ordered as in Persia, it cannot in reason be otherwise, but that there will rise in short time great profit to the dealers therein, seeing there is so great use and want thereof, as well in our country as elsewhere. And by the means of sowing and planting it in good ground, it will be far greater, better, and more plentiful than it is. Although, notwithstanding there is a great store thereof in many places of the country growing naturally and wild, which also by proof here in England, in making a piece of silk grogram, we found to be excellent good.

[It is difficult to say what plant Hariot here means, unless it be " beargrass ;" but we have never read or heard that the thin transparent outer cuticle of the leaf of that plant could be wrought into any fabric, much less, one resembling silk. Diligent search through the history of plants in Carolina, by Lawson, (no careless observer,) furnishes no aid. Nor does Brickell, who stole almost his entire book from Lawson, mention any such plant as Hariot here describes.]

Worm-silk.—In many of our journeys we found silk-worms fair and great, as big as our ordinary walnuts. [*i. e.* the cocoons.] Although it has not been our hap to have found such plenty, as elsewhere to be in the country we have heard of, yet seeing that the country does naturally breed and nourish them, there is no doubt but if art be added in planting of mulberry trees, and others, fit for them in commodious places, for their feeding and nourishing, and some of them carefully gathered and husbanded in that sort, as by men of skill is known to be necessary, there will rise a great profit in time to the Virginians, as thereof does now to the Persians, Turks, Italians and Spaniards.

Flax and Hemp.—The truth is, that of hemp and flax there is no great store in any one place together, by reason it is not planted, but as the soil does yield of itself ; and howsoever the leaf and stem or stalk do differ from ours, the stuff, by judgment of men of skill, is altogether as good as ours ; and if not, as further proof should find otherwise, we have that experience of the soil, as that there cannot be shown any reason to the contrary, but that it will grow there excellent well, and by planting will be yielded plentifully, seeing there is so much ground whereof some may well be applied to such purposes. What benefit hereof may grow in cordage and linens who cannot easily understand?

Alum.—There is a vein of earth along the sea-coast, for the space of forty or fifty miles, whereof by the judgment of some that have made trial here in England, is made good alum, of that kind which is called rock-alum. The richness of such a commodity is so well known, that I need not to say anything thereof. The same earth does also yield white copperas, *Nitrum*, and *Alumen plumeum*, but nothing so plentifully as the common alum, which be also of price and profitable.

[There is alum in North Carolina: we have by evaporation, obtained it ourselves in the form of crystals, from earth impregnated with it, in Orange county. We were not aware, however, of its presence on the coast].

Wapeih.—A kind of earth, so called by the natural inhabitants, very like to terra sigillata, and having been refined, it has been found by some of our physicians and chirurgeons to be of the same kind of virtue, and more effectual. The inhabitants use it very much for the cure of sores and wounds: there is in divers places great plenty, and in some places of a blue sort.

[The *terra sigillata* is sometimes called *terra Lemnia* or Lemnian earth, from the Isle of Lemnos in the Egean. It is also known as *sphragide*. It is an astringent medicinal earth, of fatty consistence and reddish color, used in the same cases as *bole*. In appearance it is like clay, having a smooth surface resembling agate, especially in fresh fractures. It removes impurities like soap].

Pitch, Tar, Rosin and Turpentine.—There are those kinds of trees which yield them abundantly and great store. In the very same island where we were seated, being fifteen miles of length, and five or six miles in breadth, there are few trees else but of the same kind, the whole island being full.

Sassafras.—Called by the inhabitants Winauk, a kind of wood of most pleasant and sweet smell, and of most rare virtues in physic for the cure of many diseases. It is found by experience to be far better and of more uses than the wood which is called Guiacum, or Lignum Vitæ. For the description, the manner of using, and the manifold virtues thereof, I refer you to the book of Monardes, translated and entitled in English "The joyful news from the West Indies."

Cedar.—A very sweet wood, and fine timber, whereof if nests of chests be there made, or timber thereof fitted for sweet and fine bedsteads, tables, desks, lutes, virginals, and many things else (of which there has been proof made already), to make up freight with other principal commodities, will yield profit.

Wine.—There are two kinds of grapes that the soil does yield naturally—the one is small and sour, of the ordinary bigness, as ours in England—the other far greater and of himself luscious sweet.

[It is the scuppernong that is here meant. It abounds on Roanoak island].

When they are planted and husbanded as they ought, a principal commodity of wines by them may be raised.

Oil.—There are two sorts of walnuts, both holding oil ; but the one far more plentiful than the other. When there are mills and other devices for the purpose, a commodity of them may be raised, because there are infinite store. There are also three several kinds of berries in the form of oak-acorns, which also by the experience and use of the inhabitants, we find to yield very good and sweet oil. Furthermore, the bears of the country are commonly very fat, and in some places there are many. Their fatness, because it is so liquid, may well be termed oil, and has many special uses.

Furs.—All along the sea-coast there are great store of otters, which being taken by weirs and other engines made for the purpose, will yield good profit. We hope also of marten furs, and make no doubt by the relation of the people, but that in some places of the country there are store, although there were but two skins that came to our hands. Luzernes, also, we have understanding of, although for the time we saw none.

[The otter has long since been driven out. The marten, we are inclined to think, was never among our animals. What is meant by luzernes we cannot tell].

Deerskin, dressed after the manner of chamois, or undressed, are to be had of the natural inhabitants, thousands yearly by way of traffic for trifles, and no more waste or spoil of deer than is or has been ordinarily in time before.

Civet cats.—In our travels there was found one to have been killed by a savage or inhabitant, and in another place the smell where one or more had lately been before, whereby we gather, besides than by the relation of the people, that there are some in the country. Good profit will rise by them.

[The civet-cat (viverra civetta), an animal having some resemblance to a cat or a fox, is of an ashy color, tinged with yellow, and marked with spots of a dusky hue, arranged in rows. Valuable for the civet only, and, *if ever existing in North Carolina*, probably long since extinct. Its habitat is India, Guinea, Ethiopia, and Madagascar].

Iron.—In two places of the country, specially, one about four-score, and the other six score miles from the fort or place where we dwelt, we found near the water-side the ground to be rocky, which, by the trial of a mineral man, was found to hold iron richly. It is found in many places of the country else. I know nothing to the contrary, but that it may be allowed for a good merchantable commodity, considering there the small charge for the labor and feeding of men, the infinite store of wood, the want of wood and dearness thereof in England, and the necessity of ballasting of ships.

[Of this mineral we have quantities undreamed of by Hariot, and some of the ores are very rich].

Copper.—An hundred and fifty miles into the main, in two towns, we found with the inhabitants divers small plates of copper, that had been made, as we understood, by the inhabitants that dwell further into the country, where, as they say, are mountains and rivers that yield also white grains of metal, which is to be deemed silver. For confirmation whereof, at the time of our first arrival in the country, I saw, with some others with me, two small pieces of silver grossly beaten, about the weight of a testron, hanging in the ears of a Weroance or chief lord that dwelt about four score miles from us; of whom, through inquiry, by the number of days and the way, I learned that it had come to

his hands from the same place or near, where I after understood
the copper was made, and the white grains of metal found. The
aforesaid copper we also found, by trial, to hold silver.

[We of this day are not surprised at this statement, for we know that we
  have also an abundance of this metal, and some of the ores contain
  silver.]

Pearl.—Sometimes, in feeding on muscles, we found some pearl,
but it was our hap to meet with ragges, or of a pied color, not
having yet discovered those places where we heard of better and
more plenty. One of our company, a man of skill in such matters, had gathered together from among this savage people about
five thousand, of which number he chose so many as made a fair
chain, which for their likeness and uniformity in roundness, orient-
ness, and piedness of many excellent colors, with equality in greatness, were very fair and rare, and had therefore been presented to
her majesty, had we not by casualty, and through extremity of a
storm lost them, with many things else, in coming away from the
country.

[The statement is so uniform, in all the early narratives, of the finding of
  pearls, that we are bound to believe they were met with: but we apprehend they were, for the most part, like those described by Hariot,
  obtained from muscles, and of little value. It is not credible that, if
  the natives really followed the pearl fishery advantageously, either in
  the waters of Carolina or Virginia, that the English should not have
  taken the hint, and at least made an effort to establish the business of
  pearl diving: and yet we have no account of any such enterprise. As
  to the large white pearls, which Menatonon told Lane were found in
  quantities in the country of the Chesipeans, we are inclined to believe,
  they were nothing more than the *nacre* obtained by the natives from
  the *conch*, which unquestionably was once common in our waters.]

Sweet Gums, of divers kinds, and many other apothecary drugs;
of which we will make special mention, when we shall receive it
from such men of skill in that kind, that in taking reasonable
pains shall discover them more particularly than we have done,
and than now I can make relation of, for want of the examples

I had provided and gathered, and are now lost, with other things by casualty before mentioned.

Dyes of divers kinds: There is Shoemake, [Sumach,] and used in England for black; the seed of an herb called wasebur, little small roots called by the inhabitants tangomockonomindge; which dyes are for divers sorts of red, their goodness for our English cloths remains yet to be proved. The inhabitants use them only for the dying of hair, and coloring of their faces, and mantles made of deer-skins—and also for the dyeing of rushes, to make artificial works withal in their mats and baskets; having no other thing besides that they account of, apt to use them for. If they will not prove merchantable, there is no doubt but the planters there shall find apt uses for them, as also for other colors which we know to be there.

[These dyes, with the exception of Sumach, we are unable to identify.]

Woad : a thing of great vent and uses amongst English dyers, which cannot be yielded sufficiently in our own country for spare of ground, may be planted in Virginia, there being ground enough. The growth thereof need not be doubted, when, as in the islands of the Azores, it groweth plentifully, which are in the same climate. So likewise of madder.

[Woad is a plant formerly very much used in England for making a blue dye, (*botanice*, Isatis tinctoria); now superseded by indigo.]

We carried thither sugar-canes to plant, which being not so well preserved as was requisite, and besides, the time of the year being past for their setting when we arrived, we could not make that proof of them as we desired. Notwithstanding, seeing that they grow in the same climate, in the south part of Spain, and in Barbary, our hope in reason may yet continue. So likewise for oranges and lemons. There may be planted also quinces. Whereby may grow, in reasonable time, if the action be diligently prosecuted, no small commodities in sugars, suckets, and marmalades.

[This is the first recorded instance of the attempt to introduce the culture of the sugar-cane into North Carolina. The laws of climatology were not as well understood in the days of Hariot as they are now, and he seems to have supposed that the plant which flourished on any part of the globe, in a given parallel of latitude, would of course thrive, *on that parallel*, anywhere else on the earth's surface. No mistake is more common even at this day. The isothermal line is, no where on the globe, exactly parallel to the equator, not even within the tropics. In this case, Hariot mentions the south of Spain and Barbary, as having the "same climate" as our coast of Carolina. The parallel of latitude where he was, does indeed strike, on the eastern hemisphere, somewhere about the Straits of Gibraltar ; but the line of *equal heat* (isothermal) which passes through Barbary, strikes the coast of America on the shores of Florida, and passes just along the northern coast of the gulf of Mexico, some six degrees south of the spot where Hariot was. Sugar, we know, may be cultivated in Florida and Louisiana ; and these parts of our country have, so far at least as agricultural products are concerned, a climate similar to that of southern Spain and Barbary ; but mere parallels of latitude alone cannot determine climate. The opposite sides of our own continent furnish abundant evidence of this : take the parallel of 30°, for instance, and extend it from our eastern coast, about the northern end of the peninsula of Florida, across the continent to the Pacific : it will pass through the upper part of the gulf of California, and come out upon the shores of Lower California, about two hundred miles south of San Diego. Take, now, the isothermal line on the parallel of 30° in Florida and extend it westward ; when it reaches the Pacific coast, it will be found almost identical with the tropic of Cancer, at least 650 miles south of San Diego.

So also as to oranges and lemons ; *we know* they will not come to perfection in the open air of our North Carolina climate ; and yet they grow on the same parallel in Spain.

We may, however, be excused for here digressing momentarily to say that sugar may very readily be produced in North Carolina, though not from the ordinary cane, for which the climate is too far north. But there is a plant of recent introduction into this hemisphere known commonly by the name of " Chinese sugar cane," which will flourish well in Carolina and yield abundance of sugar. It is the *Sorgho Sucre*, a plant of the cane family allied to our Indian or rather to our broom corn. It has been tried in several parts of the Union and succeeded more or less in all. It belongs primarily to China, but has for several years been largely cultivated in S. Eastern Caffraria whence it passed to France, and afterward to Algeria. There is no vegetable produced which better repays cultivation. An acre planted with it will yield a hundred bushels of seed beside many tons of stems and foliage. It abounds with saccharine matter, and furnishes beside a large quantity of solid food which is most readily consumed by horses, cattle and swine. No part of the plant is lost. From a gallon of the sap or juice, by common boiling with ordinary kitchen apparatus, a quart of molasses was obtained of good quality. The juice will yield, with proper treatment of the mill and sugar house, twenty per cent or more of crystallized sugar, and from five to eight per cent of uncrystallized sap, from which alcohol may be extracted. In a good soil it is said it will furnish twenty-five tons of fodder to the acre, and stock of all kinds will eat it greedily. The seed may be ground and made into cakes which furnish agreeable food to man, and there is no better food for fattening stock. The plant may be propagated from the seed. Even the bush or top may be utilized by conversion into brooms, and the crushed fibrous stem may be manufactured into paper. The per centage of crystallizable sugar is found to increase with the decrease of latitude. It will repay cultivation in Illinois, and we are inclined to think no climate would suit it better than that of North Carolina. Might it not be advantageously added to our agricultural productions ?*]

Many other commodities by planting may there also be raised, which I leave to your discreet and gentle consideration ; and many also may be there, which yet we have not discovered. Two more commodities of great value, one of certainty, and the other in hope, not to be planted, but there to be raised, and in short time to be provided, and prepared, I might have specified. So likewise of those commodities already set down I might have said more, as of the particular places where they are found, and best to be planted and prepared ; by what means and in what reasonable space of time they might be raised to profit, and in what proportion; but because others than well-willers might be therewithal acquainted, not to the good of the action, I have willingly omitted them, knowing that to those that are well disposed, I have uttered, according to my promise and purpose, for this part sufficient.

* The writer has the pleasure of adding, that he has procured some of the seed, and sent them to North Carolina for experiment.

THE SECOND PART OF SUCH COMMODITIES AS VIRGINIA IS KNOWN TO
YIELD FOR VICTUALS, SUSTENANCE OF MAN'S LIFE, USUALLY FED
UPON BY THE NATURAL INHABITANTS, AS ALSO BY US, DURING THE
TIME OF OUR ABODE ; AND FIRST OF SUCH AS ARE SOWED AND
HUSBANDED.

Pagatour, a kind of grain so called by the inhabitants, the
same in the West-Indies is called Maize : Englishmen call it
Guinea-wheat or Turkey-wheat, according to the names of the
countries from whence the like has been brought. The grain is
about the highness of our ordinary English pease, and not much
different in form and shape ; but of divers colors, some white,
some red, some yellow, and some blue. All of them yield a very
white and sweet flour, being used according to his kind, it makes
a very good bread. We made of the same in the country some
malt, whereof was brewed as good ale as was to be desired. So
likewise by the help of hops, thereof may be made a good beer.
It is a grain of marvelous great increase ; of a thousand, fifteen
hundred, and some two thousand fold. There are three sorts, of
which two are ripe in eleven and twelve weeks at the most, sometimes in ten, after the time they are set, and are then of height in
stalk about five or seven feet. The other sort is ripe in fourteen
weeks, and is about ten feet high ; of the stalks some bear four
heads, some three, some one, and some two ; every head containing five, six or seven hundred grains, within a few more or less.
Of these grains, besides bread, the inhabitants make victual,
either by parching them, or seething them whole until they be
broken, or boiling the flour with water into a pap. [This, as the
reader will readily perceive, is our Indian corn.]

Okindgier, called by us beans, because in greatness and partly
in shape they are like to the beans in England, saving that they
are flatter, of more divers colors, and some pied. The leaf also
of the stem is much different. In taste they are altogether as
our English pease.

Wickonzower, called by us pease, in respect of the beans, for
distinction sake, because they are much less, although in form
they little differ, but in goodness of taste much like, and are far
better than our English pease. Both the beans and pease are
ripe in ten weeks after they are set. They make them victual

either by boiling them all to pieces into a broth, or boiling them whole until they are soft, and begin to break, as is used in England, either by themselves, or mixed together; sometimes they mingle of the wheat with them; sometimes also, being whole sodden, they bruise or pound them in a mortar, and thereof make loaves or lumps of doughish bread, which they use to eat for variety.

Macoquer, according to their several forms called by us Pompions, Melons and Gourds, because they are of the like forms as those kinds in England. In Virginia such of several forms are of one taste, and very good, and do also spring from one seed. There are of two sorts: one is ripe in the space of a month, and the other in two months.

There is a herb which in Dutch is called Melden. Some of those that I describe it unto, take it to be a kind of osage; it grows about four or five feet high; of the seed thereof, they make a thick broth and pottage of a very good taste; of the stalk, by burning into ashes, they make a kind of salt-earth, wherewithal many use sometimes to season their broths; other salt they know not. We ourselves used the leaves also for pot-herbs.

There is also another great herb, in form of a marigold, about six feet in height—the head with the flower is a span in breadth. Some take it to be planta-solis, of the seeds thereof they make broth—a kind of bread and broth. [Sun-flower?]

All the aforesaid commodities for victual are set or sown, sometimes in grounds apart and severally by themselves, but for the most part together in one ground mixedly; the manner thereof, with the dressing and preparing of the ground, because I will note unto you the fertility of the soil, I think good briefly to describe.

The ground they never fatten with much dung, or any other thing, neither plough nor dig it as we in England, but only prepare it in sort as follows: A few days before they sow or set, the men with wooden instruments, made almost in form of mattocks or hoes with long handles; the women with short peckers or parers, because they use them sitting, of a foot long, and about five inches in breadth, do only break the upper part of the ground to raise up the weeds, grass and old stubble of corn-stalks with their roots. The which, after a day or two day's drying in the sun, being scraped up into many small heaps, to save them labor for carrying them away, they burn into ashes. And whereas some may think that they use the ashes for to better the ground, I say that then they would either disperse the ashes abroad, which we observed they do not, except the heaps be too great; or else would take special care to set their corn where the ashes lie, which also we find they are careless of. And this is all the husbanding of their ground that they use.

Then their setting or sowing is after this manner: First for their corn, beginning in one corner of the plot, with a pecker they make a hole, wherein they put four grains, with care that they touch not one another (about an inch asunder), and cover them with the mould again; and so throughout the whole plot, making such holes, and using them after such manner, but with this regard, that they be made in ranks, every rank differing from other half a fathom or a yard, and the holes also in every rank as much. By this means there is a yard spare ground between every hole; where, according to discretion here and there, they set as many beans and pease; in divers places also among the seeds of macoquer, melden, and planta-solis.

[We seem to have religiously adhered to this Indian mode of planting our corn : the only difference between ourselves and the natives being that we use more convenient implements in farming than they did. Nay, we have not entirely lost their fashion of placing peas between the corn-hills. Probably our best planters will say they have found no reason to depart essentially from the lessons taught the first settlers by the experience of the savage].

The ground being thus set according to the rate by us experimented, an English acre containing forty perches in length, and four in breadth, does there yield in crop or offcome of corn, beans and pease, at the least, two hundred London bushels, besides the macoquer, melden and planta-solis; when, as in England, forty bushels of our wheat yielded out of such an acre is thought to be much.

I thought also good to note this unto you, that you which shall inhabit and plant there, may know how specially that country corn is there to be preferred before ours; besides, the manifold ways in applying it to victual, the increase is so much, that small labor and pains is needful in respect of that which must be used for ours. For this I can assure you that according to the rate we have made proof of, one man may prepare and husband so much ground (having once borne corn before) with less than four and twenty hours' labor, as shall yield him victual in a large proportion for a twelvemonths, if he have nothing else but that which the same ground will yield, and of that kind only which I have before spoken of: the said ground being also but of five and twenty yards square. If need require, but that there is ground enough, there might be raised out of one and the self-same ground two harvests or offcomes; for they sow or set, and may at any time, when they think good, from the midst of March until the end of June; so that they also set when they have eaten of their first crop. In some places of the country, notwithstanding, they have two harvests, as we have heard, out of one and the same ground.

For English corn, nevertheless, whether to use or not to use it, you that inhabit may do as you shall have further cause to think best. Of the growth you need not to doubt; for barley, oats and pease, we have seen proof of, not being purposely sown, but fallen casually in the worst sort of ground, and yet to be as fair as any we have ever seen here in England. But of wheat, because it was musty and had taken salt water, we could make no trial, and of rye we had none. Thus much have I digressed, and I hope not unnecessarily: now will I return again to my course, and treat of that which yet remains appertaining to this chapter.

There is an herb which is sowed apart by itself, and is called by the inhabitants Uppowoc; in the West Indies it has divers names, according to the several places and countries where it grows and is used: the Spaniards generally call it tobacco. The leaves thereof being dried and brought into powder, they use to take the fume and smoke thereof by sucking it through pipes made of clay, into their stomach and head, from whence it purges superfluous phlegm and other gross humors, and opens all the pores and passages of the body, by which means the use thereof not only preserves the body from obstructions, but also (if any

be, so that they have not been of too long continuance) in short
time breaks them, whereby their bodies are notably preserved in
health, and know not many grievous diseases, wherewithal we in
England are often times afflicted.

[Here we find another agricultural product which is a staple in some parts
of our State. King James, who wrote his " Counterblast to Tobacco,"
would scarcely have admitted all the excellent properties of the plant
here enumerated by Hariot. Raleigh, who knew the nature of the
plant, for it had been introduced into Spain as early as 1650, ordered
his colonists to bring it home with them, and on the return of Lane's
expedition it was introduced into England, where Sir Walter himself
was the first person of station who used it. His example was soon
followed by many noblemen, and even ladies of rank. Whether the
queen smoked we cannot say, but in France, Catharine de Medici undoubtedly indulged in a pipe, and the plant was hence called " the queen's
herb." On its first introduction, it was a costly luxury, in which none
but the rich could indulge : it was worth its weight in silver. After a
time, its use became general among the common people of England,
under the influence of that singular propensity that has shown itself
among the inhabitants of almost all parts of the world to seek a seda-
tive among the vegetable productions of the earth. All have their
narcotics. The first pipes of the common people were made of a walnut shell and a straw or reed, and as early as 1610 the dramatic writers
of England, who, of course, sought " to catch the manners, living as
they rise," show us not only the existence of tobacconists' shops in
London, but also the fact of fraudulent adulteration of the article by
the dealers. Thus Ben Johnson, in " the Alchymist :"

> " This is my friend Abel, an honest fellow,
>   He lets me have good tobacco, and he does not
>   Sophisticate it with sack-lees, or oil,
>   Nor washes it in muscadel and grains,
>   Nor buries it in gravel underground,
>   Wrapped up in greasy leather," &c. &c.

How little did Hariot suppose that this Indian weed, *uppowoc*, would
ever become one of the most important articles of commercial
traffic, or prove, as it did to King James, one of the largest sources of
his royal revenue : still less did he dream that in a future day it would
be, as in France, the subject of royal monopoly, and that the monarch

of one of the first kingdoms of Europe would be the greatest tobacco-dealer in Christendom.

This uppowoc is of so precious estimation amongst them, that they think their gods are marvelously delighted therewith; whereupon sometime they make hallowed fires, and cast some of the powder therein for a sacrifice; being in a storm upon the waters, to pacify their gods, they cast some up into the air and into the water; so a weir for fish being newly set up, they cast some therein and into the air; also after an escape from danger, they cast some into the air likewise; but all done with strange gestures, stamping, sometime dancing, clapping of hands, holding up of hands, and staring up into the heavens, uttering therewithal, and chattering strange words and noises.

We ourselves, during the time we were there, used to suck it after their manner, as also since our return, and have found many rare and wonderful experiments of the virtues thereof, of which the relation would require a volume by itself; the use of it by so many of late, men and women of great calling, as else, [of others] and some learned physicians also, is sufficient witness.

And these are all the commodities for sustenance of life, that I know and can remember, they use to husband; all else that follow, are found growing naturally or wild.

OF ROOTS.

Openauk are a kind of roots of round form, some of the bigness of walnuts, some far greater, which are found in moist and marshy grounds, growing many together, one by another in ropes, as though they were fastened with a string. Being boiled or sodden, they are very good meat. Monardes called these roots, beads, or *pater nostri* of Santa Helena.

Okeepenauk are also of round shape, found in dry grounds, some are of the bigness of a man's head. They are to be eaten as they are taken out of the ground, for by reason of their dryness they will neither roast nor seethe. Their taste is not so good as of the former roots, notwithstanding for want of bread, and sometimes for variety, the inhabitants use to eat them with fish or flesh, and in my judgment they do as well as the household bread made of rye here in England.

Kaishuepenauk, a white kind of roots, about the bigness of hens' eggs, and near of that form, their taste was not so good to our seeming as of the other, and therefore their place and manner of growing not so much cared for by us; the inhabitants, notwithstanding, used to boil and eat many.

Trinaw, a kind of root much like unto that which in England is called the China root, brought from the East Indies, and we know not anything to the contrary but that it may be of the same kind. These roots grow many together in great clusters, and do bring forth a briery stalk, but the leaf in shape far unlike; which being supported by the trees it groweth nearest unto, will reach or climb the top of the highest. From these roots, while they be new or fresh, being chapt into small pieces, and stamped, is strained with water a juice that makes bread, and also being boiled, a very good spoon meat, in manner of a jelly, and is much better in taste, if it be tempered with oil. This trinaw is not of that sort, which by some was caused to be brought into England for the China root, for it was discovered since, and is in use, as is aforesaid; but that which was brought hither is not yet known, neither by us nor by the inhabitants, to serve for any use or purpose, although the roots in shape are very like.

Coscushaw, some of our company took to be that kind of root which Spaniards in the West Indies call cassava, whereupon also many called it by that name; it groweth in very muddy pools, and moist grounds. Being dressed according to the country manner, it makes a good bread, and also a good spoon meat, and is used very much by the inhabitants. The juice of this root is poison, and therefore heed must be taken before anything be made therewithal; either the roots must be first sliced and dried in the sun, or by the fire, and then being pounded into flour, will make good bread, or else, while they are green they are to be pared, cut in pieces, and stamped; loaves of the same to be laid near or over the fire until it be sour, and then being well pounded again, bread or spoon meat, very good in taste, and wholesome, may be made thereof.

Habascon is a root of hot taste, almost of the form and bigness of a parsnip; of itself it is no victual, but only a help, being boiled together with other meats.

There are also Leeks, differing little from ours in England, that grow in many places of the country, of which, when we came in places where they were, we gathered and eat many, but the natural inhabitants never.

[With the exception of the Habascon, we confess we are not able to hazard even a conjecture as to what vegetable productions of our country Hariot here alludes. Nor are we certain that we know what root he calls Habascon. It has occurred to us that he may mean *calamus* or it may be *horse-radish.*

OF FRUITS.

Chestnuts there are in divers places great store; some they use to eat raw, some they stamp and boil to make spoon meat, and with some, being sodden, they make such a manner of dough bread as they use of their beans before mentioned.

Walnuts.—There are two kinds of walnuts, and of them infinite store; in many places, where are very great woods for many miles together, the third part of the trees are walnut trees. The one kind is of the same taste and form, or little differing from ours of England, but that they are harder and thicker shelled; the other is greater, and has a very ragged and hard shell, but the kernel great, very oily and sweet. Besides their eating of them after their ordinary manner, they break them with stones, and pound then in mortars with water, to make a milk which they use to put into some sorts of their spoon meat; also among their sodden wheat, pease, beans and pompions, which makes them have a far more pleasant taste.

Medlars, a kind of very good fruit, so called by us chiefly for these respects; first in that they are not good until they be rotten, then in that they open at the head as our medlars and are about the same bigness; otherwise in taste and color they are far different, for they are as red as cherries and very sweet, but whereas the cherry is sharp sweet, they are luscious sweet.

Mutaquesunnauk, a kind of pleasant fruit almost of the shape and bigness of English pears, but that they are of a perfect red color as well within as without. They grow on a plant whose leaves are very thick, and full of prickles as sharp as needles. Some that have been in the Indies, where they have seen that kind of red dye of great price, which is called Cochineal, to grow, do describe this plant right like unto this of Metaquesunnauk; but whether it be the true Cochineal, or a bastard or wild kind, it cannot yet be certified, seeing that also, as I heard, Cochineal is not of the fruit, but found on the leaves of the plant ; which leaves for such matter we have not so specially observed. [A cactus. Prickly pear.]

Grapes there are of two sorts, which I mentioned in the merchantable commodities.

Strawberries there are as good and as great as those which we have in our English gardens.

Mulberries, Applecrabs, Hurts or *Hurtleberries,* such as we have in England.

Sacquenummener, a kind of berries almost like unto capers, but somewhat greater, which grow together in clusters upon a plant or herb that is found in shallow waters; being boiled eight or nine hours according to their kind, are very good meat and wholesome ; otherwise if they be eaten they will make a man for the time frantic or extremely sick.

There is a kind of reed which bears a seed almost like unto our rye or wheat, and being boiled is good meat.   [Wild rice?]

In our travels in some places we found wild pease like unto ours in England, but that they were less, which are also of good meat.

OF A KIND OF FRUIT OR BERRY IN FORM OF ACORNS.

There is a kind of berry or acorn, of which there are five sorts that grow on several kinds of trees; the one is called Sagatemener, the second Osamener, the third Pummuckoner.   These kind of acorns they use to dry upon hurdles made of reeds, with fire underneath, almost after the manner we dry malt in England. When they are to be used, they first water them until they be soft, and then being sodden, they make a good victual, either to eat so simply, or else being also pounded to make loaves or lumps of bread.   These be also the three kinds, of which I said before the inhabitants used to make sweet oil.

Another sort is called sapummener, which being boiled or parched, does eat and taste like unto chestnuts. They sometimes also make bread of this sort.

[The *chinguapin*, we suppose, is here referred to].

The fifth sort is called mangummenauk, and is the acorn of their kind of oak, the which, being dried after the manner of the first sorts, and afterward watered, they boil them, and their servants, or sometimes the chiefs themselves, either for variety or for want of bread, do eat them with their fish or flesh.

OF BEASTS.

Deer.—In some places there are great store : near unto the sea coast they are of the ordinary bigness of ours in England, and some less ; but farther up into the country, where there is better food, they are greater. They differ from ours only in this—their tails are longer, and the snags of their horns look backward.

Conies.—Those that we have seen, and all that we can hear of, are of a gray color, like unto hares : in some places there are such plenty that all the people of some towns make them mantles of the fur or flue of the skins of those which they usually take.

Saquenuckot and *Maquowoc*, two kinds of small beasts, greater than conies, which are very good meat. We never took any of them ourselves, but sometimes eat of such as the inhabitants had taken and brought unto us.

Squirrels, which are of a gray color, we have taken and eaten.

Bears, which are of black color. The bears of this country are good meat. The inhabitants in time of winter do use to take and eat many, so also sometimes did we. They are taken commonly in this sort : In some islands or places where they are being hunted for, as soon as they have spial of a man, they presently run away, and then, being chased, they climb and get up the next tree they can, from whence with arrows they are shot down stark dead, or with those wounds, that they may after easily be killed. We sometimes shot them down with our calivers.

I have the names of eight and twenty several sorts of beasts, which I have heard of to be here and there dispersed in the country, especially in the main, of which there are only twelve kinds that we have yet discovered; and of those that be good meat, we know only them before mentioned. The inhabitants sometimes kill the lion and eat him: and we sometimes, as they came to our hands, of their wolves or wolfish dogs, which I have not set down for good meat, lest that some would understand my judgment therein to be more simple than needeth, although I could allege the difference in taste of those kinds from ours, which by some of our company have been experimented in both.

[In Vanderdonk's Dutch history of New York, and in the travels and discoveries of John Lederer in the western parts of Virginia, we have found the *lion* named as among the animals of our continent. Here, again, Hariot speaks of the lion as an article of food among the savages of North Carolina. We presume it is scarcely necessary to say that what is usually known as the lion, the *Leo Felis* of the naturalist, is not here meant. That animal was probably never found in North America. But the genus Felis is a large one, and some of the species belonging to it are abundant enough in our country. The panther and the wild cat both belong to it. The animal to which Hariot here alludes as killed by the natives was probably one of these].

OF FOWL.

Turkey-cocks and Turkey-hens, Stockdoves, Partridges, Cranes, Herons, and in winter great store of Swans and Geese.—Of all sorts of fowl, I have the names, in the country language, of four score and six; of which number, besides those that be named, we have taken, eaten, and have the pictures as they were drawn, with the names of the inhabitants, of several strange sorts of water-fowl eight, and seventeen kinds more of land-fowl, although we have seen and eaten of many more, which, for want of leisure there for the purpose, could not be pictured; and after we are better furnished and stored upon further discovery with their strange beasts, fish, trees, plants and herbs, they shall be also published.

There are also parrots, falcons, and merlin-hawks, which, although with us they be not used for meat, yet for other causes I thought good to mention.

[The turkey is our own bird. It is the *meleagris gallo pavo* of the naturalist, from which the domesticated animal with which we are familiar is derived. It is a native of America, and was introduced into Europe in the sixteenth century. It is still found in the wild state in many parts of our country. The other hemisphere owes us a debt for potatoes and turkies, if for nothing else].

OF FISH.

For four months of the year, February, March, April and May, there are plenty of sturgeons. And also in the same months, of herrings, some of the ordinary bigness of ours in England, but the most part far greater, of eighteen, twenty inches, and some two feet in length, and better : both these kinds of fish in those months are most plentiful and in best season, which we found to be most delicate and pleasant meat.

There are also trouts, porpoises, rays, oldwives, mullets, plaices, and very many other sorts of excellent good fish, which we have taken and eaten, whose names I know not but in the country language. We have the pictures of twelve sorts more, as they were drawn in the country, with their names.

The inhabitants use to take them two manner of ways : the one is by a kind of weir made of reeds, which in that country are very strong; the other way, which is more strange, is with poles made sharp at one end, by shooting them into the fish after the manner as Irishmen cast darts, either as they are rowing in their boats, or else as they are wading in the shallows for the purpose.

There are also, in many places, plenty of these kinds which follow :—

Sea-Crabs, such as we have in England.

Oysters, some very great, and some small, some round, and some of long shape; they are found both in salt water and brackish, and those that we had out of salt water are far better than the other, as in our country.

Also *muscles*, *scallops*, *periwinkles*, and *crevises*.

Seekanauk, a kind of crusty shell-fish, which is good meat, about a foot in breadth, having a crusty tail, many legs like a crab, and her eyes in her back. They are found in shallows of water, and sometimes on the shore.

There are many *tortoises*, both of land and sea kind, their backs and bellies are shelled very thick; their head, feet and tail, which are in appearance, seem ugly, as though they were members of a serpent or venomous beast; but notwithstanding they are very good meat, as also their eggs. Some have been found of a yard in breadth and better.

And thus have I made relation of all sorts of victual that we fed upon for the time we were in Virginia, as also the inhabitants themselves, as far forth as I know and can remember, or that are specially worthy to be remembered.

THE THIRD AND LAST PART, OF SUCH OTHER THINGS AS ARE BEHOVE-FUL FOR THOSE WHO SHALL PLANT AND INHABIT, TO KNOW OF, WITH A DESCRIPTION OF THE NATURE AND MANNERS OF THE PEO-PLE OF THE COUNTRY.

OF COMMODITIES FOR BUILDING AND OTHER NECESSARY USES.

Those other things which I am more to make rehearsal of, are such as concern building, and other mechanical necessary uses, as divers sorts of trees for house and ship timber, and other uses else; also lime, stone and brick, lest that being not mentioned, some might have been doubted of, or by some that are malicious the contrary reported.

Oaks there are, as fair, straight, and tall, and as good timber, as any can be, and also great store, and in some places very great.

Walnut-trees, as I have said before, very many, some have been seen, excellent fair timber, of four and five fathom, and above fourscore feet straight without bough.

Fir-trees, fit for masts of ships, some very tall and great.

Rakiock, a kind of trees so called that are sweet wood, of which the inhabitants that were near unto us do commonly make their boats or canoes, of the form of troughs, only with the help of fire, hatchets of stones, and shells; we have known some so great being made in that sort of one tree, that they have carried well twenty men at once, besides much baggage; the timber being great, tall, straight, soft, light, and yet tough enough, I think, (besides other uses,) to be fit also for masts of ships.

[It is probably the wild poplar, or tulip-tree, to which Hariot here alludes.]

Cedar, a sweet wood good for ceilings, chests, boxes, bedsteads, lutes, virginals, and many things else, as I have also said before. Some of our company which have wandered in some places where I have not been, have made certain affirmations of *cypress*, which for such and other excellent uses is also a wood of price and no small estimation.

Maple, and also *witch-hazel*, whereof the inhabitants use to make their bows.

Holly, a necessary thing for the making of bird-lime.

Willows, good for the making of weirs and weeles to take fish after the English manner, although the inhabitants use only reeds, which, because they are so strong as also flexible, do serve for that turn very well and sufficiently.

Beech and *ash*, good for cask-hoops, and if it need require, plough work, as also for many things else.

Elm.

Sassafras-trees.

Ascopo, a kind of tree very like unto laurel, the bark is hot in taste and spicy, it is very like to that which Monardes describes to be cassia-lignea of the West Indies.

There are many other strange trees whose names I know not but in the Virginia language, of which I am not now able, neither is it so convenient for the present to trouble you with particular relation, seeing that for timber and other necessary uses I have named sufficient. And of many of the rest, but that they may be applied to good use, I know no cause to doubt.

Now for the *stone, brick and lime*, thus it is:

Near unto the sea-coast, where we dwelt, there are no kind of stones to be found, (except a few small pebbles, about four miles off,) but such as have been brought from further out of the main. In some of our voyages we have seen divers hard raggie stones, great pebbles, and a kind of gray stone, like unto marble, of which the inhabitants make their hatchets to cleave wood. Upon inquiry we heard that a little further up into the country were of all sorts very many, although of quarries they are ignorant, neither have they use of any stone whereupon they should have occasion to seek any. For, if every household have one or two to crack nuts, grind shells, whet copper, and sometimes other stones for hatchets, they have enough ; neither use they any in digging, but only for graves about three feet deep, and therefore no marvel that they know neither quarries, nor lime-stones, which both may be in places nearer than they wot of.

In the meantime until there be discovery of sufficient store in some place or other convenient; the want of you which are and shall be the planters therein may be as well supplied by brick, for the making whereof, in divers places of the country, there is clay both excellent good, and plenty, and also by lime made of oyster shells, and of others burnt, after the manner as they use in the Isles of Thanet and Shippy ; and also in divers other places of England, which kind of lime is well known to be as good as any other. And of oyster-shells there is plenty enough ; for besides divers other particular places where are abundance, there is one shallow sound along the coast, where for the space of many miles together in length, and two or three miles in breadth, the ground is nothing else, being but half a foot under water for the most part.

Thus much I can say furthermore of stones, that about one hundred and twenty miles from our fort near the water in the side of a hill, was found by a gentleman of our company, a great vein of hard ragge stones, which I thought good to remember unto you.

[It is pleasant to remark how late experience has verified all that is here said by this truthful and accurate observer. Stone does not exist where he was, but has been found in abundance in the interior, just such as he here describes it to be. There is also " clay both excellent good and plenty " from which bricks have long been made ; and until within a comparatively recent period all the lime used in the eastern part of the state was obtained from burning oyster shells, of which there are large deposits on the coast side of the state.]

OF THE NATURE AND MANNERS OF THE PEOPLE.

It rests I speak a word or two of the natural inhabitants, their natures and manners, leaving large discourse thereof until time more convenient hereafter ; now only so far forth, as that you may know, how that they in respect of troubling our inhabiting and planting, are not to be feared, but that they shall have cause both to fear and love us, that shall inhabit with them.

They are a people clothed with loose mantles made of deer skins, and aprons of the same round about their middles, all else naked, of such a difference of stature only as we in England; having no edge tools or weapons of iron or steel to offend us withal, neither know they how to make any; those weapons that they have, are only bows made of Witch-hazel, and arrows of reeds, flat edged truncheons also of wood about a yard long; neither have they any thing to defend themselves but targets made of sticks wickered together with thread.

Their towns are but small, and near the sea coast but few, some containing but ten or twelve houses, some twenty; the greatest that we have seen has been but of thirty houses; if they be walled, it is only done with barks of trees made fast to stakes, or else with poles fixed upright and close one by another.

Their houses are made of small poles, made fast at the tops in round form after the manner as is used in many arbors in our gardens of England, in most towns covered with barks, and in some with artificial mats made of long rushes, from the tops of the houses down to the ground. The length of them is commonly double to the breadth, in some places they are but twelve and sixteen yards long, and in other some we have seen of four and twenty.

In some places of the country, one only town belonged to the government of a Weroance or chief Lord, in other some two or three, in some six, eight, and more; the greatest Weroance that yet we had dealing with, had but eighteen towns in his government, and able to make not above seven or eight hundred fighting men at the most. The language of every government is different from any other, and the further they are distant, the greater is the difference.

[The difference generally we apprehend was for the most part that of various dialects of the same mother tongue. Though we are inclined to think that there were *two* mother languages within the limits of North Carolina. The one was Algonquin and the other Iroquois. When Manteo, who was a native of Croatan island on the sea shore near Ocracoke, accompanied Lane up the Roanoak and was near the borders of Virginia, he understood the speech of the tribes in that region so well, that he knew the meaning of their threats, and warned the English that they were about to discharge a volley of arrows upon them. Our materials for the study of these languages, we regret to say, are limited: we have but a few words and phrases furnished by Smith, and a short comparative vocabulary by Lawson. Our best labors with these have led us to the conclusion we have expressed above of *two* mother tongues. We think too that dialects of the Iroquois preponderated in that part of the country seen by the English settlers. The Tuscarora and Coranine speech were both Iroquois. That very warlike race (the Iroquois) we are inclined to think had at some period, prior to the arrival of the Europeans, driven away a branch of what Smith calls the Susquehannocks who in his day were on the shores of the Chesapeak, and whom we take to have been Algonquins. But the subject is one of so much obscurity that it is hardly safe to do more than hazard a conjecture. We know, however, that between the Tuscarora and Wococon languages, there is very little verbal relationship, while between the former and the Pamptico (Coranines) the case is otherwise. We regret the more that our researches in this department have been so fruitless, because, as every Indian name has a definite meaning, a fuller understanding of the languages might have afforded valuable aid in settling localities wherever the name was descriptive of the place, as in the Iroquois dialects it generally is. But we get no such aid; we find indeed that in the Pamptico tongue, *Chuwon* meant *paint*, and *Ronoak* signified *Peak* or Wampum. Possibly they found some coloring substance, clay perhaps, on the Chowan; and fancy might too hastily conjecture that they made peak of the muscle shells in the Roanoak, though this latter is very improbable as *they* called the river, not Roanoak, but *Moratoc.* They knew no river by the name Roanoak; the island bore that name; and there was, as before remarked, the town of *Ohanoak.* It was once asserted, and that before ethnology had entered into the patient labor of research into the languages of our continent, that the number of different tongues in America was immense; but more recent and careful investigation has satisfactorily shown that here, as in the other hemisphere, while the dialects are indeed numerous, the matrices from which they spring may be reduced to a comparatively small number; and we think that we have traced some of these most unmistakably to Northern Asia. Still there are dialects of different mother tongues both in North and South America, for which we account, satisfactorily to ourselves at least, by the evidence which has convinced us of different times and modes of settlement from widely different localities.]

Their manner of wars amongst themselves is either by sudden surprising one another most commonly about the dawning of the day, or moon-light, or else by ambushes, or some subtil devices. Set battles are very rare, except it fall out where there are many trees, where either party may have some hope of defence, after the delivery of every arrow, in leaping behind some or other.

If there fall out any wars between us and them, what their fight is likely to be, we having advantages against them so many manner of ways, as by our discipline, our strange weapons and devices else, especially ordinance great and small, it may easily be imagined, by the experience we have had in some places, the turning up of their heels against us in running away was their best defence.

In respect of us they are a people poor, and for want of skill and judgment in the knowledge and use of our things, do esteem our trifles before things of greater value. Notwithstanding, in their proper manner (considering the want of such things as we have) they seem very ingenious; for, although they have no such tools, nor any such crafts, sciences and arts as we, yet in such things as they do, they show excellent wit. And by how much they upon due consideration shall find our manner of knowledges and crafts to exceed theirs in perfection, and speed for doing or execution, by so much the more is it probable that they should desire our friendship and love, and have the greater respect for pleasing and obeying us. Whereby may be hoped, if means of good government be used, that they may in short time be brought to civility and the embracing of true religion.

Some religion they have already, which, although it be far from the truth, yet being as it is, there is hope it may easier and sooner be reformed.

They believe that there are many gods, which they call Mantoac, but of different sorts and degrees, one only chief and great God, which has been from all eternity. Who, as they affirm, when he purposed to make the world, made first other gods of a principal order, to be as means and instruments to be used in the creation and government to follow, and after the sun, moon and stars as petty gods, and the instruments of the other order more principal. First (they say) were made waters, out of which by the gods was made all diversity of creatures that are visible or invisible.

[We here meet with a striking fact, which must have often forced itself upon the notice of the student of paganism. It is this, that most commonly among such idolaters as have furnished evidence of progress in intelligence and in devising material comforts, though they may have an abundance of gods of wood and stone, yet they have also almost uniformly what Hariot here calls "one only chief and great God, which hath been from all eternity," and *of which they make no outward or visible representation.*

"It is a remarkable fact," says our accomplished countryman, Mr. Prescott, "that many, if not most of the rude tribes inhabiting the vast American continent, however disfigured their creeds may have been in other respects by a childish superstition, had attained to the sublime conception of one Great Spirit, the creator of the universe, who, immaterial in his own nature, was not to be dishonored by an attempt at visible representation, and who, pervading all space, was not to be circumscribed within the walls of a temple].

For mankind they say a woman was made first, which, by the working of one of the gods, conceived and brought forth children; and in such sort, they say, they had their beginning. But how many years or ages have passed since, they say they can make no relation, having no letters nor other such means as we to keep records of the particularities of times past, but only tradition from father to son.

They think that all the gods are of human shape, and therefore they represent them by images in the forms of men, which they call Kewasowak, one alone is called Kewas : them they place in houses appropriate or temples, which they call Machicomuck, where they worship, pray, sing, and make many times offering unto them. In some machicomuck we have seen but one kewas, in some two, and in other some three. The common sort think them to be also gods.

They believe also the immortality of the soul, that after this life, as soon as the soul is departed from the body, according to the works it has done, it is either carried to heaven the habitacle of gods, there to enjoy perpetual bliss and happiness, or else to a great pit or hole, which they think to be in the further parts of their part of the world toward the sunset, there to burn continually : the place they call Popogusso.

For the confirmation of this opinion, they told me two stories of two men that had been lately dead and revived again, the one happened but few years before our coming into the country, of a wicked man, (who, having been dead and buried, the next day the earth of the grave being seen to move, was taken up again), who made declaration where his soul had been, that is to say, very near entering into Popogusso, had not one of the gods saved him, and gave him leave to return again, and teach his friends what they should do to avoid that terrible place of torment. The other happened in the same year we were there, but in a town that was sixty miles from us, and it was told me for strange news, that one being dead, buried, and taken up again as the first, showed that, although his body had laid dead in the grave, yet his soul was alive, and had traveled far in the long broad way ; on both sides whereof grew most delicate and pleasant trees, bearing more rare and excellent fruits than ever he had seen before, or was able to express, and at length came to most brave and fair houses, near which he met his father that had been dead before, who gave him great charge to go back again, and show his friends what good they were to do to enjoy the pleasures of that place, which when he had done he should after come again.

What subtilty soever be in the weroances and priests, this opinion worketh so much in many of the common and simple sort of people, that it makes them have great respect to their governors, and also great care what they do, to avoid torment after death, and to enjoy bliss ; although, notwithstanding there is punishment ordained for malefactors, as stealers, whoremongers, and other sorts of wicked doers, some punished with death, some with forfeitures, some with beating, according to the greatness of the facts.

And this is the sum of their religion, which I learned by having special familiarity with some of their priests. Wherein they were not so sure grounded, nor gave such credit to their traditions and stories, but through conversing with us they were brought into great doubts of their own, and no small admiration for ours, with earnest desire in many, to learn more than we had means for want of perfect utterance in their language to express.

Most things they saw with us, as mathematical instruments, sea-compasses, the virtue of the load-stone in drawing iron, a perspective-glass, whereby was shown many strange sights, burning-glasses, wild fireworks, guns, books, writing and reading, spring-clocks, that seem to go of themselves, and many other things that we had were so strange unto them, and so far exceeded their capacities to comprehend the reason and means how they should be made and done, that they thought they were rather the works of gods than of men, or at the least wise they had been given and taught us of the gods. Which made many of them to have such opinion of us, as that if they knew not the truth of God and religion already, it was rather to be had from us whom God so specially loved, than from a people that were so simple, as they found themselves to be in comparison of us. Whereupon greater credit was given unto that we spake of concerning such matters.

Many times, and at every town where I came, according as I was able, I made declaration of the contents of the Bible, that therein was set forth the true and only God, and his mighty works, that therein was contained the true doctrine of salvation through Christ, with many particularities of miracles and chief points of religion, as I was able then to utter, and thought fit for the time. And although I told them the book materially and of itself was not of any such virtue, as I thought they did conceive, but only the doctrine therein contained, yet would many be glad to touch it, to embrace it, to kiss it, to hold it to their breasts and heads, and stroke over all their body with it, to show their hungry desire of that knowledge which was spoken of.

The Weroance with whom we dwelt, called Wingina, and many of his people, would be glad many times to be with us at our prayers, and many times call upon us, both in his own town, and also in others whither he sometimes accompanied us, to pray and sing psalms, hoping thereby to be partaker of the same effects which we by that means also expected.

[These passages, we may hope, will furnish ample refutation of the mis-
representations of Anthony a Wood, on the subject of Hariot's religious opinions. We learn here that he *prayed*, and further, that in
every town where he went, to the best of his ability, he taught those
poor heathen the truths of the Bible, and especially, " the true doctrine
of salvation through Christ."]

Twice this Weroance was so grievously sick that he was like to
die, and as he lay languishing, doubting of any help by his own
priests, and thinking he was in such danger for offending us and
thereby our God, sent for some of us to pray and be a means to
our God that it would please him either that he might live, or
after death dwell with him in bliss, so likewise were the requests
of many others in the like case.

On a time also when their corn began to wither, by reason of a
drought which happened extraordinarily, fearing that it had come
to pass by reason that in something they had displeased us, many
would come to us and desire us to pray to our God of England,
that he would preserve their corn, promising that when it was
ripe we also should be partakers of the fruit.

There could at no time happen any strange sickness, losses,
hurts, or any other cross unto them, but that they would impute
to us the cause or means thereof, for offending or not pleasing us.
One other rare and strange accident, leaving others, will I mention before I end, which moved the whole country that either
knew or heard of us, to have us in wonderful admiration.

There was no town where we had any subtle device practiced
against us, we leaving it unpunished or not revenged, (because we
sought by all means possible to win them by gentleness,) but that
within a few days after our departure from every such town the
people began to die very fast, and many in short space, in some
towns about twenty, in some forty, and in one six score, which in
truth was very many in respect of their numbers. This happened
in no place that we could learn, but where we had been, where
they used some practice against us, and after such time. The
disease also was so strange, that they neither knew what it was,
nor how to cure it, like by report of the oldest men in the country never happened before, time out of mind. A thing specially

observed by us, as also by the natural inhabitants themselves. Insomuch, that when some of the inhabitants which were our friends, and especially the Weroance Wingina, had observed such effects in four or five towns, to follow their wicked practices, they were persuaded that it was the work of our God through our means, and that we by him might kill and slay whom we would without weapons, and not come near them. And thereupon when it had happened that they had understanding that any of their enemies had abused us in our journeys, hearing that we had wrought no revenge with our weapons, and fearing upon some cause the matter would so rest, did come and intreat us that we would be a means to our God that they as others that had dealt ill with us might in like sort die, alleging how much it would be for our credit and profit, as also theirs, and hoping furthermore that we would do so much at their requests in respect of the friendship we professed them.

Whose entreaties, although we showed that they were ungodly, affirming that our God would not subject himself to any such prayers and requests of men, that indeed all things have been and were to be done according to his good pleasure as he had ordained, and that we, to show ourselves his true servants, ought rather to make petition for the contrary, that they with them might live together with us, be made partakers of his truth, and serve him in righteousness, but notwithstanding in such sort, that we refer that, as all other things, to be done according to his divine will and pleasure, and as by his wisdom he had ordained to be best.

[Here again the correct religious views of Hariot are presented, and we are obliged to admit that Wood seems to have forgotten his own duty as a professed Christian, in bearing, as he has done, false witness against his neighbor.]

Yet because the effect fell out so suddenly, and shortly after according to their desires, they thought nevertheless it came to pass by our means, and that we in using such speeches unto them, did but dissemble the matter, and therefore came into us to give us thanks in their manner, that although we satisfied them not in promise, yet in deeds and in effect we had fulfilled their desires.

This marvelous accident, in all the country wrought so strange opinions of us, that some people could not tell whether to think us gods or men, and the rather because that all the space of their sickness, there was no men of ours known to die, or that was specially sick; they noted also that we had no women amongst us, neither that we did care for any of theirs.

Some therefore were of opinion that we were not born of women, and therefore not mortal, but that we were men of an old generation many years past, then risen again to immortality.

Some would likewise seem to prophecy, that there were more of our generation yet to come and kill theirs, and take their places, as some thought the purpose was, by that which was already done. Those that were immediately to come after us they imagined to be in the air, yet invisible and without bodies, and that they, by our entreaty, and for the love of us, did make the people to die in that sort as they did, by shooting invisible bullets into them.

To confirm this opinion, their physicians (to excuse their ignorance in curing the disease) would not be ashamed to say, but earnestly make the simple people believe, that the strings of blood they sucked out of the sick bodies, were the strings wherewithal the invisible bullets were tied and cast. Some also thought that we shot them ourselves out of our pieces, from the place where we dwelt, and killed the people in any town that had offended us, as we listed, how far distant from us soever it were. And other some said, that it was the special work of God for our sakes, as we ourselves have cause in some sort to think no less, whatsoever some do, or may imagine to the contrary, specially some astrologers, knowing of the eclipse of the sun which we saw the same year before our voyage thitherward, which unto them appeared very terrible. And also of a comet which began to appear but a few days before the beginning of the said sickness. But to exclude them from being the special causes of so special an accident, there are further reasons than I think fit at this present to be alleged. These their opinions I have set down the more at large, that it may appear unto you that there is good hope they may be brought, through direct dealing and government, to the embracing of the truth, and consequently to honor, obey and love us.

And although some of our company, towards the end of the

year, showed themselves too fierce in slaying some of the people in some towns, upon causes that on our part might easily enough have been borne withal, yet notwithstanding, because it was on their part justly deserved, the alteration of their opinions generally and for the most part concerning us is the less to be doubted. And whatsoever else they may be, by carefulness of ourselves, need nothing at all to be feared.

The best nevertheless in this, as in all actions besides, is to be endeavored and hoped, and of the worst that may happen notice to be taken with consideration, and as much as may be eschewed.

THE CONCLUSION.

Now I have (as I hope) made relation not of so few and small things, but that the country (of men that are indifferent and well disposed) may be sufficiently liked if there were no more known than I have mentioned; which doubtless and in great reason is nothing to that which remains to be discovered, neither as to the soil, nor commodities. As we have reason to gather by the difference we found in our travels, for although all which I have before spoken of, have been discovered and experimented not far from the sea-coast, where was our abode and most of our traveling, yet sometimes as we made our journeys further into the main and country, we found the soil to be fatter, the trees greater and to grow thinner, the ground more firm and deeper mould, more and larger champains, finer grass, and as good as ever we saw any in England; in some places rocky and far more high and hilly ground, more plenty of their fruits, more abundance of beasts, the more inhabited with people, and of greater policy and larger dominions with greater towns and houses.

Why may we not then look for in good hope, from the inner parts, of more and greater plenty, as well of other things, as of those which we have already discovered. Unto the Spaniards happened the like in discovering the main of the West Indies. The main also of this country of Virginia, extending some ways so many hundreds of leagues, as otherwise than by the relation of the inhabitants we have most certain knowledge of, where yet no Christian prince has any possession or dealing cannot but yield many excellent commodities, which we in our discovery have not yet seen.

What hope there is else to be gathered of the nature of the climate, being answerable to the island of Japan, the land of China, Persia, Jewry, the island of Cyprus and Candy, the south parts of Greece, Italy and Spain, and of many other notable and famous countries, because I mean not to be tedious, I leave to your own consideration.

Whereby also the excellent temperature of the air there at all seasons, much warmer than in England, and never so vehemently hot, as sometimes is under and between the tropics, or near them, cannot be known to you without further relation.

For the wholesomeness thereof, I need to say but thus much— that for all the want of provision, as first of English victual, excepting for twenty days, we lived only by drinking water, and by the victual of the country, of which some sorts were very strange unto us, and might have been thought to have altered our temperatures in such sort as to have brought us into some grievous and dangerous diseases. Secondly, the wants of English means, for the taking of beasts, fish and fowl, which by the help only of the inhabitants and their means could not be so suddenly and easily provided for us, not in so great number and quantities, nor of that choice as otherwise might have been to our better satisfaction and contentment. Some want also we had of clothes. Furthermore, in all our travels, which were most specially and often in the time of winter, our lodging was in the open air upon the ground. And yet I say for all this, there were but four of our whole company (being one hundred and eight) that died all the year, and that but at the latter end thereof, and upon none of the aforesaid causes. For all four, especially three, were feeble, weak and sickly persons before ever they came thither, and those that knew them much marveled that they lived so long being in that case, or had adventured to travel.

[The colonists reached Roanoak island on the 17th of August, and remained until the 18th of the following June. September is one of the most unwholesome months of the year in the eastern part of the state, as then bilious fevers are most prevalent and fatal. It is, therefore, matter of surprise that there should have been so small a mortality as but four persons out of one hundred and eight, when we consider what must have been the unavoidable exposure of the colonists. These four, too, seem not to have died from any peculiarity of the climate. Has the country become less salubrious, or were the English preserved in health from living (as they seem to have done) on much the same food as that used by the natives?]

Seeing, therefore, the air there is temperate and wholesome, the soil so fertile, and yielding such commodities, as I have before mentioned, the voyage also thither to and fro being sufficiently experimented to be performed twice a year with ease, and at any season thereof, and the dealing of Sir Walter Raleigh so liberal in large giving and granting land there, as is already known, with many helps and furtherances else (the least that he has granted has been five hundred acres to a man only for the adventure of his person). I hope there remains no cause whereby the actions should be misliked.

If that those which shall thither travel to inhabit and plant be but reasonably provided for the first year, as those are which were transported the last, and being there, do use but that diligence and care that is requisite, and as they may with ease; there is no doubt, but for the time following, they may have victuals that are excellent, good and plenty enough; some more English sorts of cattle also hereafter, as some have been before and are there yet remaining, may, and shall be (God willing) thither transported. So, likewise, our kinds of fruits, roots and herbs, may be there planted and sowed, as some have been already, and prove well, and in short time also they may raise so much of those sorts of commodities which I have spoken of, as shall both enrich themselves, as also others that shall deal with them.

And this is all the fruits of our labors that I have thought necessary to advertise you of at this present. What else concerns the nature and manners of the inhabitants of Virginia, the number with the particularities of the voyages thither made, and of the actions of such as have been by Sir Walter Raleigh therein, and there employed, many worthy to be remembered as of the first discoverers of the country, of our general, for the time, Sir Richard Greenvil, and after his departure of our governor there

Master Ralph Lane, with divers other directed and employed under their government; of the captains and masters of the voyages made since for transportation, of the governor and assistants of those already transported, as of many persons, accidents, and things else, I have ready in a discourse by itself in manner of a chronicle, according to the course of times, which, when time shall be thought convenient, shall be also published.

[This " discourse, in manner of a chronicle," we fear is irrecoverably lost. Coming from the pen of such an intelligent and honest eye-witness as Hariot, it would to us of this day be invaluable. Many of Hariot's MSS. went into the possession of the Duke of Northumberland : from him they descended to the Earl of Egremont, and in 1784 were at his seat of Petworth. Is it not worth an effort to ascertain if this be among them ?]

Thus referring my relation to your favorable constructions, expecting good success of the action, from him which is to be acknowledged the author and governor, not only of this, but of all things else, I take my leave of you, this month of February, one thousand five hundred and eighty-seven.

No. 7.

THE FOURTH VOYAGE

MADE TO

VIRGINIA,

WITH THREE SHIPS, IN THE YEAR

1587.

WHEREIN WAS TRANSPORTED THE SECOND COLONY.

———

[Reprinted from HAKLUYT, *Vol. III., page* 280].

In the year of our Lord, fifteen hundred and eighty-seven, Sir Walter Raleigh intending to persevere in the planting of his country of Virginia, prepared a new colony of one hundred and fifty men to be sent thither, under the charge of John White, whom he appointed Governor, and also appointed unto him twelve assistants, unto whom he gave a charter, and incorporated them by the name of Governor and Assistants of the city of Raleigh in Virginia.

[The distinguishing features in this effort seem to have been an attempt at the establishment of regular government, and the presence of females in the expedition. Both these imply the hope and intention of *permanent* settlement, though not (as we learn from the future narrative) on the island of Roanoak. What the precise form of government was under the charter of " the Governor and Assistants of the city of Raleigh in Virginia," we cannot now discover.

But as to this company thus chartered, it furnishes proof of a change in Raleigh's mode of proceeding for the settlement of his colonies. He seems to have resolved that it was expedient to associate with him in interest, others, who stimulated by the hope of pecuniary returns, either advanced money as " adventurers," or went out themselves to establish and transact business, with the intent seemingly of making shipments to England of the products of the colony. We find, under date of January 7th, 1587, which was some three or four months before this voyage by White, an instrument executed by Raleigh, whereby, without divesting himself entirely of his interest, he permitted others to *share* with him in the privileges conferred by his patent. This document has been preserved by Hakluyt, and is reprinted in Hazard's state papers, vol. I. p. 42.

Under the charter of Elizabeth, which forms the first document of this volume, bearing date March 25th, 1584, certain rights and privileges were granted, which, divested of the technicalities of legal phraseology used in the grant, may in plain language be described as follows:

1. Power was given to Raleigh and his assigns by the queen, freely to search for, occupy and enjoy forever, such remote and barbarous lands, not already possessed by any Christian people, as to him might seem good ; and he was to have in them all such rights and prerogatives as the patent proceeded to grant.

2. He was at liberty to take with him to such lands and leave there for inhabitants, as many of the people of England as chose willingly to accompany him for that purpose.

3. He was to enjoy in fee-simple all the soil of the lands he might thus discover, and might convey any part of it in fee-simple, or otherwise, to those who accompanied him (they remaining, however, in the queen's allegiance) and reserving also to the queen one fifth of all the gold and silver that might be found in such lands. The queen was to be acknowledged as sovereign.

4. He had power to repel and drive out any who, without his license, entered on his lands to make settlement, or planted themselves within six hundred miles of any place where he had made a settlement, or might make one within six years from the date of his grant. In thus repelling he might surprise and take such intruders prisoners, and destroy their ships and property. In other words, might make war upon them.

5. The children of all English subjects born in any of his colonies should enjoy all the rights and privileges of persons born in England.

6. For the preservation of peace and good order, power was given him to correct, punish, govern and rule, at his discretion, all the colonists both in criminal and civil cases, and to this end he had power to make laws, provided they did not contravene the Christian faith, and were made as conformable as circumstances allowed to the laws of England.

7. Power was given him, under the supervision of certain English officials of high rank to export from England all such goods and commodities as might be necessary for the relief and support of his colonists.

8. If, however, at any time, he or his followers should rob or spoil by sea or land, or commit unlawful hostilities against the subjects of any power at peace with England; he should on demand by his own sovereign, within a limited time, make full satisfaction to the party injured; failing which, he and his should be out of the queen's protection, and might be pursued and treated as an enemy by the government of the party robbed, &c., just as if they were not the queen of England's subjects.

This is the substance of his patent, and it will be seen that under it he possessed a qualified sovereignty.

When he formed the corporation with a charter, known as " the Governor and Assistants of the city of Raleigh in Virginia," of which White here speaks, he acted alone, under the powers conferred by the sixth paragraph of the foregoing abstract of his patent. Having, however, thus formed the corporation, he next proceeded, by indenture to make certain individuals " free of the corporation," in other words, members of it under the powers conferred in the third paragraph.

VOL. I.—13

13

The indenture therefore sets forth substantially as follows :—

1. Sir Walter Raleigh, as the grantor, and describes him as "Chief Governor of *Assamocomoc*, alias *Wingandacoa*, alias *Virginia*."

2. The grantees, who are divided into two classes. The first class numbers nineteen, and they are described as "merchants of London, and adventurers to Virginia aforesaid." These remained at home, and adventured or risked their money only in the hands of their factors or agents whom they sent out or selected from those bound on the voyage. The second class numbers thirteen, and consists of the individuals who we learn from White's narrative went on the voyage, and constituted the "Governor and Assistants" of the new city of Raleigh. These are described as "late of London, gentlemen," not as merchants.

The instrument then recites that to these latter, whom he constitutes the "Governor," &c. of the corporation, he grants such powers as his original charter conferred on him in transporting settlers, inhabiting the country, making provision for its government, &c. It then proceeds to declare that the other nineteen grantees, "adventurers as aforesaid, purposing and intending to be made, free of the corporation, company and society lately made by the said Sir Walter Raleigh, in the city of Raleigh, intended to be erected and builded" in Virginia, do "adventure divers and sundry sums of money, merchandises and shipping, munition, victual, and other commodities" into Virginia.

It then recites that, in consideration of this adventure, Sir Walter grants to them a perfectly unrestricted and free trade forever to any settlements he may now have or make by future discovery in America. He also grants them a donation of £100, to be invested by them as an adventure in any mode they please, the profits thereof to be applied by them in Virginia, "in planting the Christian religion, and advancing the same," and for "the common utility and profit of the inhabitants thereof."

He then exempts them from all duties or customs on their commerce, and from all rents, subsidies, &c., generally, and finally covenants to execute any further instrument the law may require to define and secure in perpetuity the rights of the corporation he has created. It will thus be seen that he made no *general* transfer of all his rights under the original patent ; but simply created a corporation on very liberal terms, and thus induced capitalists to become members of it, in the hope that under the impulse of individual interest, a portion of their funds would be so used as to benefit the colony as well as prove profitable to themselves. This is what is commonly called "the assignment of his patent." In this he showed his usual sagacity ; for if he could convince London merchants that their money, employed in Virginia, would yield a return, he was very certain that, this proving true, Virginia colonies would not only grow, but very soon exhibit a self-supporting power within themselves.

It may gratify the curiosity of the reader, if we subjoin the names of those who constituted the corporators of " the city of Raleigh in Virginia," that was never built. It is well to know who those were that helped (even at the risk of loss) in the series of trials that finally planted an English colony in the southern part of the United States. The " nineteen" who remained at home were Thomas Smith, afterward Sir Thomas Smith, who, as treasurer, had much to do with the settlement of Jamestown, William. Sanderson, Walter Bayly, William Gamage, Edmund Neville, Thomas Harding, Walter Master, Thomas Martin, Gabriel Harris, William George, William Stone, Henry Fleetwood, John Gerrard, Robert Macklyn, Richard Hakluyt, Thomas Hoode, Thomas Wade, Richard Wright, and Edmund Walden.

In a rare old tract, giving the names, and sums respectively subscribed, of " adventurers" to the Virginia colony at Jamestown, at a later period, I find no less than *ten* of the names mentioned above, viz., Smith, Bayly, Neville, Martin, Harris, Stone, Fleetwood, Hakluyt, Wade and Wright.

The " thirteen" other grantees, who, with the exception of two, Nichols and Fulwood, came to this country, were John Whyte, Governor, Roger Bayly, Ananias Dare, Christopher Cooper, John Sampson, Thomas Steevens, William Fulwood, Roger Pratt, Dyonisius Harvie, John Nichols, George Howe, James Platt and Simon Fernando. Of these we read no more after this voyage, for most of this colony, consisting of one hundred and twenty-one, were never found after White left them for England. All perished or became incorporated among the savages, with the exception of such as returned home with White.]

April.—Our fleet, being in number three sails, viz :—the Admiral, a ship of one hundred and twenty tons, a fly-boat, and a pinnace, departed the six and twentieth of April from Portsmouth, and the same day came to anchor at the Cowes in the Isle of Wight, where we stayed eight days.

May.—The fifth of May, at nine o'clock at night, we came to Plymouth, where we remained the space of two days.

The eighth we weighed anchor at Plymouth, and departed thence for Virginia.

The sixteenth, Simon Ferdinando, master of our Admiral, lewdly forsook our fly boat, leaving her distressed in the Bay of Portugal.

[We know but little of this Simon Fernando, or Ferdinando, save that he proved a treacherous villain. He was one of those named in the list of "assistants" to the governor, and was, beside, the sailing master of the largest ship in the little squadron. These circumstances increased his power of doing mischief. Williamson says he had been *twice* before on the coast of Carolina as a pilot. That he was on the first voyage with Amadas and Barlowe, is proved by the insertion of his name at the close of Barlowe's narrative, as one of his company. There is no evidence that he was with Lane's colonists during their stay of one year, though he may have been in the fleet, under Grenville, which brought them : and so also he may have been on board the relief ship of 1586, or in Grenville's fleet on his second visit, made in the same year. But whether he had been there before, once only, or twice, certain it is, that on this voyage of White he manifested no little perfidy, from the very commencement of the voyage. Thus, we find him deserting one of the vessels in the Bay of Portugal, telling falsehoods about the island of Santa Cruz, refusing to stop at Hispaniola, lying repeatedly about supplies to be obtained at various West India islands, nearly losing the vessel on Cape Fear shoals, and finally preventing the return of White and the colonists to the ship when they landed at Roanoak island to look for the colonists left there by Grenville. He professed to be on very friendly terms with the Spanish governor of Hispaniola, and his own name would indicate, that if not by birth a Spaniard, he was of Spanish descent. It is therefore possible that he may have been secretly working in the interests of Spain. Had he permitted White and his companions, after visiting Roanoak island, to return on board, we probably should have been saved the sad reflections occasioned by musing on the mysterious fate of the one hundred and twenty human beings, men, women and children, who constituted White's colony. Sir Walter's instructions to White were merely to stop at Roanoak long enough to look for the men Grenville had left and then to proceed to the Chesapeak, and there make a settlement. What must have been the worse than savage cruelty of heart that could thus abandon women and children on a spot which had proved the scene of former failures, and the unfitness of which for colonizing had been made but too well known to Fernando by his own personal experience on the coast ?]

June.—The nineteenth we fell in with Dominica, and the same evening we sailed between it and Guadaloupe : the twenty-first, the fly-boat also fell in with Dominica.

The twenty-second we came to an anchor at an island called Santa Cruz, where all the planters were set on land, staying there till the twenty-fifth of the same month. At our first landing on this island, some of our women and men, by eating small fruit like green apples, were fearfully troubled with a sudden burning in their mouths, and swelling of their tongues so big, that some of them could not speak. Also a child, by sucking one of those women's breasts, had at that instant his mouth set on such a burning, that it was strange to see how the infant was tormented for the time, but after twenty-four hours, it ware away of itself.

Also, the first night of our being on this island, we took five great tortoises, some of them of such bigness, that sixteen of our strongest men were tired with carrying one of them but from the sea-side to our cabins. In this island we found no watering-place but a standing pond, the water whereof was so evil, that many of our company fell sick with drinking thereof, and as many as did but wash their faces with that water, in the morning before the sun had drawn away the corruption, their faces did so burn and swell, that their eyes were shut up, and they could not see in five or six days, or longer.

The second day of our abode there, we sent forth some of our men to search the island for fresh water, three one way, and two another way. The governor, also, with six others, went up to the top of a high hill to view the island, but could perceive no sign of any men, or beasts, nor any goodness, but parrots and trees of Guiacum. Returning back to our cabins another way, we found in the descent of a hill certain potsherds of savage making, made of the earth of that island ; whereupon it was judged that this island was inhabited with savages, though Fernando had told us for certain the contrary. The same day, at night, the rest of our company very late returned to the governor. The one company affirmed that they had seen in a valley eleven savages, and divers houses half a mile distant from the steep, or top of the hill where they stayed. The other company had found running out of a high rock a very fair spring of water, whereof they brought three bottles to the company ; for before that time we drank the stinking water of the pond.

The same second day, at night, Captain Stafford, with the pinnace, departed from our fleet, riding at Santa Cruz, to an island called Beake, lying near St. John, being so directed by Ferdinando, who assured him he should there find great plenty of sheep. The next day, at night, our planters left Santa Cruz and came all aboard, and the next morning after, being the 25th of June, we weighed anchor and departed from Santa Cruz.

The seven and twentieth we came to anchor at Cottea, where we found the pinnace riding at our coming.

The twenty-eighth we weighed anchor at Cottea, and presently came to anchor at St. Johns in Musketo's Bay, where we spent three days unprofitably in taking in fresh water, spending in the meantime more beer than the quantity of the water came unto.

July.—The first day we weighed anchor at Musketo's Bay, where were left behind two Irishmen of our company, Darbie Glaven and Dennis Carrell, bearing along the coast of St. Johns till evening, at which time we fell in with Ross Bay. At this place Ferdinando had promised we should take in salt, and had caused us before to make and provide as many sacks for that purpose as we could. The governor, also, for that he understood there was a town in the bottom of the bay, not far from the salt hills, appointed thirty shot, ten pikes and ten targets, to man the pinnace, and to go aland for salt. Ferdinando perceiving them in readiness, sent to the governor, using great persuasions with him not to take in salt there, saying that he knew not well whether the same were the place or not ; also, that if the pinnace went into the bay, she could not, without great danger, come back till the next day at night, and that if in the meantime any storm should rise, the Admiral were in danger to be cast away. Whilst he was thus persuading, he caused the lead to be cast, and having craftily brought the ships in three fathoms and a half water, he suddenly began to swear, and tear God in pieces, dissembling great danger, crying to him at the helm, Bear up hard, bear up hard ! So we went off, and were disappointed of salt by his means.

The next day, sailing along the west end of St. John, the

governor determined to go aland in St. German's Bay, to gather young plants of oranges, pines, mameas and plantanos, to set at Virginia, which we knew might easily be had, for that they grow near the shore, and the places where they grew, well known to the governor and some of the planters, but our Simon denied it, saying he would come to an anchor at Hispaniola and there land the governor, and some other of the assistants with the pinnace, to see if he could speak with his friend Alanson, of whom he hoped to be furnished both of cattle, and all such things as we would have taken in at St. John; but he meant nothing else, as it plainly did appear to us afterwards.

The next day after, being the third of July, we saw Hispaniola, and bear with the coast all that day, looking still where the pinnace should be prepared to go for the place where Ferdinando's friend Alanson was; but that day passed, and we saw no preparation for landing in Hispaniola.

The fourth of July, sailing along the coast of Hispaniola until the next day at noon, and no preparation yet seen for the staying there, we having knowledge that we were past the place where Alanson dwelt, and were come up with Isabella; hereupon Ferdinando was asked by the Governor whether he meant to speak with Alanson, for the taking in of cattle and other things, according to his promise, or not; but he answered that he was now passed the place, and that Sir Walter Raleigh told him, the French ambassador certified him that the king of Spain had sent for Alanson into Spain, wherefore he thought him dead, and that it was to no purpose to touch there in any place, at this voyage.

The next day we left sight of Hispaniola, and hauled off for Virginia, about four o'clock in the afternoon.

The sixth of July we came to the Island Caycos, wherein Ferdinando said were two salt ponds, assuring us if they were dry we might find salt to shift with, until the next supply, but it proved as true as finding of sheep at Baque. In this island, whilst Ferdinando solaced himself ashore, with one of the company in part of the island, others spent the latter part of that day in other parts of the island, some to seek the salt ponds, some fowling, some hunting swans, whereof we caught many. The next day early in the morning we weighed anchor, leaving Caycos, with good hope, that the first land that we saw next should be Virginia.

About the sixteenth of July we fell in with the main of Virginia, which Simon Ferdinando took to be the island of Croatoan, where we came to anchor, and rode there two or three days ; but finding himself to be deceived, he weighed and bare along the coast, where in the night, had not Captain Stafford been more careful in looking out, than our Simon Fernando, we had been all cast away upon the breach, called the Cape of Fear ; for we were come within two cables' length upon it : such was the carelessness and ignorance of our master.

The two and twentieth of July we arrived safe at Hatorask, where our ship and pinnace anchored ; the Governor went aboard the pinnace, accompanied with forty of his best men, intending to pass up to Roanoak forthwith, hoping there to find those fifteen Englishmen, which Richard Greenvill had left there the year before, with whom he meant to have conference, concerning the state of the country, and savages, meaning after he had so done, to return again to the fleet and pass along the coast, to the bay of Chesepiok, where we intended to make our seat and fort, according to the charge given us among other directions in writing, under the hand of Sir Walter Raleigh ; but as soon as we were put with our pinnace from the ship, a gentleman by the means of Ferdinando, who was appointed to return for England, called to the sailors in the pinnace, charging them not to bring any of the planters back again, but to leave them in the island, except the Governor, and two or three such as he approved ; saying that the summer was far spent, wherefore he would land all the planters in no other place. Unto this were all the sailors, both in the pinnace and ship, persuaded by the master, wherefore it booted not the Governor to contend with them, but passed to Roanoak, and the same night, at sun-set, went aland on the island, in the place where our fifteen men were left, but we found none of them, nor any sign that they had been there, saving only we found the bones of one of those fifteen, which the savages had slain long before.

The three and twentieth of July the Governor with divers of his company walked to the north end of the island, where master

Ralph Lane had his fort, with sundry necessary and decent dwelling houses, made by his men about it, the year before, where we hoped to find some signs, or certain knowledge of our fifteen men. When we came thither, we found the fort razed down, but all the houses standing unhurt, saving that the neather (outer) rooms of them, and also of the fort, were overgrown with melons of divers sorts, and deer within them, feeding on those melons; so we returned to our company, without hope of ever seeing any of the fifteen men living.

The same day order was given that every man should be employed for the repairing of those houses, which we found standing, and also to make other new cottages, for such as should need.

The twenty-fifth, our fly-boat and the rest of our planters arrived all safe at Hatorask, to the great joy and comfort of the whole company: but the master of our Admiral, Ferdinando, grieved greatly at their safe coming, for he purposely left them in the Bay of Portugal, and stole away from them in the night, hoping that the master thereof, whose name was Edward Spicer, for that he never had been in Virginia, would hardly find the place, or else being left in so dangerous a place as that was, by means of so many men of war, as at that time were abroad, they should surely be taken or slain; but God disappointed his wicked pretences.

The eight and twentieth, George Howe, one of our twelve assistants, was slain by divers savages, which were come over to Roanoak, either of purpose to espy our company, and what number we were, or else to hunt deer, whereof were many in the island. These savages being secretly hidden among high reeds, where oftentimes they find the deer asleep, and so kill them, espied our man wading in the water above, almost naked, and without any weapon, save only a small forked stick, catching crabs therewithal, and also being strayed two miles from his company, and shot at him in the water, where they gave him sixteen wounds with their arrows; and after they had slain him with their wooden swords, they beat his head in pieces and fled over the water to the main.

On the thirtieth of July, Master Stafford and twenty of our men passed by water to the island of Croatoan, with Manteo, who had his mother and many of his kindred dwelling in that island, of whom we hoped to understand some news of our fifteen men, but especially to learn the disposition of the people of the country towards us, and to renew our old friendship with them.

At our first landing they seemed as though they would fight with us, but perceiving us begin to march with our shot towards them, they turned their backs and fled. Then Manteo, their countryman, called to them in their own language, whom, as soon as they heard, they returned, and threw away their bows and arrows, and some of them came unto us, embracing and entertaining us friendly, desiring us not to gather or spoil any of their corn, for that they had but little. We answered them that neither their corn nor any other thing of theirs should be diminished by any of us, and that our coming was only to renew the old love, that was between us and them at the first, and to live with them as brethren and friends; which answer seemed to please them well, wherefore they requested us to walk up to their town, who there feasted us after their manner, and desired us earnestly that there might be some token or badge given them of us, whereby we might know them to be our friends, when we met them anywhere out of the town or island. They told us further, that for want of some such badge, divers of them were hurt the year before, being found out of the island by Master Lane and his company, whereof they showed us one, which at that very instant lay lame, and had been laying of that hurt ever since; but they said, they knew our men mistook them, and hurt them instead of Wingina's men, wherefore they held us excused.

[We have already mentioned that Lawson, in his map of 1709, marks as "*Croatan*," the *main* land lying west of Roanoak island, in the present county of Tyrrel; some of the modern maps apply to this region the same name; but this paragraph is important as showing that this was *not* the region known to the early voyages and colonists as Croatan. It is here expressly called an *island*, and we know it to have been on the coast, because Sir Francis Drake's fleet was first seen from it on the open sea, approaching from the south. Of the early Indian name applied to what is now Tyrrel county, there can be no doubt. On the map of Amadas and Barlowe, the first ever made of the country, it is called *Dasamonguepeuk*, and this name is continued on many of the subsequent old maps. If we may hazard a conjecture as to the later application of the name "Croatan" to Tyrrel, we would suggest that possibly it may have been caused in this wise.

From the future story of White we learn that it was agreed between him and the colonists, before his departure for England, that should they remove from Roanoak before his return, they should carve in some conspicuous place the name of the place to which they had gone. On his return, he found carved the word "Croatan." We also learn from his narrative, that the purpose was entertained, even before he left the colony, that it should "*remove* fifty miles further up *into the main.*" The nearest main land to them was Tyrrel, and Lawson (whose map, by the way, is the *first* to call Tyrrel Croatan) may have been induced by the words "into the main" to suppose that, carrying out their avowed intention to go further into the interior, if forced to remove at all, they would make for the nearest point of the main land; and that this therefore must be "Croatan" which they had designated as the point of their destination. But he overlooked the important fact that White, in his relation, (which we suppose Lawson to have seen,) did not at all understand Tyrrel to be meant by "Croatan;" for he expressly says, "I greatly joyed that I had found a certain token of their safe being at Croatoan, which is the place where *Manteo* was born, and the savages of *the island* our friends." He then relates his attempt to *sail* to the island, on the open sea, and the fact of his ships being driven off the coast by a storm.]

August.—The next day we had conference further with them, concerning the people of Secotan, Aquascogoc, and Pomeiok, willing them of Croatoan to certify the people of those towns, that if they would accept our friendship, we would willingly receive them again, and that all unfriendly dealings past on both parts, should be utterly forgiven and forgotten. To this the chief men of Croatoan answered, that they would gladly do the best they could, and within seven days bring the Weroances and chief Governors of those towns with them, to our Governor at Roanoak, or their answer. We also understood of the men of Croatoan, that our man, master Howe, was slain by the remnant of Wingina's men dwelling then at Dasamonguepeuk, with whom Wanchese kept company; and also we understood by them of Croatoan, how that the fifteen Englishmen left at Roanoak the year before, by Sir Richard Greenvill, were suddenly set upon by thirty of the men of Secota, Aquoscogoc, and Dasamonguepeuk, in manner following. They conveyed themselves secretly behind the trees, near the houses where our men carelessly lived, and having perceived that of those fifteen they could see but eleven only, two of those savages appeared to the eleven Englishmen, calling to them by friendly signs that but two of their chief men should come unarmed to speak with those two savages, who seemed also to be unarmed. Wherefore two of the chiefest of our Englishmen went gladly to them; but whilst one of those savages traitorously embraced one of our men, the other with his sword of wood, which he had secretly hidden under his mantle, struck him on the head and slew him, and presently the other eight and twenty savages shewed themselves; the other Englishman perceiving this fled to his company, whom the savages pursued with their bows and arrows, so fast that the Englishmen were forced to take the house, wherein all their victual and weapons were; but the savages forthwith set the same on fire, by means whereof our men were forced to take up such weapons, as came first to hand, and without order to run forth among the savages, with whom they skirmished above an hour. In this skirmish another of our men was shot into the mouth with an arrow, where he died; and also one of the savages was shot into the side by one of our men, with a wild fire arrow, whereof he died presently. The place where they fought was of great advantage to the savages, by means of the thick trees, behind which the savages through their nimbleness, defended themselves, and so offended our men with their arrows, that our men, being some of them hurt, retired fighting to the water side where their boat lay, with which they fled towards Hatorask. By that time they had rowed but a quarter of a mile, they espied their four fellows coming from a creek thereby, where they had been to fetch oysters; these four they received into their boat, leaving Roanoak, and landed on a little island on the right hand of our entrance into the harbor of Hatorask, where they remained a while, but afterward departed, whither as yet we know not.

[We have here the fate of Sir Richard Greenville's fifteen men. They were all killed by the savages or drowned. Probably, when they left "the little island" near "the harbor of Hatorask" they attempted in their frail craft to coast down to Croatoan, where they knew they had friends, and perished by the way.]

Having now sufficiently dispatched our business at Croatoan, the same day we departed friendly, taking our leave, and came aboard the fleet at Hatorask.

The eighth of August, the Governor having long expected the coming of the Weroances of Pomeiok, Aquascocog, Secota, and Dasamonguepeuk, seeing that the seven days were past, within which they promised to come in, or to send their answers by the men of Croatoan, and no tidings of them heard, being certainly also informed by those men of Croatoan, that the remnant of Wingina his men, which were left alive, who dwell at Dasamonguepeuk, were they which had slain Geo. Howe, and were also at the driving of our eleven Englishmen from Roanoak, he thought to defer the revenge thereof no longer. Wherefore the same night, about midnight, he passed over the water, accompanied with Captain Stafford, and twenty-four men, whereof Manteo was one, whom we took with us to be our guide to the place where those savages dwelt, where he behaved himself toward us as a most faithful Englishman.

The next day, being the ninth of August, in the morning so early that it was yet dark, we landed near the dwelling place of our enemies, and very secretly conveyed ourselves through the woods, to that side, where we had their houses between us and the water, and having espied their fire and some sitting about it, we presently set upon them; the miserable souls herewith amazed, fled into a place of thick reeds, growing fast by, where our men perceiving them, shot one of them through the body with a bullet, and therewith we entered the reeds, among which we hoped to acquit their evil doing towards us; but we were deceived, for those savages were our friends, and were come from Croatoan to gather the corn and fruit of that place, because they understood our enemies were fled immediately after they had slain George Howe, and for haste had left all their corn, tobacco and pompions standing in such sort, that all had been devoured of the birds, and deer, if it had not been gathered in time; but they had like to have paid dearly for it, for it was so dark, that they being naked, and their men and women appareled all so like others, we knew not but that they were all men, and if that one of them which was a Weroance's wife had not had a child at her back, she had been slain instead of a man, and as hap was, another savage knew master Stafford, and ran to him, calling him by his name, whereby he was saved. Finding ourselves thus disappointed of our purpose, we gathered all the corn, pease, pompions, and tobacco, that we found ripe, leaving the rest unspoiled, and took Menatoan's wife, with the young child, and the other savages with us over the water to Roanoak. Although the mistaking of these savages somewhat grieved Manteo, yet he imputed their harm to their own folly, saying to them, that if their Weroances had kept their promise in coming to the Governor at the day appointed, they had not known that mischance.

The thirteenth of August, our savage Manteo, by the commandment of Sir Walter Raleigh, was christened in Roanoak, and called Lord thereof, and of Dasamonguepeuk, in reward of his faithful service.

The eighteenth, Eleanor, daughter to the governor, and wife to Ananias Dare, one of the assistants, was delivered of a daughter in Roanoak, and the same was christened there the Sunday following, and because this child was the first christian born in Virginia, she was named Virginia. By this time our ships had unladen the goods and victuals of the planters, and began to take in wood and fresh water, and to new caulk and trim them for England: the planters also prepared their letters and tokens to send back into England.

These baptisms of Manteo, and the infant child of Mr. Dare, suggest the inquiry whether there was a clergyman among the colonists. There is no prefix or suffix to any in the list of colonists' names that would seem to imply the presence of a minister of religion. This, however, is not conclusive, because the use of such a term as "reverend" as indicating the profession, was not in that day common. There may have been a clergymen among the colonists, even though no title is affixed to his name; and, as Sir Walter gave positive orders, before the expedition sailed, that Manteo should be baptized when he reached America, it is not probable that, with the prevalent religious opinions of his day on the subject of baptism, he permitted it to sail without a chaplain. We know that one was sent with the first colony to Jamestown. The matter is of some little moment to southrons, because it has been very much the fashion to consider the southern colonies of Virginia and the Carolinas as composed of "godless gangs;" and to insinuate, if not assert, that all the piety and morals in the country were introduced by the holier men of northern settlements. God forbid that we should deny the existence of very sincere piety in many of the northern colonists; but they did not have it all. A careful study of contemporaneous authorities will show that the reverent fear and worship of God was by no means wanting either on Roanoak or at Jamestown. Hariot tells us of the daily prayers of Lane's colony, and the early history of Jamestown brings out beautifully as fine a picture of ministerial character, faithfulness and zeal in Hunt, Whitaker and others, as the christian would desire. The religion of these men, however, was not used as capital, political or otherwise: they sought not to trade on it; but were content to feel it and live accordingly. Had they been asked "if they had any religion?" they probably would have answered as a late excellent prelate did—"none *to speak of.*" The fact here recorded in the text is further interesting, because this was the first christian sacrament ever administered by protestants in America].

Our two ships, the Lion and the Fly-boat, almost ready to depart, the 21st of August, there arose such a tempest at the north-east, that our admiral, then riding out of the harbor, was forced to cut his cables and put to sea, where he lay beating off and on six days before he could come to us again, so that we feared he had been cast away, and the rather, for that at the time the storm took them, the most and best of their sailors were left aland.

At this time some controversies arose between the governor and assistants about choosing two out of the twelve assistants, which should go back as factors of the company into England; for every one of them refused, save only one, which all other thought not sufficient; but at length, by much persuading of the governor, Christopher Cooper only agreed to go for England; but the next day, through the persuasion of divers of his familiar friends, he changed his mind, so that now the matter stood as at the first.

The next day, the twenty-second of August, the whole company, both of the assistants and planters, came to the governor, and with one voice requested him to return himself into England, for the better and sooner obtaining of supplies, and other necessaries for them; but he refused it, and alleged many sufficient causes why he would not: the one was, that he could not so suddenly return back again without his great discredit, leaving the action and so many whom he partly had procured through his persuasions to leave their native country, and undertake that voyage; and that some enemies to him and the action, at his return into England, would not spare to slander falsely both him and the action, by saying he went to Virginia, but politicly, and to no other end but to lead so many into a country, in which he never meant to stay himself, and there to leave them behind him. Also, he alleged, that seeing they intended to remove fifty miles further up into the main presently, he being then absent, his stuff and goods might be both spoiled, and most of them pilfered away in the carriage; so that at his return he should be either forced to provide himself of all such things again, or else at his coming again to Virginia find himself utterly unfurnished, whereof already he had found some proof, being but once from them but three days. Wherefore he concluded that he would not go himself.

The next day, not only the assistants, but divers others, as well women as men, began to renew their requests to the governor again, to take upon him to return into England for the supply and dispatch of all such things as there were to be done, promising to make him their bond under all their hands and seals for the safe preserving of all his goods for him at his return to Virginia, so that if any part thereof were soiled or lost, they would see it restored to him, or his assignees, whensoever the same should be missed and demanded, which bond, with a testimony under their hands and seals, they forthwith made and delivered into his hand. The copy of the testimony I thought good to set down:

"May it please you, her majesty's subjects of England, we your friends and countrymen, the planters in Virginia, do by these presents let you and every of you understand, that for the present and speedy supply of certain our known and apparent lacks and needs, most requisite and necessary for the good and happy planting of us, or any other in this land of Virginia, we all of one mind and consent, have most earnestly entreated, and incessantly requested JOHN WHITE, governor of the planters in Virginia, to pass into England, for the better and more assured help and setting forward of the foresaid supplies; and knowing assuredly that he both can best, and will labor and take pains in that behalf for us all, and he not once but often refusing it, for our sakes, and for the honor and maintenance of the action, has at last, though much against his will, through our importunities, yielded to leave his government and all his goods among us, and himself in all our behalves to pass into England, of whose knowledge and fidelity in handling this matter, as all others, we do assure ourselves by these presents, and will you to give all credit thereunto, the twenty-fifth of August, 1587."

The governor being at the last, through their extreme entreating, constrained to return into England, having then but a half a day's respite to prepare himself for the same, departed from Roanoak the seven and twentieth of August in the morning, and the same day about midnight came aboard the Fly-boat, who already had weighed anchor, and rode without the bar, the admiral riding by them, who but the same morning was newly come thither again. The same day both the ships weighed anchor and set sail for England. At this weighing their anchor, twelve of the men which were in the Fly-boat were thrown from the capstan, which by means of a bar that broke, came so fast about upon them that the other two bars thereof struck and hurt most of them so sore, that some of them never recovered it; nevertheless, they assayed presently again to weigh their anchor, but being so weakened with the first fling, they were not able to weigh it, but were thrown down and hurt the second time. Wherefore, having in all but fifteen men aboard, and most of them by this unfortunate beginning so bruised and hurt, they were forced to cut their cable and lose their anchor, nevertheless they kept company with the admiral until the seventeenth of September, at which time we fell in with Corvo and saw Flores.

September.—The eighteenth, perceiving of all our fifteen men

11

in the Fly-boat there remained but five, which by means of the former mischance, were able to stand to their labor, and that the admiral meant not to make any haste for England, but to linger about the island of Tercera for purchase, the Fly-boat departed for England with letters, where we hoped by the help of God to arrive shortly ; but by that time we had continued our course homeward about twenty days, having had sometimes scarce and variable winds, our fresh water also by leaking almost consumed, there arose a storm at north-east, which for six days ceased not to blow so exceedingly, that we were driven further in those six than we could recover in fifteen days, in which time others of our sailors began to fall very sick, and two of them died, the weather also continued so close, that our master sometimes in four days together could see neither sun nor star, and all the beverage we could make, with stinking water, dregs of beer, and lees of wine which remained, was but three gallons, and therefore now we expected nothing but by famine to perish at sea.

October.—The sixteenth of October we made land, but we knew not what land it was, bearing in with the same land at that day : about sunset we put into a harbor where we found a hulk of Dublin, and a pinnace of Hampton riding, but we knew not as yet what place this was, neither had we any boat to go ashore, until the pinnace sent off their boat to us with six or eight men, of whom we understood we were in Smerwick in the west part of Ireland : they also relieved us presently with fresh water, wine and other fresh meat.

The eighteenth the governor and the master rode to *Dingen a Cushe*, five miles distant, to take order for the new victualing of our Fly-boat for England, and for relief of our sick and hurt men ; but within four days after, the boatswain, the steward, and the boatswain's mate, died aboard the Fly-boat, and the 28th the master's mate and two of our chief sailors were brought sick to Dingen.

November.—The first, the governor shipped himself in a ship called the *Monkey*, which at that time was ready to put to sea from Dingen for England, leaving the Fly-boat and all his company in Ireland. The same day we set sail, and on the third day we fell in with the north side of the Land's End, and were shut up the Severn, but the next day we doubled the same for Mount's Bay.

The fifth, the governor landed in England at Martasew, near St. Michael's Mount in Cornwall.

The eighth we arrived at Hampton, where we understood that our consort, the Admiral, was come to Portsmouth, and had been there three weeks before; and also that Ferdinando, the master, with all his company were not only come home without any purchase, but also in such weakness by sickness and death of their chiefest men, that they were scarce able to bring their ship into harbor, but were forced to let fall anchor without, which they could not weigh again, but might all have perished there, if a small bark by great hap had not come to them to help them. The names of the chief men that died are these—Roger Large, John Matthew, Thomas Smith, and some other sailors, whose names I knew not at the writing hereof. Anno Dom., 1587.

The names of all the men, women and children, which safely arrived in Virginia, and remained to inhabit there 1587.

Anno regni Reginæ Elizabethæ 29.

John White,	Clement Taylor,	Thomas Butler,
Roger Baily,	William Sole,	Edward Powell,
Ananias Dare,	John Cotsmur,	John Burdon,
Christopher Cooper,	Humphrey Newton,	James Hynde,
Thomas Stevens,	Thomas Colman,	Thomas Ellis,
John Sampson,	Thomas Gramme,	William Browne,
Dionys. Harvie,	Mark Bennett,	Michael Myllet,
Roger Prat,	John Gibbes,	Thomas Smith,
George Howe,	John Stilman,	Richard Kemme,
Simon Fernando,	Robert Wilkinson,	Thomas Harris,
Nicholas Johnson,	John Tydway,	Richard Taverner,
Thomas Warner,	Ambrose Viccars,	John Earnest,
Anthony Cage,	Edmund English,	Henry Johnson,
John Jones,	Thomas Topan,	John Starte,
William Willes,	Henry Berry,	Richard Darige,
John Brooke,	Richard Berry,	William Lucas,
Cutbert White,	John Spendlove,	Arnold Archard,
John Bright,	John Hemmington,	John Wright,

William Dutton,
Maurice Allen,
William Waters,
Richard Arthur,
John Chapman,
William Clement,
Robert Little,
Hugh Tayler,
Richard Wildye,
Lewes Wotton,
Michael Bishop,
Henry Browne,
Henry Rufoote,
Richard Tomkins,
Henry Dorrell,
Charles Florrie,
Henry Mylton,
Henry Paine,
Thomas Harris,
William Nichols,
Thomas Phevens,
John Borden,
Thomas Scot,
Peter Little,
John Wyles,
Bryan Wyles,
George Martyn,

Hugh Pattenson,
Martin Sutton,
John Farre,
John Bridger,
Griffin Jones,
Richard Shabedge,
James Lasie,
John Cheven,
Thomas Hewet,
William Berde.

———

Women.
Eleanor Dare,
Margery Harvie,
Agnes Wood,
Winnifred Powell,
Joyce Archard,
Jane Jones,
Elizabeth Glane,
Jane Pierce,
Audry Tappan,
Alice Chapman,
Emma Merimoth,
—— Colman,
Margaret Lawrence,
Joan Warren,
Jane Mannering,

Rose Payne,
Elizabeth Viccars.

———

Boys and Children.
John Sampson,
Robert Ellis,
Ambrose Viccars,
Thomas Archard,
Thomas Humfrey,
Thomas Smart,
George Howe,
John Prat,
William Wythers.

———

*Children Born in
Virginia.*
Virginia Dare,
—— Harvie.

———

Savages.
Manteo,
Towaye,
that were in England
and returned home to
Virginia with them.

[We have here one hundred and twenty-one names, and sad it is to think,
that with the exception of White and Fernando, we know not the fate
of another individual here named. Seventeen of this list were women,
and from the similarity of name only, we infer that ten had husbands
among the colonists. In like manner, from name alone, we suppose
that six at least of those enumerated among the " boys and children"
were with their parents.]

No. 8.

THE FIFTH VOYAGE

OF

M. JOHN WHITE,

INTO THE

WEST INDIES,

AND PARTS OF AMERICA CALLED

VIRGINIA,

IN THE YEAR

159..

———

[*Reprinted from* HAKLUYT, *Vol. III., page* 288.]

*To the worshipful and my very friend, Master Richard Hakluyt,
much happiness in the Lord :*

SIR,—As well for the satisfying of your earnest request, as the
performance of my promise made unto you at my last being with
you in England, I have sent you (although in a homely style, especially for the contentation of a delicate ear,) the true discourse of
my last voyage into the West Indies, and parts of America called
Virginia, taken in hand about the end of February, in the year of
our redemption 1590. And what events happened unto us in this
our journey, you shall plainly perceive by the sequel of my discourse. There were at the time aforesaid three ships absolutely
determined to go for the West Indies, at the special charges of
Mr. John Wattes, of London, merchant. But when they were
fully furnished and in readiness to make their departure, a general
stay was commanded of all ships throughout England. Which,
so soon as I heard, I presently (as I thought it most requisite) acquainted Sir Walter Raleigh therewith, desiring him that, as I
had at sundry times before, been chargeable and troublesome unto
him, for the supplies and reliefs of the planters in Virginia; so
likewise that by his endeavor, it would please him at that instant
to procure license for those three ships to proceed on with their
determined voyage, that thereby the people in Virginia (if it were
God's pleasure) might speedily be comforted and relieved without
further charges unto him.—Whereupon, he by his good means
obtained license of the queen's majesty, and order to be taken
that the owner of these ships should be bound unto Sir Walter
Raleigh or his assigns in three thousand pounds, that those three
ships, in consideration of their releasement, should take in and
transport a convenient number of passengers, with their furni-
tures and necessaries, to be landed in Virginia. Nevertheless,
that order was not observed, neither was the bond taken according
to the intention aforesaid. But rather in contempt of the aforesaid
order, I was, by the owner and commanders of the ships, denied
to have any passengers, or any thing else transported in any of
the said ships, saving only myself and my chest; no, not so much
as a boy to attend upon me, although I made great suit and earnest entreaty, as well to the chief commanders as to the owner of
the said ships. Which cross and unkind dealing, although it very

much discontented me, notwithstanding, the scarcity of time was such that I could have no opportunity to go unto Sir Walter Raleigh with complaint: for the ships, being then all in readiness to go to the sea, would have been departed before I could have made my return. Thus, both governors, masters and sailors, regarding very smally the good of their countrymen in Virginia, determined nothing less than to touch at those places, but wholly disposed themselves to seek after purchase and spoils, spending so much time therein, that summer was spent before we arrived at Virginia. And when we were come thither, the season was so unfit and weather so foul, that we were constrained of force to forsake that coast, having not seen any of our planters, with loss of one of our ship-boats, and seven of our chiefest men: and also with loss of three of our anchors and cables, and most of our casks with fresh water left on shore, not possible to be had aboard. Which evils and unfortunate events (as well to their own loss as to the hindrance of the planters in Virginia) had not chanced, if the order set down by Sir Walter Raleigh had been observed, or if my daily and continual petitions for the performance of the same might have taken any place. Thus may you plainly perceive the success of my fifth and last voyage to Virginia, which was no less unfortunately ended than frowardly begun, and as luckless to many as sinister to myself. But I would to God it had been as prosperous to all, as noisome to the planters; and as joyful to me as discomfortable to them. Yet, seeing it is not my first crossed voyage, I remain contented. And, wanting my wishes, I leave off from prosecuting that whereunto I would to God my wealth were answerable to my will. Thus, committing the relief of my discomfortable company, the planters in Virginia, to the merciful help of the Almighty, whom I most humbly beseech to help and comfort them, according to His most holy will, and their good desire, I take my leave. From my house at Newtown, in Kilmore, the 4th of February, 1593.

Your most well-wishing friend,

JOHN WHITE.

The twentieth of March, the three ships, the *Hopewell*, the *John Evangelist*, and the *Little John*, put to sea from Plymouth with two small shallops.

The twenty-fifth at midnight, both our shallops were sunk, being towed at the ship's stern by the boats' in . negligence.

On the thirteenth, we saw ahead of us that part of the coast of Barbary, lying east of Cape Cantyn, and the Bay of Asophi.

The next day we came to the Isle of Mogadore, where rode, at our passing by, a pinnace of London, called the Moonshine.

April.—On the first of April we anchored in Santa Cruz road, where we found two great ships of London, lading in sugar, of whom we had two ship boats to supply the loss of our shallops.

On the second we set sail from the road of Santa Cruz for the Canaries.

On Saturday the fourth we saw Alegranza, the east isle of the Canaries.

On Sunday the fifth of April we gave chase to a double fly-boat, the which, we also the same day fought with, and took her, with loss of three of their men slain, and one hurt.

On Monday the sixth we saw Grand Cararie, and the next day we landed and took in fresh water on the south side thereof.

On the ninth we departed from Grand Canarie, and framed our course for Dominica.

The last of April we saw Dominica, and the same night we came to an anchor on the south side thereof.

May.—The first of May in the morning, many of the savages came aboard our ships in their canoes, and did traffic with us; we also the same day landed and entered their town from whence we returned the same day aboard without any resistance of the savages, or any offence done to them.

The second of May our Admiral and our pinnace departed from Dominica, leaving the John, our Vice-admiral, playing off and on about Dominica, hoping to take some Spaniard outward bound to the Indies; the same night we had sight of three small islands, called Los Santos, leaving Guadaloupe and them on our starboard.

The third we had sight of S. Christopher's Island, bearing north-east and by east of us.

On the fourth we sailed by the Virgins, which are many broken islands, lying at the east end of St. John's Island; and the same day towards evening, we landed upon one of them, called Blanca, where we killed an incredible number of fowls; here we stayed but three hours, and from thence stood upon the shore northwest, and having brought this island southeast of us, we put, towards night, through an opening or swatch, called The passage, lying between the Virgins, and the east end of St. John; here the pinnace left us and sailed on the southside of St. John.

The fifth and sixth the Admiral sailed along the north side of St. John, so near the shore that the Spaniards discerned us to be men of war, and therefore made fires along the coast as we sailed by; for so their custom is, when they see any men of war on their coasts.

The seventh we landed on the northwest end of St. John, where we watered in a good river, called Yaguana, and the same night following we took a frigate of ten tons coming from Gwathanelo, laden with hides and ginger. In this place Pedro, a mulatto, who knew all our state, ran from us to the Spaniards.

On the ninth we departed from Yaguana.

The thirteenth we landed on an island, called Mona, whereon were ten or twelve houses inhabited of the Spaniards; there we burned and took from them a pinnace, which they had drawn a ground and sunk, and carried all her sails, masts and rudders into the woods, because we should not take her away; we also chased the Spaniards over all the island; but they hid themselves in caves, hollow rocks, and bushes, so that we could not find them.

On the fourteenth we departed from Mona, and the next day after we came to an island, called Saona, about five leagues distant from Mona, lying on the south side of Hispaniola near the east end; between these two islands we lay off and on four or five days, hoping to take some of the Domingo fleet doubling this island, as a nearer way to Spain than by Cape Tyburon, or by Cape St. Anthony.

On Thursday, being the nineteenth, our Vice-admiral, from whom we departed at Dominica, came to us at Saona, with whom we left a Spanish frigate, and appointed him to lie off and on other five days between Saona and Mona to the end aforesaid;

then we departed from them at Saona for Cape Tyburon. Here I was informed that our men of the Vice-admiral, at their departure from Dominica, brought away two young savages, which were the chief Cacique's sons of that country and part of Dominica; but they shortly after run away from them at Santa Cruz Island, where the Vice-admiral landed to take in ballast.

On the twenty-first the admiral came to the Cape Tyburon, where we found the John Evangelist our pinnace staying for us, where we took in two Spaniards almost starved on the shore, who made a fire to our ships as we passed by. Those places, for a hundred miles in length, are nothing else but a desolate and mere wilderness, without any habitation of people, and full of wild bulls and boars and serpents.

The twenty-second, our pinnace came also to an anchor in Alligator Bay at Cape Tyburon. Here we understood of M. Lane, captain of the pinnace, how he was set upon with one of the king's gallies belonging to Santo Domingo, which was manned with four hundred men, who, after he had fought with him three or four hours, gave over the fight and forsook him, without any great hurt done on either part.

The twenty-sixth, the John, our vice-admiral, came to us to Cape Tyburon, and the frigate which we left with him at Jasna. This was the appointed place where he should attend for the meeting with the Santo Domingo fleet.

On Whitsunday evening, at Cape Tyburon, one of our boys ran away from us, and at ten days' end returned to our ships almost starved for want of food. In sundry places about this part of Cape Tyburon we found the bones and carcases of divers men, who had perished (as we thought) by famine in those woods, being either straggled from their company or landed there by some men of war.

June.—On the fourteenth of June, we took a small Spanish frigate, which fell amongst us so suddenly as he doubled the point of the bay of Cape Tyburon, where we rode, so that he could not escape us. This frigate came from Santo Domingo, and had but three men in her, the one was an expert pilot, the other a mountaineer, and the third a vintner, who escaped all out of prison at Santo Domingo, purporting to fly to Yaguana, which is a town in the west parts of Hispaniola, where many fugitive Spaniards are gathered together.

The seventeenth, being Wednesday, Captain Lane was sent to Yaguana with his pinnace and a frigate to take a ship, which was there taking in freight, as we understood by the old pilot, whom we had taken three days before.

The twenty-fourth, the frigate returned from Captain Lane at Yaguana, and brought us word to Cape Tyburon that Captain Lane had taken the ships, with many passengers and negroes in the same, which proved not so rich a prize as we hoped for; for that a Frenchman of war had taken and spoiled her before we came. Nevertheless, her loading was thought worth a thousand or thirteen hundred pounds, being hides, ginger, cannafistula, copper-pans and cassavi.

July.—The second of July, Edward Spicer, whom we left in England, came to us at Cape Tyburon, accompanied with a small pinnace, whereof one H. Harps was captain. And the same day we had sight of a fleet of fourteen sail, all of Santo Domingo, to whom we presently gave chase; but they upon the first sight of us fled, and, separating themselves, scattered here and there; wherefore we were forced to divide ourselves, and so made after them until twelve o'clock at night. But then, by reason of the darkness, we lost sight of each other, yet in the end the Admiral and the Moonlight happened to be together the same night, at the fetching up of the Vice-Admiral of the Spanish fleet, against whom the next morning we fought and took him, with loss of one of our men and two hurt, and of theirs, four slain and six hurt. But what had become of our vice-admiral, our pinnace and prize, and two frigates, in all this time, we were ignorant.

The third of July, we spent about rifling, rummaging and fitting the prize to be sailed with us.

The sixth of July, we saw Jamaica, the which we left on our larboard, keeping Cuba in sight on our starboard.

Upon the eighth of July, we saw the island of Pinos, which lies on the south side of Cuba, nigh unto the west end or cape called Cape St. Anthony. And the same day we gave chase to a frigate, but at night we lost sight of her, partly by the slow sail-

ing of our Admiral, and lack of the Moonlight, our pinnace, whom
Captain Cook had sent to the cape the day before.

On the eleventh we came to Cape St. Anthony, where we
found our consort, the Moonlight, and her pinnace abiding for our
coming ; of whom we understood that the day before there passed
by them twenty-two sail, some of them of the burden of three
hundred, and some four hundred tons, laden with the king's
treasure from the main, bound for Havana : from this eleventh of
July until the twenty-second, we were much becalmed, and the
wind being very scarce, and the weather exceeding hot, we were
much pestered with the Spaniards we had taken, wherefore we
were driven to land all the Spaniards saving three ; but the place
where we landed them was of their own choice on the south side
of Cuba near unto the Organs and Rio de Puercos.

The twenty-third we had sight of the Cape of Florida, and the
broken islands called the Martyrs.

The twenty-fifth, being St. James' day, in the morning, we fell
in with the Matanzas, a headland eight leagues towards the east
of Havana, where we purposed to take fresh water in, and make
our abode two or three days.

On Sunday, the twenty-sixth of July, plying to and fro between
the Matanzas and Havana, we were espied of three small pinnaces of St. John de Ulloa, bound for Havana, which were exceeding richly laden. These three pinnaces came very boldly up unto
us, and so continued until they came within musket-shot of us.
And we supposed them to be Captain Harp's pinnace, and two
small frigates taken by Captain Harp ; wherefore we showed
them our flag. But they, presently upon the sight of it, turned
about and made all the sail they could from us toward the shore,
and kept themselves in so shallow water, that we were not able
to follow them, and therefore gave them over with expense of
shot and powder to no purpose. But, if we had not so rashly set
out our flag, we might have taken them all three, for they would
not have known us before they had been in our hands. This chase
brought us so far to leeward as Havana ; wherefore, not finding
any of our consorts at Matanzas, we put over again to the Cape
of Florida, and from thence through the channel of Bahama.

On the twenty-eighth, the Cape of Florida bare west of us.

The thirtieth, we lost sight of the Coast of Florida, and stood to sea, for to gain the help of the current, which runneth much swifter afar off, than in sight of the coast. For, from the cape to Virginia, all along the shore, are none but eddy currents, setting to the south and southwest.

The thirty-first, our three ships were clearly disbacked, [sic.] the great prize, the Admiral and the Moonshine, but our prize being thus disbacked departed from us without taking leave of the Admiral or consort, and sailed directly for England.

August.—On the first of August the wind scanted, and from thence forward, we had very foul weather, with much rain, thundering and great spouts, which fell round about us nigh unto our ships.

The third, we stood again in for the shore, and at midday we took the height of the same. The height of that place we found to be thirty-four degrees of latitude. Towards night we were within three leagues of the low sandy islands west of Wokokon. But the weather continued so exceeding foul, that we could not come to an anchor nigh the coast, wherefore we stood off again to sea until Monday, the ninth of August.

On Monday, the storm ceased, and we had very great likelihood of fair weather; therefore we stood in again for the shore, and came to an anchor at eleven fathoms, in thirty-five degrees of latitude, within a mile of the shore, where we went on land on the narrow sandy island, being one of the islands west of Wokokon; in this island we took in some fresh water, and caught great store of fish in the shallow water. Between the main (as we supposed) and that island it was but a mile over, and three or four feet deep in most places.

On the twelfth, in the morning, we departed from thence, and toward night we came to an anchor at the northeast end of the island of Croatoan, by reason of a breach which we perceived to lie out two or three leagues into the sea; here we rode all that night.

The thirteenth, in the morning, before we weighed our anchor, our boats were sent to sound over this breach; our ships riding at the side thereof at five fathoms; and a ship's length from us we found but four and a quarter, and then deepening and shallowing for the space of two miles; so that sometimes we found five fathoms, and by and by seven, and within two casts with the lead, nine, and then eight, next cast five, and then six, and then four, and then nine again and deeper, but three fathoms was the least, and two leagues off from the shore. This breach is in thirty-five degrees and a half, and lays at the very northeast point of Croatoan, where goes a fret out of the main sea into the inner waters which part the islands and the main land.

The fifteenth of August, towards evening, we came to an anchor at Hatorask, in thirty-six degrees and one-third, in five fathoms water, three leagues from the shore. At our first coming to anchor on this shore, we saw a great smoke rise in the isle Roanoak, near the place where I left our colony in the year 1587, which smoke put us in good hope that some of the colony were there expecting my return out of England.

[This description presents a truthful picture of our coast, even as it now is, northward of Cape Lookout. There still, in the sultry heats of August, the water-spouts rise off Cape Hatteras, (we have seen no less than three at once); there are the long sandy islands that fringe the coast, the shallow, deceptive and ever shifting inlets, and the never-ending diversity of soundings. And these things have not only long been so, but we fear must long continue. There is no gradual, *permanent* sloping from the shore, of the land under the sea. The sandy bed there is in continual agitation, and were its surface suddenly uncovered, it would doubtless present striking inequalities of hill and valley. Our coast, from Cape Fear to our northern boundary, presents the two sides of a triangle, of which Cape Hatteras is the apex. The wind from northeast or southeast has nothing to obstruct its terrific sweep, while from north, northwest, and west, it pours its fury on the waters of the sounds just within the low islands of our coast, *between which are all our inlets,* and stirring up the sandy beds of their troubled waters, produces their ever-shifting shoals, and makes their changeful bars. The ocean tide from without meets the wind-driven waters from within, and in the shock of their collision, at the point of contact, drops the suspended sediment that makes the bar and shoal. We are exempt from the operation of these physical causes only where, as at Beaufort, *there is no sound behind the inlet,* and the coast changing its direction, and running from east to west, forms a sheltered cove with an exclusively southern aspect; and is protected from the ocean's assaults by the great natural breakwater of Cape Lookout on the northeast ; while by its strong eddy current arising from its cove-formed site, it sends the sands of southern and southeastern winds to form the shoals of Hatteras. If proof be needed of this, it is furnished in the fact that those shoals extend now much further into the ocean than they did at an earlier period. A similar state of things, existing, though not to an equal degree, on the south side of Brunswick county, would, but for counteracting causes, produce similar effects. The breakwater of Cape Fear is there, and the aspect is southern, and there is no sound behind the coast ; but there is the *Cape Fear river bringing down its sands and soil, through a distance of many miles, to meet the ocean-tide and make its deposit on the coast.* Hence the obstruction in the *entrance* to the Cape Fear : within, the water is, for the most part, deep enough, up to a considerable distance.]

The sixteenth and next morning, our two boats went ashore, and Captain Cooke, and Captain Spicer, and their company with me, with intent to pass to the place at Roanoak, where our countrymen were left. At our putting from the ship we commanded our master-gunner to make ready two minions and a falcon well loaded, and to shoot them off with reasonable space between every shot, to the end that their reports might be heard to the place where we hoped to find some of our people. This was accordingly performed, and our two boats put off unto the shore ; in the admiral's boat we sounded all the way and found from our ship until we came within a mile of the shore, nine, eight, and seven fathoms ; but before we were half way between our ships and the shore we saw another great smoke to the southwest of Kindriker's [Kendrick's] mounts ; we therefore thought good to go to that second smoke first ; but it was much further from the harbor where we landed, than we supposed it to be, so that we were very sore tired before we came to the smoke. But that which grieved us more was that, when we came to the smoke, we found no man nor sign that any had been there lately, nor yet any fresh water in all this way to drink. Being thus wearied with this journey, we returned to the harbor where we left our boats, who in our absence had brought their cask ashore for fresh water ; so we deferred our going to Roanoak until the next morning, and caused some of those sailors to dig in those sandy hills for fresh water, whereof we found very sufficient. That night we returned aboard with our boats and our whole company in safety.

The next morning, being the seventeenth of August, our boats and company were prepared again to go up to Roanoak, but Captain Spicer had then sent his boat ashore for fresh water, by means whereof it was ten o'clock aforenoon before we put from our ships which were then come to an anchor within two miles of the shore. The Admiral's boat was half way toward the shore, when Captain Spicer put off from his ship. The Admiral's boat first passed the breach, but not without some danger of sinking, for we had a sea broke into our boat which filled us half full of water, but by the will of God and careful steerage of Captain Cook we came safe ashore, saving only that our furniture, victuals, match and powder were much wet and spoiled. For at this time the wind blew at northeast and direct into the harbor so great a gale, that the sea broke extremely on the bar, and the tide went very forcibly at the entrance. By that time our Admiral's boat was hauled ashore, and most of our things taken out to dry, Captain Spicer came to the entrance of the breach with his mast standing up, and was half passed over, but by the rash and indiscreet steerage of Ralph Skinner his master's mate, a very dangerous sea broke into their boat and overset them quite; the men kept the boat, some in it and some hanging on it, but the next sea set the boat on ground, where it beat so, that some of them were forced to let go their hold, hoping to wade ashore, but the sea still beat them down, so that they could neither stand nor swim, and the boat twice or thrice was turned keel upward, whereon Captain Spicer and Skinner hung until they sunk and were seen no more. But four that could swim, kept themselves in deeper water and were saved by Captain Cook's means, who so soon as he saw their oversetting, stripped himself and four others that could swim very well, and with all haste possible rowed unto them and saved four. They were eleven in all, and seven of the chiefest were drowned, whose names were Edward Spicer, Ralph Skinner, Edward Kelley, Thos. Bevis, Hance, the surgeon, Edward Kilborne, Robert Coleman. This mischance did so much discomfort the sailors, that they were all of one mind not to go any further to seek the planters; but in the end, by the command

and persuasion of me and Captain Cook, they prepared the boats, and seeing the captain and me so resolute, they seemed much more willing. Our boats and all things filled again, we put off from Hatorask, being the number of nineteen persons in both boats ; but before we could get to the place where our planters were left, it was so exceeding dark, that we overshot the place a quarter of a mile, where we espied towards the north end of the island the light of a great fire through the woods, to the which we presently rowed : when we came right over against it, we let fall our grapnel near the shore and sounded with a trumpet a call, and afterwards many familiar English tunes of songs, and called to them friendly ; but we had no answer, we therefore landed at daybreak, and coming to the fire we found the grass and sundry rotten trees burning about the place. From hence we went through the woods to that part of the island directly over against Dasamonguepeuk, and from thence we returned by the water side round about the north point of the island, until we came to the place where I left our colony in the year 1586. In all this way we saw in the sand the print of the savage's feet of two or three sorts trodden in the night ; and, as we entered up the sandy bank, upon a tree, in the very brow thereof were curiously carved these fair Roman letters, C. R. O., which letters presently we knew to signify the place, where I should find the planters seated, according to a secret token agreed upon between them and me at my last departure from them ; which was, that in any way they should not fail to write or carve on the trees or posts of the doors the name of the place where they should be seated ; for at my coming away they were prepared to remove from Roanoak fifty miles into the main. Therefore at my departure from them in An. 1587, I willed them, that if they should happen to be distressed in any of those places, that then they should carve over the letters or name a cross † in this form ; but we found no such sign of distress. And, having well considered of this, we passed toward the place where they were left in sundry houses, but we found the houses taken down, and the place very strongly enclosed with a high palisado of great trees, with curtains and flankers, very fort-like ; and one of the chief trees or posts at the right side of the entrance had the bark taken off, and five feet from the ground, in fair capital letters, was graven CROATOAN, without any cross or sign of distress; this done, we entered into the palisado, where we found many bars of iron, two pigs of lead, four iron-fowlers, iron locker-shot, and such like heavy things thrown here and there, almost overgrown with grass and weeds. From thence we went along by the water side toward the point of the creek, to see if we could find any of their boats or pinnace, but we could perceive no sign of them, nor any of the last falcons or small ordinance which were left with them at my departure from them. At our return from the creek, some of our sailors meeting us, told us that they had found where divers chests had been hidden, and long sithence [since] digged up again and broken up, and much of the goods in them spoiled and scattered about, but nothing left of such things as the savages knew any use of, undefaced. Presently Captain Cooke and I went to the place which was in the end of an old trench, made two years past by Captain Amadas, where we found five chests that had been carefully hidden of the planters, and of the same chests three were my own, and about the place many of my things spoiled and broken, and my books torn from the covers, the frames of some of my pictures and maps rotten and spoiled with rain, and my armor almost eaten through with rust: this could be no other than the deed of the savages, our enemies at Dasamonguepeuk, who had watched the departure of our men to Croatoan, and as soon as they were departed, digged by every place where they suspected anything to be buried; but although it much grieved me to see such spoil of my goods, yet on the other side I greatly joyed that I had safely found a certain token of their safe being at Croatoan, which is the place where Manteo was born, and the savages of the island our friends.

When we had seen in this place so much as we could, we returned to our boats, and departed from the shore toward our ships, with as much speed as we could; for the weather began to be overcast, and very likely that a foul and stormy night would ensue. Therefore the same evening, with much danger and labor, we got ourselves aboard, by which time the wind and sea were so greatly risen that we doubted our cables and anchors would scarcely hold until morning, wherefore the captain caused the boat to be manned with five lusty men, who could swim all well, and sent them to the little island on the right hand of the harbor to bring aboard six of our men, who had filled our cask with fresh water: the boat the same night returned aboard with our men, but all our casks, ready filled, they left behind, impossible to be had aboard without danger of casting away both men and boats; for this night proved very stormy and foul.

The next morning it was agreed by the captain and myself, with the master and others, to weigh anchor, and go for the place at Croatoan, where our planters were; for that then the wind was good for that place, and also to leave that cask with fresh water on shore in the island until our return. So then they brought the cable to the capstan, but when the anchor was almost apeak the cable broke, by means whereof we lost another anchor, wherewith we drove so fast into the shore, that we were forced to let fall a third anchor, which came so fast home hat the ship was almost aground by Kenrick's mounts; so that v were forced to let slip the cable, end for end. And if it had not chanced that we had fallen into a channel of deeper water, closer by the nore than we accounted of, we could never have gone clear of the point that lies to the southward of Kenrick's mounts. Being thus clear of some dangers, and gotten into deeper waters, but not without some loss; for we had but one cable and anchor left us of four, and the weather grew to be fouler and fouler; our victuals scarce, and our cask and fresh water lost; it was therefore determined that we should go for St. John or some other island to the southward for fresh water. And it was further purposed, that if we could any ways supply our wants of victuals and other necessaries, either at Hispaniola, St. John, or Trinidad, that then we should continue in the Indies all the winter following, with hope to make two rich voyages of one, and at our return to visit our countrymen at Virginia. The captain and the whole company in the Admiral (with my earnest petitions) thereunto agreed, so that it rested only to know what the master of the Moonlight, our consort, would do herein. But when we demanded them if they would accompany us in that new determination, they alleged that their weak and leaky ship was not able to continue it; wherefore the same night we parted, leaving the Moonlight to go directly for England, and the admiral set his course for Trinidad, which course we kept two days.

[It will hence be seen that the colony under White, who had left Roanoak for Croatoan, was seen no more by Englishmen. What had become of them? No man can, with certainty, answer; but any man can readily conjecture what must have been the misery of these poor creatures, as sickening under "hope deferred," they looked from day to day, but looked in vain for the return of White. They knew nothing of the troubled state of England which prevented his coming, and the mother must have looked sorrowfully upon her child as each setting sun closed another day of suffering and disappointment, and wept as she thought of the starvation of her offspring. The probability is that, driven by want of supplies, perhaps also by the savage enemy, they sought an asylum among their friends the Hatteras Indians at Croatoan. These natives, in the days of Lawson, more than an hundred years after the times of which we write, were wont to tell a story (we quote from Lawson) "that several of their ancestors were white people, and could talk in a book as we do; the truth of which is confirmed by gray eyes being found frequently among these Indians, and no others. They value themselves extremely for their affinity to the English, and are ready to do them all friendly offices. It is probable that this settlement miscarried for want of timely supplies from England, or through the treachery of the natives; for we may reasonably suppose that the English were forced to cohabit with them for relief and conversation; and that in process of time they conformed themselves to the manners of their Indian relations." This tradition of the Hatteras Indians may possibly shadow forth the fate of the unfortunate colonists of White. At any rate, if there be truth in it at all, and we see no reason to doubt it, we know of no other English colony, in North Carolina, to whom such a story could apply. That under Amadas and Barlowe was but an exploring party, and returned home after a stay of two months; that under Lane was, after one year's stay, carried back by Sir Francis Drake: the fifteen left by Greenville were killed or drowned, such was the Indian story; and the only other colony on Roanoak island was this under White, the fate of which is confessedly uncertain. We are inclined to think that, driven by starvation, such as survived the famine, were merged into the tribe of friendly Indians at Croatoan; and, alas! lost, ere long, every vestige of christianity and civilization; and thus those who came to shed light on the darkness of paganism, in the mysterious providence of God, ended by relapsing themselves into the heathenism they came to remove. It is a sad picture of poor human nature].

On the eighteenth the wind changed, and it was set on foul weather every way; but this storm brought the wind west and northwest, and blew so forcibly that we were able to bear no sail, but our fore-course half-mast high, wherewith we ran upon the wind per force, the due course for England, for that we were driven to change our first determination for Trinidad, and stood for the islands of Azores, where we purposed to take in fresh water, and also there hoped to meet with some Englishmen of war about those islands, at whose hands we might obtain some supply of our wants. And thus continuing our course for the Azores, sometimes with calm and sometimes with very scarce wind, on the fifteenth of September the wind came south southeast, and blew so exceedingly that we were forced to lie by all that day. At this time by account we judged ourselves to be about twenty leagues to the west of Cuervo and Flores, but about night the storm ceased, and fair weather ensued.

On Thursday, the seventeenth, we saw Cuervo and Flores, but we could not come to anchor that night, by reason the wind shifted.

The next morning, being the eighteenth, standing in again with Cuervo, we escried a sail ahead of us, to whom we gave chase; but when we came near him, we knew him to be a Spaniard, and hoped to make sure purchase of him; but we understood at our speaking with him, that he was a prize, and of the Domingo fleet, already taken by the John, our consort, in the Indies. We learned also of this prize, that our Vice-Admiral and pinnace had fought with the rest of the Domingo fleet, and had forced them with their admiral to flee unto Jamaica, under the fort for succor, and some of them ran themselves aground, whereof one of them they brought away, and took out of some others so much as the time would permit. And further we understood of them, that in their return from Jamaica, about the Organs, near Cape St. Anthony, our Vice-Admiral met with two ships of the main land, come from Mexico, bound for Havana, with whom he fought; in which fight our Vice-Admiral's lieutenant was slain, and the captain's right arm stricken off, with four other of his men slain, and six-

teen hurt. But in the end he entered, and took one of the Spanish ships, which was so sore shot by us under water, that before
they could take out her treasure, she sunk; so that we lost thirteen pipes of silver, which sunk with her, besides much other
rich merchandise. And in the meantime the other Spanish ships
being pierced with nine shot under water, got away, whom our
Vice-Admiral intended to pursue; but some of their men in the
top made certain rocks, which they saw above water near the
shore, to be gallies of Havana, and Carthagena, coming from
Havana, to rescue the two ships, wherefore they gave over their
chase, and went for England. After this intelligence was given
us by this our prize, he departed from us and went for England.

On Saturday, the nineteenth of September, we came to an
anchor near a small village on the north side of Flores, where we
found riding five English men-of-war, of whom we understood
that our Vice-Admiral and prize were gone thence for England.
One of those five was the Moonlight, our consort, who, upon the
first sight of our coming into Flores, set sail and went for England, not taking any leave of us.

On Sunday, the twentieth, the Mary Rose, admiral of the
queen's fleet, wherein was General Sir John Hawkins, stood in
with Flores, and divers other of the queen's ships, namely, the
Hope, the Nonpareil, the Rainbow, the Swiftsure, the Foresight,
with many other good merchant ships of war, as the Edward
Bonaventure, the Merchant Royal, the Amity, the Eagle, the
Dainty of Sir John Hawkins, and many other good ships and
pinnaces, all attending to meet with the king of Spain's fleet,
coming from Terrafirma of the West Indies.

The twenty-second of September we went aboard the Rainbow,
and towards night we spake with the Swiftsure, and gave him
three pieces. The captains desired our company; wherefore we
willingly attended on them, who at this time, with ten other
ships, stood for Fayal. But the general, with the rest of the fleet,
were separated from us, making two fleets, for the sure meeting
with the Spanish fleet.

On Wednesday, the twenty-third, we saw Gratiosa, where the
admiral and the rest of the queen's fleet were come together. The
admiral put forth a flag of counsel, in which was determined that

MAP
of INDIAN LOCALITIES
in N. Carolina
1584

VIRGINIA

GATES

CAMDEN

CURRITUCK

PASQOTANK

PERQUIMONS

WEAPEMEOC

CHOWAN

Chowan R.

Chawanook
Ohanoac
Muscamunge
Melackwend

BERTIE

Chepanock

ALBEMARLE SOUND

Roanoke or
Moratoc R.

MARTIN

WASHINGTON

TYRREL

DASAMONGUEPEUC

Dasamonguepeuc

Trinity Harbor according
to Nuremberg & M.
New Inlet
probably entrance
of the English

ATLANTIC OCEAN

BEAUFORT

Pamlico

HYD

L. Pungupo
or Matamuskeet
Pamled

PAMLICO SOUND

Cape Hatteras
or Amadas
Hatteras Inlet
of the English Pilot 1737

PAMTICO R.

POMOUIK

Ocracoke Inlet

JONES

Aguascogog

Wokokon
or
Ocracoke

Croatan
Nuremberg &
Map 1666

Cedar Inlet

CARTERET

Cape Lookout

ATLANTIC

Scale of Statute Miles
10 5 0 10 20 30

Drawn by G. Schröeter.   Lith of W. noe.

the whole fleet should go for the main, and spread themselves on the coast of Spain and Portugal, so far as conveniently they might, for the sure meeting of the Spanish fleet in those parts.

The twenty-sixth we came to Fayal, where the admiral, with some other of the fleet anchored, other some plyed up and down between that and the Pico until midnight, at which time the Antony shot off a piece, and weighed, showing his light; after whom the whole fleet stood to the east, the wind at northeast by east.

On Sunday, the twenty-seventh, towards evening, we took our leave of the admiral and the whole fleet, who stood to the east. But our ship, accompanied with a fly-boat, stood in again with St. George, where we purposed to take in more fresh water, and some other fresh victuals.

On Wednesday, the thirtieth of September, seeing the wind hang so northerly, that we could not attain the island of St. George, we gave over our purpose to water there, and the next day framed our due course for England.

October.—The second of October, in the morning, we saw St. Michael's Island on our starboard quarter. The 23d, at 10 of the clock, before noon, we saw Ushant, in Brittany.

On Saturday, the twenty-fourth, we came in safety, God be thanked, to an anchor in Plymouth.

[This ends our documentary history of the earlier attempts at colonization under Raleigh and his associates. We now proceed in our effort to condense, into the form of continuous narrative, the facts gathered from the materials we have presented to the reader, in the previous pages.]

NARRATIVE.

1584—1591.

CHAPTER I.

First English Colony in America planted in North Carolina.—Sir Walter Raleigh.—
Expedition of Amadas and Barlowe in 1584.—Inlet at which they probably entered
not Ocracoke. — Interview and friendly intercourse with the natives. — River
" Occam."—Roanoak Island.—Return of the expedition to England with two of the
natives.—Name of Virginia applied by Queen Elizabeth to the lands discovered.—
Second expedition, under Sir Richard Greenville, sent by Raleigh in 1585.—Its
arrival at Roanoak Island.—Sir Richard's return to England.—The command de-
volves on Ralph Lane.—Discoveries of the colonists.—Plot of the savages to massacre
the English.—Defeated by Lane.—Return of the expedition with Sir Francis Drake,
after one year's residence in Carolina.

THAT portion of the United States included within the limits
of North Carolina, may justly claim the honor of having received
the first English colony that was planted in the western hemisphere. The story of its trials, its disasters, and final failure,
carries us back to a memorable period in England's history; and
derives additional interest from its association with the life of
one of the most remarkable men in an age, when remarkable
men were by no means uncommon. The reign of Elizabeth and
the career of Sir Walter Raleigh, present to the historian of
North Carolina the first actors in the early scenes of which that
State has been the theatre.

It was the lot of Sir Walter Raleigh (as it commonly is that of
public men possessing great energy of character) to occupy no
middle position in the eyes either of friend or foe. The exaggera-
tions of friendship raised him perhaps as much above the dead
level of humanity as the revilings of hatred placed him below it.
The devoted affection of his adherents was equaled only by the
intense enmity of his foes. And yet, after all due allowance is

made for partiality on the one hand, and prejudice on the other, the dispassionate mind settles down in the conviction that Sir Walter Raleigh was, both morally and intellectually, a very remarkable man. Truly has it been said that "no Englishman of his age possessed so various or so extraordinary qualities."[*] Remarkable for the boldness of his designs, he sought only large and magnificent results; and to produce these, he called into exercise the calmest self-possession, the most indomitable courage, a perfectly wonderful faculty of meeting unexpected obstacles with means and expedients adopted at the moment, and an industry that never tired in the pursuit of his end.

Thoroughly loyal, as we believe, and with a heart devoted to the prosperity of his country, he brought to his task as a legislator and statesman, the soundest practical wisdom, united to a comprehensiveness of design which by its very magnitude often startled his more timid companions. The power of Spain was then at its height, and was the only dangerous rival to the splendid career of England in the course of nautical enterprise on which she was then just entering. All Raleigh's plans aimed, therefore, at the humiliation of Spain, and probably no Englishman of his day contributed more than he did with sword and tongue and pen to establish the supremacy of his country over her haughty rival.

A judicial murder at length closed, on the scaffold, the career of this gifted man, who to the last exhibited the qualities which ennoble human nature. But we have already spoken of him so fully on a previous page, that no more need be said here; and we trust an apology for the little that has been offered will suggest itself in the thought, that it scarcely seems meet to commence a history of North Carolina without some notice, however brief, of the character of a noble, though not faultless man, who planted the first English colony on our shores, and whose remembrance has been honorably and gratefully perpetuated in the name of her capital, by the State which he first sought to bring within the pale of civilization. It was a just and appropriate tribute paid by posterity to his fair fame, alike honorable to the

---

* 1 Bancroft, 123.

memory of him on whom it was conferred, and to those who, too
far removed from his times to be affected by prejudice, were
better fitted, calmly and dispassionately, to appreciate the virtues
of a great man, whose very faults, for the most part, flowed from
the excess of his noble and generous emotions.

"The 27 day of Aprill, in the yeere of our redemption, 1584,"
(so runs the record*) two barks, under the respective commands
of Philip Amadas and Arthur Barlowe, and "well furnished with
men and victuals," sailed from the west of England on a voyage
of discovery to that large portion of the continent of America,
afterward known under the general name of Virginia. These
barks had been fitted out, and the voyage undertaken at the sole
charge of Sir Walter Raleigh, whose active mind and enterprising
spirit prompted him readily to enter into the schemes of distant
colonization, which at that time agitated in a greater or less degree nearly all the maritime powers of Europe. It was only in
the previous year that his step-brother, Sir Humphrey Gilbert,
had perished, on his return voyage from the northern part of our
continent; but, undismayed by the sad event, Raleigh resolved
to seek on our more southern shores a milder climate, and there
to colonize. It was not difficult to obtain from the queen of
England the necessary patent. Elizabeth was too wise to dis-
countenance an extension of her dominions; and the wild dreams
of immense wealth to be gathered from the new world doubtless
afforded a stimulus alike potent both to sovereign and subjects.

By this patent, which was to continue six years, Raleigh was
made lord proprietor of his discoveries, with almost unlimited
powers.†

On the fourth of July, according to the calendar of that day,
the two barks arrived upon the coast of North Carolina. The
land which was thus first made was situated between Cape Lookout and Cape Hatteras, and is now known as Ocracoke Island, in
the county of Carteret. Finding no entrance from the sea, the
barks sailed along the coast, a distance of one hundred and twenty
miles, and entered, with some difficulty, the first inlet that was
found, probably New inlet, or some other near it, now filled up

---

* 3 Hakluyt, 246.—Ante. p. 70.
† 1 Hazard's State Papers, pp. 33—38.—Ante, p. 11.

by the sand from the sea. In the account furnished to Sir Walter by Amadas and Barlowe, they represent the island of Roanoke as distant but seven leagues from the inlet through which the vessels entered, and the present New inlet seems best to answer that description.* Here a landing was made and formal possession taken of the country, and the party now for the first time discovered that the land along which they had been coasting was not the continent, but a narrow island, from which it was separated by a strait of considerable length. By the side of this island, the voyagers remained two days without seeing any of the natives:—on the third day, a small boat containing three persons was perceived approaching from the north. It landed on the island, a short distance from the barks, and two of the individuals remaining with the boat, the third, without any manifestation of fear, advanced along the beach toward the vessels. The officers rowed to the shore and met him, and with his own consent carried him on board, where he received presents of clothing and food. Returning to his own boat, he pushed out into the strait and commenced fishing; in half an hour he had filled his boat, with which he returned to land, and by way of requital for the hospitality he had experienced, he divided his fish into two portions, and intimating by signs that each vessel should take a portion, he then departed. Thus friendly was the first intercourse between the whites and the natives of North Carolina: would that the progress of our story could show that these amicable relations were never afterward interrupted.

The visit above related led, on the next day, to the arrival of many boats, in one of which was *Granganimeo*, the brother of the king, *Wingina*, who ruled over the territory around, which the English supposed, though erroneously, was called *Wingandacoa*.† His visit was not without the rude dignity and state in which barbarous royalty was there wont to assert its supremacy ; and in his case, as in that of many more civilized kings and nobles, its distinguishing feature consisted in an arbitrary appropriation to himself of all that benevolence or policy induced the adventurers to offer as gifts to his attendants. His deportment, how-

* 3 Hakluyt, 247 ; Vide Ante, p. 71, *et seq.*

† Vide Ante, p. 78.

ever, was most friendly, and by all the expressive signs he could devise, he intimated to the strangers that he considered them as one with himself. He contrived to communicate to the English that the king, his brother, had been badly wounded in battle, and that he therefore was present as his representative. A petty traffic then commenced between the parties, in which an exchange was made of skins for shining tin platters and copper kettles ; but at no price would the white men gratify the anxious desire of the savages to possess axe, hatchet or sword.

After a few days, *Granganimeo* repeated his visit, when his wife and children accompanied him with entire confidence; and, in truth, the intercourse on both sides seems to have been characterized by mutual good will, during the whole period of the communication between the parties.

At length, after several visits had brought them into familiar acquaintance, it was resolved by the English commanders to make an attempt at exploration; and accordingly Amadas with seven men embarked in a boat and proceeded northwardly up a river, as he terms it, which was called *Occam*. It is needless to say, to one acquainted with the country in which the voyagers were, that it was not a *river* on which they floated. An inspection of the map will show the island of Roanoke lying between Pamtico and Albermarle sounds; on the eastern side of the island runs a narrow strait, which unites the waters of the two sounds, and it was probably this which they mistook for a river; as, according to their relation, pursuing their course, on the river, they reached on the next evening the northern part of the island, which, to voyagers coming from the south, was attainable no otherwise than through this strait.* It is also highly probable that they may have supposed Albermarle sound, lying on the northern side of Roanoak Island, and stretching away westwardly beyond their knowledge, to have been a part of the "river" Occam. At the northern end of the island they found an Indian village, in which *Granganimeo* resided: he, however, was from home, but his wife received them with a warmth of hospitable kindness, evidently intended as a reciprocation of the civility she had met with on her visits to them. Here they were informed of

* Vide Ante, p. 73.

the existence of other towns on the main land, of which it has long been supposed, but erroneously, that the site of one only is known. This one was *Pomeiock*, which it has been conjectured stood near the mouth of Gibbs' creek, in the present county of Hyde. The English, however, made no further explorations at this time, and the accounts of the natives to them present little more than barbarous names connected with descriptions of so much uncertainty, that it is impossible, from the facts of this first voyage alone, to ascribe localities to all the places they enumerated.

The adventurers were too few in number to attempt a settlement; they contented themselves, therefore, with making observations of the region immediately around them, and with questioning the natives as to the interior of the country; and sailing at once for England, reached it about the middle of September, 1584, after an absence of a little less than five months; on their return, they were accompanied by two of the natives, *Manteo* and *Wanchese*.*

The voyagers had met with but little of privation or hardship; they had visited Carolina at a season when her summer seas and exuberant vegetation presented her in the most favorable aspect, and it is therefore not surprising that the accounts they rendered to their employer, should have depicted an almost earthly paradise. The queen heard their glowing descriptions, and, proud of their discovery, conferred upon the imaginary fairy land the fanciful name of Virginia, in allusion to her own maiden state.

It was not long, before Raleigh (who about this time was knighted) obtained an act of parliament confirming his discovery, and resolved upon sending out another expedition. The highly colored representations of the previous voyagers readily brought around him a multitude willing to emigrate, and form a permanent settlement. He enlisted in the enterprise his kinsman, Sir Richard Greenville, and to him he intrusted the command of the seven vessels which formed the expedition. One hundred and eight colonists were on board; of whom some probably had been on the former voyage, and it is certain that Amadas and Manteo returned in the little fleet.†

---

* The only authority for the voyage is 3 Hakluyt, 246—Vide Ante, p. 70.

† 3 Hakluyt 254 and 257. Ante, p. 89.

On the 9th day of April, 1585, the vessels sailed from Plymouth (the largest of the fleet being of one hundred and forty tons) and after cruising against the Spaniards in the West Indies, on the 26th of June it came to anchor at Ocracoke, then called *Wocokon*, but no mention is made of any attempt here to enter at the inlet, with the larger vessels. In a short time a messenger was dispatched to Roanoke island to inform King *Wingina* of the arrival of the colonists, and *Manteo* was sent over to the main land. After the lapse of a few days he returned accompanied by the old friend of Amadas, *Granganimeo*, the king's brother. During the absence of *Manteo*, Sir Richard Greenville, accompanied by a considerable number of men, including those of most importance in the expedition, passed over the sound from Ocracoke, *in boats*, and discovered the town of *Pomeiok*, (which as already stated, is supposed to have been at the mouth of Gibbs' creek) together with several others; and penetrating into the interior, came upon a lake called by the natives *Paquipe*, and now known as Mattamuskeet Lake, in Hyde county. On this expedition of Greenville's the first interruption of harmony between the English and natives occurred. A silver cup had been stolen by one of the savages, and not being returned according to promise, one of the Indian towns was burned, and all the corn growing near it was destroyed. This, it must be confessed, was a heavy retribution for a comparatively venial offence. After having made the discovery of *Secotan* and examined Hatteras, Sir Richard Greenville sailed for England on the 25th of August, having remained in the country two months.*

Upon the departure of Sir Richard Greenville, the command devolved upon Ralph Lane (a man of worth and distinguished as a soldier, and whom Chalmers calls "a person of prudence and spirit,") who had come out with the fleet for the purpose of superintending the colony. He found himself at the head of one hundred and eight men, among whose names we read those of Amadas (who was "Admiral of the country,") and Thomas Hariot, a sensible and judicious observer of what was around him, and known to science as the inventor of the system of notation in modern Algebra. Both Lane and Hariot have left behind them

* 3 Hakluyt p. 253. Ante, p. 89.

their narratives, and from them we gather the material of our story.[*]

The colonists having fortified themselves on the island of Roanoke, which they made head-quarters, directed their explorations toward the south, the north, the west and the southwest. The most remote point to which they traveled south was Secotan, about eighty miles distant from the island, on the coast of what is now Carteret county. To the northward they went to Elizabeth river which empties into Chesapeake bay below Norfolk. Of the existence of this bay they became fully convinced, though they never entered it. Passing westwardly up Albemarle Sound they came to the river *Chawanook*, now Chowan; this they ascended to a point a little below the junction of the Meherrin and Nottoway by which it is formed. It will thus be seen that they passed along the borders of the present counties of Perquimans, Chowan, Bertie, Gates and Hertford. Proceeding still further to the westward, they discovered the mouth of the *Moratoc* river, now known as the Roanoke, up which they ascended for four days, making but little progress against the current, and being reduced to live upon a pottage, made of the meat of their dogs with the leaves of the sassafras tree. In this part of the expedition, the presence of *Manteo* proved of no small service in putting them on their guard against the hostile attacks of the Indians, which his knowledge of their language enabled him to discover as being intended.

To understand the cause of this contemplated attack, the reader should be informed, that the feelings of King *Wingina* had undergone a total change. His brother, *Granganimeo*, who always continued friendly to the whites, died a few days after his visit with *Manteo*. Death also, ere long, removed *Ensenore*, the father of the king; and in the loss of these two influential natives, the English were deprived of their best friends. Upon the removal of *Granganimeo*, *Wingina*, who changed his name to *Pemisapan*, resolved to accomplish by stratagem the destruction of the colony. Preserving externally the most friendly relations, he attempted to deceive Lane by the most extravagant representations of rich mines to be reached by ascending the Roanoke, and stated

[*] 3 Hakluyt, pp. 255—266. Ante, pp. 103—146.

16

that the river itself gushed forth from a rock so near a sea situated to the westward, that in high winds the surge dashed over into the fountain. The banks of the river he represented as filled with ore, the art of refining which, he said, was understood by the natives. Lane thought it his duty to investigate the truth of all this by personal examination, and the artful savage, having secretly dispatched to the tribes on the Roanoke information that Lane would visit them with hostile purposes, saw with delight the victim move toward the snare that had thus cunningly been provided.

Pemisapan seems to have been so certain of the destruction of Lane, that he originated a rumor during his absence that he had been either killed or starved. But when he returned, bringing with him, as a sort of hostage, the favorite son of one of the most powerful inland native kings, and when the faithful *Manteo* related how little fear the English manifested of any enemy, and how cheerfully they endured the severest privations, *Pemisapan* deemed it prudent for a time to suspend his devices. The possession by Lane of the young Indian prince was in furtherance of a measure he contemplated, which, with the knowledge he possessed, was not wanting in good judgment, and which, if executed, might have anticipated by some years the settlement of the first Virginia colony at Jamestown. Lane had discovered that his locality on Roanoke Island was by no means advantageous : he had, in his exploration of the Chowan and of the parts northeast of it, become fully satisfied of the existence among the *Chesepiook* tribe of Indians of the great bay which, by a slight corruption of its original name, we call Chesapeake. He was daily expecting a reinforcement of the colony from England, and on its arrival his plan was to send a portion of the colony northward by sea with directions to find the entrance into the bay and to enter ; while he, proceeding with the residue of the company, designed to go in boats up the Chowan river, thence to cross overland and meet the party who should have entered the bay. Thus he hoped to accomplish the purpose of finding a better harbor than that at Roanoke Island, and of selecting a more suitable site for the colony. The father of the Indian prince was to furnish him with guides for the overland journey, a portion of which was also to be through the territory subject to him. The non-arrival in time of the anticipated reinforcement from England alone prevented Lane from attempting the enterprise. We of this day can perceive the possibility, in the hands of resolute men, of its complete success.*

After the return of Lane, a variety of circumstances soon convinced him that, notwithstanding the pretended friendship of *Wingina*, no reliance could be placed on him, and he was therefore watched with sleepless vigilance. The necessities of the English compelled them to divide their company into smaller parties for the purpose of procuring sustenance until the expected supplies from England should arrive. Thus one party was detached to Croatan and another to Hatteras, to live upon shell-fish, while a third was sent weekly over to the main land to find sustenance in cassada and oysters. *Wingina* was quick to perceive the advantages which these separations afforded him. Under pretence of solemnly celebrating his father's funeral rites, he devised a scheme for assembling, without suspicion, several hundred natives, who might, at a given signal, extirpate the English at a blow. Unfortunately for the success of his plot, he relied too confidently on the co-operation of the Indian prince, *Skyco*, whom Lane held as a hostage. The prince had once attempted to escape, and Lane had in consequence confined him and threatened him with the loss of his head : *Pemisapan* had interceded for his life, and Lane, seeming to yield to his entreaties, had granted it. *Pemisapan* hence supposed that he might safely confide his scheme to *Skyco ;* but he, who from the kind treatment he had received at the hands of all the English, had become perfectly friendly and contented with his condition, informed Lane of all that *Pemisapan* had revealed ; and his story was very soon after confirmed by one of *Pemisapan's* own men, who voluntarily communicated a history of the plot to Lane.

The governor immediately took measures to counteract it, and, resorting to stratagem, entrapped *Pemisapan* with eight of his head men, and put them to death. A few days after, the agreeable intelligence reached him from his party at Croatan that Sir Francis Drake's fleet had arrived off the coast. Upon communi-

* Ante, p. 115.

cating with Drake, he made to Lane two offers : he proposed either to leave a ship, pinnace and boats, with sufficient men and provisions, to stay and make further discoveries, and then bring the whole colony to England if they should desire it ; or, if they preferred returning home at once, he offered them all a free passage.   They desiring to remain, gladly accepted the first offer, but had scarcely received the ship, without the provisions, when a violent and unusual storm drove some of the vessels to sea ; and that designed for the colonists, narrowly escaping destruction, was seen by them no more until they reached England.   Drake then renewed his offer of another ship or a return passage : the latter was now accepted, and the whole colony (which during its stay had lost but four men) embarked on the 18th of June, and on the 28th of July, 1586, reached Portsmouth in safety, leaving no English colony on the shores of North America.*

* A summarie and true discourse of Sir Francis Drake's West Indian voyage. London, 1652, pp. 39, 40.

CHAPTER II.

Character of Ralph Lane.—Arrival of Supply Ship.—Unable to find the Colonists—She returns to England.—Arrival of Sir Richard Greenville with three ships.—Finding no trace of Lane's company, he returns, leaving fifteen men on Roanoak Island.—In 1587, a colony sent out by Raleigh under John White.—Women sent in this expedition.—A form of government established for the colony.—Directions by Raleigh that they shall settle on Chesapeake Bay.—White and the planters abandoned on Roanoak Island.—Manteo, a faithful Indian, baptized by Raleigh's orders.—Birth of the first English child in America.—Governor White, at the request of the colonists, returns to England for supplies.—Sign agreed on that he might know their condition, and where they were when he should return.—Troubles in England prevented his return until 1590.—Never found the colonists.—Their probable fate.—Imaginary sketch of the daily life of Lane's colonists.—Starvation of White's company.—Obstacles in the way of successful colonization.

UPON a review of the perils by which the colony under Lane was surrounded, and of his conduct in the midst of them, he scarcely deserves the reproach of a modern writer who has said he "did not possess the qualities suited to his station."[*] And though his return to England is not to be stigmatized as "a precipitate desertion,"[†] yet it may justly be a source of regret that he did not remain a little longer; inasmuch as we now know, what he could not have foreknown, that supplies for his relief were actually then on the way to him. Sir Walter Raleigh, much too noble to forget the men whom he had planted in the wilderness of North Carolina, fitted out a ship in 1586 solely to carry to them abundant supplies. Unfortunately, however, she did not reach the seat of the colony until the latter part of June, at which time Lane and his men had embarked in Drake's fleet.

The commander of the supply ship, having for some time sought in vain for his countrymen, returned to England. About a fortnight after his departure, Sir Richard Greenville (who had commanded in the former expedition) arrived on the coast with three

* 1 Bancroft's United States, 115.
† Ibid, 117.—Vide Ante, p. 138, et seq,

other ships.   Disappointed in his expectation of finding the supply ship, and fruitlessly examining in person the shores of the
sound and rivers for the colony under Lane, he gave over the
search.   Unwilling, however, to relinquish the possession of that
which Englishmen had once held, he landed fifteen men, with a
supply of provisions for two years, on Roanoke Island, and
returned to England.*

Under the combined influences of such untoward events, most
men, in the situation of Sir Walter Raleigh, would have desisted
entirely from an enterprise which thus far had cost much, and
yielded no return ; but not so with him.   The enthusiasm of the
English people was somewhat abated by the ill success of Lane's
attempt, but the accounts published by Hariot of the natural
advantages of the country were such as to induce men to embark
in further plans of colonization ;† and accordingly, in the year
1587, Raleigh prepared a new set of adventurers, consisting of
one hundred and seventeen souls, under the charge of John White
as governor, and on the 26th of April, in that year, they sailed in
three vessels from Portsmouth, fitted out in part at the expense of
Raleigh. There were two particulars connected with this attempt
worthy of notice ; the first was the presence of women and children.   The proprietary very justly supposed that their presence
would form a tie to the soil not easily to be broken by the colonists.   A husband and father would not leave wife and children
behind him, and the difficulty of removing a family presented an
almost insurmountable obstacle to the departure of its head.
Agricultural pursuits and permanency of settlement were therefore likely to result from the presence of these females, who were
in number seventeen.   The other particular worthy of notice is
the provision made for government in this settlement, which it
was hoped would be thus rendered permanent. The chief, White,
had associated with him eleven of the colonists, as counsellors
and assistants, and to the twelve were given a letter of instructions, and a charter incorporating them as "the Governor and
Assistants of the City of Raleigh, in Virginia:" for as yet the
name, Carolina, was unknown.   Sir Walter had also, distant as

* Ante, p. 145.
† Hariot's Narrative ; Ante, p. 146.

he was from the scene, discovered the superior advantages of the Chesapeake bay, and therefore directed the settlement to be made on its shores.

On the 16th of July they made the coast of North Carolina, and narrowly escaping shipwreck on Cape Fear, on the 22d they arrived at Hatteras. Immediately, the governor with forty men proceeded to Roanoke Island in search of the fifteen men who had been left by Sir Richard Greenville in the previous year. After finding them, his purpose was to return to the fleet, and proceed northwardly to Chesapeake bay, according to his instructions. Scarcely, however, had he left the ship, before those on board charged the seamen in the pinnace with the governor to bring back none of the planters, but to leave them on Roanoke Island. Remonstrance on the part of the governor proved fruitless, because the commander of the ship was impatient to renew a profitable traffic in the West Indies, and thus the colony under White was, much against his will, forced, by necessity, to attempt a settlement on Roanoke Island, the scene of Lane's failure.

On reaching the island, he sought in vain for the fifteen men, and the only vestige even that they had been there, was found in the discovery of the bones of one human being. The next day, White with some of his men walked to the northern part of the island, where Lane had erected his fort and dwellings, hoping there to meet with some traces of the fifteen left by Greenville. On his arrival at the spot he found the fort demolished, but the dwellings were yet standing, and their only tenants were the deer who were quietly feeding on the melons that luxuriantly grew in and about them. The unfortunate fifteen, as he subsequently learned from some of the natives, had been attacked by the savages; when the survivors, betaking themselves to their boat, had fled to a little island near Hatteras, where they remained a short time, and then departed, whither no one knew, but probably for Croatan, and this is all that was ever learned of their fate.

White, submitting to the necessities of his position, immediately gave orders for repairing the houses left by Lane, and for erecting more for the accommodation of those whom he knew would be sent from the ships, and on their arrival found himself at the head of ninety-one men, seventeen women and nine children. Among these men were some who had been with Lane, and proved themselves to be men indeed : the colony, as we shall presently see, was probably not without its clergyman, and the faithful *Manteo*, who was among them, had by this time become in heart an Englishman. In this he presented a remarkable contrast to *Wanchese*, who, it will be remembered, had been his companion on his first voyage to England ; and who, after his return, was as notorious for his hostility as *Manteo* was for his fidelity.

The mother and kindred of *Manteo* lived on the island of Croatan, and thither, very soon, a visit was made by the faithful Indian and a party of the English, who endeavored, through the instrumentality of the islanders, to establish friendly relations with the inhabitants on the main land : but the effort was in vain. In truth, the greater portion of the Indians around, manifested implacable ill will, and had already murdered one of the assistants, who had incautiously strayed alone from the settlement on Roanoke island.

On the 13th of August, by direction of Raleigh, given before leaving England, *Manteo* was baptized, (being probably the first native of this continent who ever received this sacrament at the hands of the English) and was also called Lord of Roanoke and of Dasamonguepeuk, as the reward of his fidelity. A few days after, another event, not without interest in the little colony, occupied the attention of all; and doubtless in no small degree enlisted the sympathies of the female portion of the adventurers. On the 18th of August, Eleanor, the daughter of Governor White, and wife of Mr. Dare, one of the assistants, gave birth to a daughter, the first child born of English parents upon the soil of the United States. On the Sunday following, in commemoration of her birth-place, she was baptized by the name of VIRGINIA.

Governor White remained but thirty-six days in North Carolina. As the period approached for the return of the ships, the colonists, who felt most sensibly their dependence on England, and perceived also a considerable reduction in their supplies, applied with one voice to the governor to return in their behalf to the mother country and procure relief. Actuated by very honorable feelings, he for a long time refused, but at length overcome by their unanimous and earnest supplications, he consented to go, leaving behind him in the persons of his daughter and her child, ties strong enough to give zeal to his efforts and hasten his return. Before he left, however, it seems to have been understood that the colony should remove from Roanoke Island and settle on the main land : and as, at his return, he might be at some loss to find them it was further agreed that in the event of their departure, during his absence, they should carve, on some post or tree the name of the place whither they had gone ; and if in distress, they were to carve above it, a cross.

When White reached England, he found the whole kingdom alarmed by a threatened invasion from Spain. Raleigh, Greenville and Lane, the three individuals most likely to aid in the relief of the colony, were all members of the council of war, and their time was fully occupied by their duties. Raleigh, however, soon found leisure to fit out a small fleet for the relief of the colony, but ere it could sail, owing to the formidable armament of Spain, every ship was impressed, and Sir Richard Greenville, who was to have commanded the expedition to Carolina, was summoned to attend Sir Walter to Cornwall and train troops there. Governor White, however, with Raleigh's aid succeeded in obtaining two barks with which he sailed on the 22d of April. These vessels, however, were more anxious to fight the Spaniards than to reach the colony ; both were so much disabled in their encounters with the enemy, that they were obliged to return to England, and never made the contemplated voyage. This delay was fatal to the poor colonists of Roanoke.

When the Spanish Armada had been defeated and England once more breathed in peace, Sir Walter found himself too much reduced in means to prosecute his purposes. Forty thousand pounds, a sum in our day nearly equivalent to two hundred thousand, had been expended by him, for which he had never received the smallest return. But he resolved still to do what he could for the accomplishment of his end : he had used the privilege of his patent to form a company of merchants and adventurers to carry on the work of colonization. But the company languished, because it wanted the energy and liberality of a spirit like Raleigh's. It was not until the 20th of March, 1590, that Governor White embarked in three ships to seek his colony and his children. Much time was lost on the voyage, and the sandy islands of the Carolina coast were not seen until the beginning of the succeeding August. White found the island of Roanoke a desert. As he approached he sounded a signal trumpet, but no answer was heard to disturb the melancholy stillness that brooded over the deserted spot. What had become of the wretched colonists? No man may with certainty say: for all that White found to indicate their fate was a high post bearing on it the letters CRO, and at the former site of their village he found a tree which had been deprived of its bark and bore in well cut characters the word CROATAN.* There was some comfort in finding no cross carved above the word, but this was all the comfort the unhappy father and grandfather could find. He of course hastened back to the fleet, determined instantly to go to Croatan, but a combination of unpropitious events defeated his anxious wishes; storms and a deficiency of food forced the vessels to run for the West Indies for the purpose of refitting, wintering and returning; but even in this plan White was disappointed and found himself reluctantly compelled to run for the western islands and thence for England. Thus ended the effort to find the lost colony; they were never heard of. That they went to Croatan, where the natives were friendly, is almost certain; that they became gradually incorporated with them is probable from the testimony of a historian who lived in North Carolina and wrote in 1714:—"The Hatteras Indians who lived on Roanoke Island or much frequented it, tell us," (says he) "that several of their ancestors were white people and could talk in a book, as we do; the truth of which is confirmed by gray eyes being found frequently amongst those Indians, and no others. They value themselves extremely for their affinity to the English, and are ready to do them all friendly offices. It is probable that this settlement miscarried for want of timely supplies from England; or through the treachery of the natives, for we may reason-

---

* "The stump of a live oak, said to have been the tree on which this word was cut, was shown as late as the year 1778 by the people of Roanoke Island. It stood at the distance of about six yards from the shore of Shalonbas bay, on the land then owned by Daniel Baum. This bay is formed by Ballast point and Baum's point." 1 *Martin's History*, p. 35 *note*.

ably suppose that the English were forced to cohabit with them, for relief and conversation; and that in process of time, they conformed themselves to the manners of their Indian relations, and thus we see how apt human nature is to degenerate." * This slight vestige of the ultimate fate of White's colony concludes the history of Sir Walter Raleigh's noble but unavailing efforts; and when we resume our story, we shall have to pass over an interval of some years, leaving meanwhile the wilderness on which we have looked to the roughness of its natural state, and the occupancy of its savage inhabitants. When the scene next opens upon us, it will be indeed upon the same theatre, but the actors will be very different, and will have entered by a different way.

Scanty as are the materials afforded us for judging of the daily life of these adventurous colonists, still, upon a close review of the incidents we have here been relating, imagination may readily sketch a picture from mere casual remarks in their stories, the chief features of which will undoubtedly be true. It is easy to believe, for instance, of Lane's company, that though some were, as Hariot has described them, such as "by reason of their bad natures" were "worthily punished;" and some of that class "which had little understanding, less discretion, and more tongue than was needful," and some who, having been reared in the comfort of cities, sighed for the enjoyments they had left behind; yet that, in the mass, they were a bold, hardy set, gathered, for the most part, from England's rough specimens of humanity of that day, and kept in subordination and awe by the rigorous military discipline of the times. It was the fashion of Englishmen of that age to look up to their superiors in rank and station with a submission and deference which we, probably, should think not far removed from abject servility. Perhaps, too, the strong common sense, which is certainly an ingredient in the English national character, may have led most of the colonists to feel that their safety depended on submission to their leaders; especially as those leaders were men whom they could respect, and in whom they could have confidence. Lane was a soldier accustomed to command: his story shows him to have been both prompt and brave, and these are captivating qualities among the people: his

* Lawson's History of Carolina, p. 62.

counsellors were Amadas the sailor, "admirall of the countrie," the energetic and indefatigable Captain Stafford, and the philosophical naturalist Hariot. These were men who, doubtless, taught their inferiors to respect and obey Lane, by obeying and respecting him themselves; and it is worthy of note that, in all these early narratives, we have no hint that among the colonists, after landing, any act of *severe* discipline was required or administered during their stay.

Again, Lane took care to keep all employed. We can readily fancy them, summoned by early beat of drum from the rude log-huts which formed their settlement, and assembling to that "daily prayer" which Hariot tells us was their wont. There was Lane, probably in light armor—for armor was the fashion of that day—with Amadas and Stafford and Hariot, and there too was a motley group of stern-faced, rough-looking Englishmen, probably not of the cleanest, mingled perhaps with the wild natives (for Hariot lets us know that sometimes the savage was present at their prayers), and presently the Amen! of their devotions is succeeded by their morning meal, when the various detachments scatter to their allotted duties. Here is a party embarking, under Amadas, it may be, in their light shallops either for exploration or food. There goes another party under Captain Stafford for Croatan, to conclude some unfinished business with Manteo's friendly countrymen. But all the natives are not like Manteo's countrymen; so here, perchance, comes from the court of guard the armed watchmen of the day with their swords and cumbersome match-locks, who take their several stations, not forgetting by the way to see that their mounted culverins are in order, and watching every speck on the waters that may, by possibility, prove a prowling enemy or an approaching boat. Some too are off, it may be, to observe and give their labor to the little plots of ground where Hariot tells us they had sown or planted English vegetables; and we may almost fancy that we see their lips smile and their eyes sparkle as they mark, peeping above ground, some well-known inmate of the kitchen-garden at home, which looks to them like an old friend in this far-off wilderness, and sends their busy memories back to some loved old homestead in one of the quiet dells of dear old England. And here, too, is our philosopher, who, it may be, is thoughtfully botanizing; or, perchance, learning from some savage what he can gather of the country yet unseen; or, better still, teaching the untutored mind of that poor child of the forest the story of a heavenly country bought for him by Christ; for all these things, we learn from his story, that at times he did. There was no wearisome monotony among them, for they were fighting the battle of life at a disadvantage. Every faculty was obliged to be active. And then, when day had closed and evening brought back some party of explorers for instance, we have no difficulty in imagining the group of eager questioners and listeners who gathered around to hear the new stories of their traveled companions. Rough but brave men, for the most part, were these colonists under Lane, and let us honor them, at least, for the courage with which they encountered privations and hardships.

But they could be pioneers only, for they had among them none of the gentler sex. They were but laying foundations that others might come in and help them to built thereon. But Providence saw fit to call *them* all away; and now, under White, another set of actors is on the stage, even that "lost" colony whose sad story we have told already. And here are women and children. Daily life, we may imagine, was somewhat different now. The men are probably not so rough-visaged and so untidy. They have been partially humanized by the gentleness of woman and the caresses of children. True, they have a hard battle to fight, but they have also a stake to fight for. But, alas! here is an enemy more to be dreaded than even the vindictive and treacherous savage—*starvation!* And now the father wishes that wife and children were but in safety in the land whence he brought them. He can suffer himself, but it unmans him to see them suffer. That skeleton child for whom the mother has starved herself in vain; he has laid it in its coffin and buried it in the ground, and he turns sadly away from the task of comforting its desolate mother; for his own heart is breaking: that mother must go next. Domestic life was monotonous enough now. It was one long sad gaze over the waters: the eye might strain itself over the sea, but it looked in vain for the coming ship. No vessel ever came. "Hungry famine had them in the wind," and gaunt spectacles of suffering humanity, attenuated almost to transparency, flitted like ghosts around. The spectral crew vanished by degrees, how, God knoweth ; and whether they found a grave in the ocean's depths, or on the land, is reserved for the revelations of that day when "the earth and the sea shall give up their dead."

And yet this latter colony was better and more wisely planned than that under Lane. It had some light from the past experience of those who had been before and had\ now gone again: Amadas and Stafford were both there. It had the comfort and salutary influence of woman's presence, without which no colony can succeed. It had a system of government which, if not perfect, was probably, in the main, equitable and at least sufficient to preserve order. It had beside, many more individuals of respectability and station in society than Lane's had. But it had not Sir Walter Raleigh as the single mind to direct and provide for it ; and in the villainy of Fernando, the pilot, it had its worst evil in the deprivation of its supplies. It was the inscrutable will of Heaven that it should not succeed. This is nearly all that man can say of its melancholy failure.

True, indeed, we may see the ill effects then, of some of the erroneous opinions, but too prevalent even at this day, on the subject of planting colonies : but these alone will not explain the loss of White's colony.

Thus, we find no mention made of individual ownership acquired in the land cultivated : none of the stimulus created in man by the consideration that he is improving his own property ; no awakening of forethought for the comfort of that period when age should overtake the colonist, and call for a repose from labor, to be enjoyed on the fruits of earlier industry. All, as far as appeared, labored for the benefit of a common stock out of which all were to live. Now, however such a system may answer for a short time in the beginning, in exploration for instance, it is not a system to insure success, when permanent settlement is once begun. The history of colonization presents no instance of success under such a system, because such a plan runs counter to human nature : it leaves out of view that consideration of personal interest which is left by Heaven in man, as a stimulus to exertion. There is too much equality in the return made alike to laborious toil and evasive idleness: industry is taxed to supply the deficiencies of indolence; and community of interest is not likely to produce economy of expenditure. Hence the plan is soon not merely seen, but felt to be inequitable, and men are not apt to make a prosperous community where they are treated unjustly. The colonization of Virginia, some twenty years later, commenced on this defective system. It never prospered until men were permitted to secure an individual right in their land and their labor.

Again: too little attention, probably, was paid to individual character in the selection of colonists. Doubtless, this was then as it is now, in some degree, unavoidable. The affluent, and the possessors of moderate comfort, in the home of their youth, are not likely to sever all ties and cross an ocean to people a wilderness. There must ordinarily be some strong moral influence to prompt such men to remove. But it is from among such men only, refined by culture, accustomed to some comforts, and disciplined, by their position, to orderly habits, and a proper respect for lawful authority, that good colonists are likely to come. Such men only, meet privations with a cheerful spirit, and seek to supply their deficiencies. The outcasts of London prisons and the sweepings of London kennels, then as now, doubtless could furnish their quota to every ship-load of adventurers. The dissipated scions of respectable families were gladly sent off, lest they should finally tarnish ancestral honors by a felon's fate at home: the inmates of the vile slums and alleys of the metropolis were but too glad to escape the grasp of violated law; to leave a country where they had nothing to gain and every thing to lose, because they had reached an infamy and attained to a notoriety in guilt, which left them no further hope of committing crime with impunity. In short, we may not doubt, that some of the earliest colonists belonged to that class which the poet has described as "the cankers of a long peace, and a calm world."

But we are inclined to think that these causes would not have prevented the successful establishment of White's colony, had it not been subjected to the horrors of famine. Time and experience would probably have corrected the evils we have named; but for starvation there was no remedy; and so, after the toil and suffering of years, the expenditure of much precious treasure, and the loss of still more precious life, the waves of Albermarle rolled, as of old, their ripples up the deserted island beach, and the only voice heard was that of the fitful winds, as they sighed through the forests of Roanoke, and broke upon the stillness of nature's rough repose. The white man was there no longer.